A HANDBOOK TO
TWENTIETH-CENTURY
MUSICAL SKETCHES

This indispensable handbook explains how scholars and students should work with and think about the composer's working manuscripts. Over the past quarter-century, the scholarly study of autograph sources has exploded and nowhere is this more true than in the field of twentieth-century music. And yet, few if any courses or seminars broach the subject of sketch studies and the skills required to examine the manuscripts. This book surveys the knowledge necessary to work efficiently in archives and libraries housing this material and with the skills and techniques specifically related to sketch studies: transcription, reconstructing sketchbooks, deciphering handwriting, dating documents. It deals with the music of important twentieth-century composers and presents visual examples of manuscripts from the collections of world renowned institutions such as the Paul Sacher Foundation. The book aims to make the work of both researchers and students more efficient and rewarding.

PATRICIA HALL is Associate Professor of Music Theory at the Department of Music, University of California, Santa Barbara. She is the author of *A View of Berg's 'Lulu' through the Autograph Sources* (1997). She has also contributed to several works including *The Cambridge Companion to Berg* (1997) and has written articles and reviews for a number of journals.

FRIEDEMANN SALLIS is Professor at the Département de musique, Université de Moncton. He is the author of *An Introduction to the early works of György Ligeti* (1996). He also contributed to *Music of the Twentieth-Century Avant-Garde* (ed. L. Sitsky, 2002) and has published numerous articles on music of the nineteenth and twentieth centuries.

A HANDBOOK TO TWENTIETH-CENTURY MUSICAL SKETCHES

EDITED BY
PATRICIA HALL AND FRIEDEMANN SALLIS

CAMBRIDGE
UNIVERSITY PRESS

PUBLISHED BY THE PRESS SYNDICATE OF THE UNIVERSITY OF CAMBRIDGE
The Pitt Building, Trumpington Street, Cambridge, United Kingdom

CAMBRIDGE UNIVERSITY PRESS
The Edinburgh Building, Cambridge, CB2 2RU, UK
40 West 20th Street, New York, NY 10011– 4211, USA
477 Williamstown Road, Port Melbourne, VIC 3207, Australia
Ruiz de Alarcón 13, 28014 Madrid, Spain
Dock House, The Waterfront, Cape Town 8001, South Africa

http://www.cambridge.org

First published 2004

Printed in the United Kingdom at the University Press, Cambridge

Typeface Adobe Garamond 11/14 pt.   *System* LaTeX 2_ε [TB]

A catalogue record for this book is available from the British Library

ISBN 0 521 80860 X hardback

to our students

Contents

Illustrations

Acknowledgements

This book was originally conceived by Patricia Hall as an ideal text for a course she has taught since 1999 on twentieth-century sketches and autographs. Many of the topics for the book correspond to subjects covered in this course – subjects we thought would be valuable to anyone studying twentieth-century sketches and autographs. In this regard, we must first thank the authors of this book, who, as dedicated teachers and researchers, took time from their busy schedules to contribute to this pedagogical endeavour. At Cambridge University Press we were also very fortunate to have Penny Souster guiding and encouraging this project. Special thanks go to Ulrich Mosch and the Paul Sacher Foundation for their generous contribution and we would also like to thank the Alban Berg Stiftung, the Archivio Luigi Nono, the Bartók Archives, the Hindemith Institute and the John Cage Trust for allowing us to reproduce their holdings.

In its planning stage (at a cafeteria in Basle, Switzerland), we very much benefited from Tomi Mäkelä's suggestions on possible authors and topics and sincerely thank him for his contribution. We heartily thank J. Bradford Robinson and Michael Graubart for their translations and John Boulay for his competent work on the translation of the two chapters submitted in French. We are deeply grateful to Marion Macfarlane for scrupulously correcting all the translated chapters and also for her expert advice. We would like to thank the Direction générale des technologies of the Université de Moncton and particularly Léo Blanchard for the time and energy invested in preparing the plates and examples presented in this book. Finally, we could not have completed this project without the help of our research assistants. In the final rush to submit the manuscript to Cambridge, Katherine Schroeder was a Godsend, sending files electronically to Moncton, contacting authors, and checking footnotes. We would also like to thank Élise Malinge, Myrianne Dubé, Mylène Ouellette, Renée Fontaine and Serge-André Comeau for their assistance at various stages of this project. Similarly, William Koseluk kindly produced the musical examples for chapters 9 and 12.

The research for this book was funded by the Austrian-American Fulbright Commission, the Social Sciences and Humanities Research Council of Canada, a General Research Grant from the University of California, Santa Barbara and grants from the Faculté des arts et des sciences sociales as well as the Faculté des études supérieures et de la recherche of the Université de Moncton.

Copyright materials are reproduced as follows:

Plates 1.2–2 were reproduced by kind permission of the Hindemith Institute. Plates 2.1–4, 7.1–5 and 10.1–4 were reproduced by kind permission of the Paul Sacher Foundation. Plate 4.1 was reproduced by kind permission of the Paul Sacher Foundation and Editio Musica Budapest on behalf of the composer. Plates 4.2–4.5 were reproduced by kind permission of the Paul Sacher Foundation and the composer. Plate 5.1 was reproduced by kind permission of the Archivio Luigi Nono. Plates 8.1–6 were reproduced by kind permission of the Austrian National Library and the Alban Berg Stiftung. Plates 9.1–6 were reproduced by kind permission of the Bartók Archives of the Institute for Musicology of the Hungarian Academy of Sciences. Plates 12.1 and 12.5 were reproduced by kind permission of G. Schirmer and Associated Music Publishers. Plates 12.2–4 were reproduced by kind permission of the Paul Sacher Foundation and the composer. Plates 13.1–3 were reproduced by kind permission of the Paul Sacher Foundation and the composer. Plates 14.1–4 were reproduced by kind permission of the John Cage Trust.

Introduction

Friedemann Sallis and Patricia Hall

Over the past quarter-century, the scholarly study of autograph sources has exploded and nowhere is this more true than in the field of twentieth-century music. A cursory examination of the list of institutions devoted to the promotion and study of the work of twentieth-century composers (found at the end of this book) shows that their number increased dramatically during this period. Whereas only a handful of such institutions were established in the decades following the Second World War, between 1990 and 2000 no less than fifteen opened their doors and many of these contain massive manuscript collections.

The study of manuscript material is not a recent phenomenon. Western culture has been collecting, conserving and scrutinising these documents since at least the fourteenth century. During the Renaissance, the working manuscript of writers and visual artists gradually obtained a permanent position as the step before the finished work, attesting to five centuries of remarkable continuity in terms of tools and procedures.[1] Some of the oldest surviving examples are those of humanists such as Petrarch and Leonardo da Vinci. Indeed, the very idea that a sketch or a draft has some value and should be conserved is intimately linked with the emergence of our modern concept of the work of art. Not surprisingly, our current interest for the composer's sketches can be traced back to the beginning of the Romantic period, a time when the musical work of art finally came into its own.[2]

In North America, the annual summer trek to archives and foundations housing manuscript collections has now become a standard feature of academic calendars and in some quarters these excursions have acquired the status of a 'rite of passage' for doctoral candidates. And yet, most students and many colleagues are ill-prepared to deal with the tasks and challenges facing them as they embark on a study of sketch material. Few if any courses or seminars broach the subject of sketch studies and the skills required to examine manuscripts, creating what one astute observer has called a 'methodological black hole'. The result is lost time and frustrating experiences for the visiting researcher, the archivist and the host institution. This book seeks to address this problem by providing useful information, which is intended to make the work of both colleagues and students more efficient and rewarding.

The first chapter presents a survey of themes related to the study of the sketch material of twentieth-century composers. Giselher Schubert and Friedemann Sallis ask to what extent sketches should be seen as preliminary documents and thus tributary to a work or work project (no matter how ill-defined), or whether they can be understood as texts in their own right. These opposing view-points have been part of sketch studies throughout the twentieth century and they continue to shape how we think about them to this day.

The following chapters can be roughly divided into two sections. The first (chapters 2–6) deals with the knowledge and skills necessary to work efficiently in archives or other institutions housing manuscript material. Some of the most critical work of research projects involving autographs is completed before leaving home. Benefiting from years of experience as a musicologist at the Paul Sacher Foundation, Ulrich Mosch presents invaluable advice for those preparing for a prolonged period of work in an archive. The conservation of original documents is of course the primary responsibility of every archive and library. In chapter 3 Therese Muxeneder looks at the impact this vocation can have on the researcher's work. She examines the composition of paper and how it ages, as well as providing advice on how to handle fragile autographs. The terminology we use to describe and classify the composer's working manuscripts is discussed in chapter 4. Friedemann Sallis also looks at the concepts underlying this terminology and how these concepts have changed as they passed from the nineteenth to the twentieth century. Erika Schaller carefully walks the reader through the complexities of cataloguing sketch material and highlights the advantages of using database technology for this purpose. Equipment and supplies required for the digital preservation of information contained in manuscript source material is now both readily available and affordable, though still not widely used. William Koseluk's essay presents photographic methods and an analysis of various computer scanning options as well as a survey of graphic software and various distribution methods.

The second half of the book (chapters 7–14) is devoted to issues and techniques pertinent to the study of sketch material. Each chapter focuses on a work or a selection of works by one or two composers. Using two sketches by Anton Webern, Regina Busch begins this section with a detailed examination of theoretical and practical aspects of transcription. Researchers are frequently confronted with the tasks of reconstructing sketchbooks and deciphering a composer's hastily written annotations. Patricia Hall's essay presents pragmatic techniques for overcoming these difficulties, which all scholars will find useful. Putting his renowned knowledge of Béla Bartók's autographs to good use, László Somfai examines the problem of establishing a chronology of undated sketches. In chapter 10, Tomi Mäkelä takes a fresh look at the importance of sound colour and instrumentation in twentieth-century music and proposes a method for the systematic study of this aspect of Igor Stravinsky's music. Pascal Decroupet exhaustively analyses the evolution of serial technique in the 1950s and 1960s and demonstrates how the sketch material of Pierre Boulez and Karlheinz Stockhausen provides us with new perspectives on their work. In chapter 12, Denis Vermaelen discusses the significance of Elliott Carter's pre-compositional strategies and their impact on the completed work. In the penultimate chapter, Ross Feller assesses the impact of music-writing software on the working methods of Brian Ferneyhough. Finally, Larry Austin reports on his recomposition of John Cage's *Williams Mix* using the composer's manuscript material and computer technology.

Notwithstanding the division of the book into two sections, the essays presented here also relate to one another in multiple ways forming a network of interconnections within which the reader will discover a number of possible links. For instance, profiting from his long experience with Paul Hindemith's autographs, Giselher Schubert presents the advantages and disadvantages of publishing sketch material in facsimile and in transcription. These points are then taken up and examined in great detail by Regina Busch. The chapters dealing with the impact of computer technology on archival practice (chapters 5 and 6) and on the working methods of composers (chapters 13 and 14) constitute another obvious example. An important thread running through much of the book are questions concerning the interpretation of sketch material and how knowledge gained from the study of sketches can enhance our understanding of a given composer's music.

In preparing this book we made a conscious effort to overstep disciplinary, cultural and linguistic boundaries. Sketch studies are best situated in that space where the history and theory of music overlap. Problems of analysis and context are inseparably bound up in the composer's working documents: examining them usually requires a broadly based, holistic approach.[3] The musicological and theoretical perspectives brought to this project by the editors reflect this belief. To be sure, the book presents neither a history nor a theory of sketch studies, though we do hope that it will be considered an important step in both of these directions.

Seven of the book's chapters were initially submitted in German and French. Walter Benjamin observed that fidelity and freedom are built into the very nature of translation.[4] He was referring to the translation of poetry; however his point is well taken here. During the past three years we have attempted to set the content of the original versions in clear, readable English and are grateful for the patient collaboration of our foreign-language contributors during this long and at times arduous process. We would also note, together with Benjamin, 'that no translation would be possible if in its ultimate essence it strove for likeness to the original. For in its afterlife – which could not be called that if it were not a transformation and a renewal of something living – the original undergoes a change.'[5]

We remind the reader that, notwithstanding the traditional practice of most major publishing houses, the translations included in this book should be considered as unnecessary crutches. As Ulrich Mosch and Patricia Hall underline in their respective chapters, sketch studies require a thorough knowledge of the composer's first language, no matter how little known it may be outside of the area in which it is spoken. We would stress that an adequate knowledge of important regional and minority languages (for instance German in Central Europe, French in Canada and Spanish in the USA) is also absolutely necessary. Foreign-language competence is essential not only to be able to understand the remarks, words and abbreviations which normally accompany the composer's musical notation, but also because sketches constitute a highly idiosyncratic system of signs, which must be deciphered as though one were learning a new language. Thus the acquisition of a second or a third language provides the scholar with a broad range of aptitudes and capabilities which will prove indispensable in the course of the research project. If the problem of second- and third-language competence is not exclusively North American, it is nonetheless particularly acute on that continent. Though North American universities habitually require a second language in their doctoral programs, real competence is often sorely lacking.

Sketch studies have been and will no doubt remain a locus for controversy. The benefits of studying the composer's working documents have been both wildly exaggerated[6] and summarily dismissed.[7] Douglas Johnson's old argument concerning their relevance for analysis now seems tinged with that naivety we often attribute to ideas from another age.[8] Sketches, like the works or work projects to which they may pertain, are deeply contextualised phenomena and it is wistful thinking to assume that either a sketch or a published score can simply be read or analysed at face value. We believe that it is time to put this argument to rest. The question is not whether sketch material will be used for analysis, but rather how this should be done. Sketch studies have become and will no doubt remain a permanent fixture of both the history and analysis of music for the foreseeable future and it is within this perspective that the book was conceived.

CHAPTER I

Sketches and sketching

Giselher Schubert and Friedemann Sallis

SKETCHES AND THE WORK

In the visual arts, the sketch possesses a completely autonomous aesthetic value, which can neither be attained nor overtaken by the completed work. The precarious balance between content and expressive means in Paul Cézanne's sketches and studies of the *Mont Sainte-Victoire* (1902–6) allows them to be apprehended as works in their own right without necessarily referring to other, more complete, versions of the same painting.[1] Traditionally, no such claim can be made for the composer's preliminary working documents. As a rule, they are understood to be unfinished, open and provisional: the first unsure attempts to notate ideas, the significance of which remains uncertain. As opposed to sketches in the visual arts, the content of musical sketches is normally projected towards a completed composition, even in those cases where the work is missing because it has not survived, was not completed or was never written down in the first place. There are of course compositions whose titles include the term 'sketch'. From a thematic, melodic, rhythmic and formal point of view, Claude Debussy's *D'un Cahier d'Esquisse* for piano (1903) is an extraordinarily subtle work. In this case, however, the term 'sketch' refers to a compositional principle, which the composer controls and forms technically. It has nothing to do with the working documents used to compose the work.

Contradicting this more traditional view is the position that all sketch material, no matter how preliminary, should be accorded an independent status, which is lost when this material is uncritically subsumed within the bounds of a work or work project. This position understands sketching as a relatively autonomous process, not necessarily limited to demands or contingencies existing outside of the process itself. In this light, sketching represents the utopia of unhindered musical imagination developing on its own terms. Over the past half-century, this latter position has been indirectly reinforced by attempts to create innovative forms based on open work-concepts and more recently by the emergence of so-called post-modern approaches to the understanding of art and culture. Be that as it may, these contradictory positions are built into the very foundation of sketch studies. In the following pages we shall examine how we use sketch material to better understand music and how these contradictory positions affect this usage.

SKETCHES, ANALYSIS AND HERMENEUTICS

The scientific basis for the study of sketches first emerged during the early twentieth century and is intimately bound up with an important paradigm shift in aesthetics. While some scholars took Friedrich Nietzsche's position – that the completeness of a work of art cannot be accounted for in the information contained in the composer's working documents – others fixed their attention on the multitude of potentialities always present in the creative process and of which only a small portion emerge in the finished work. From this latter perspective, the isolated, self-contained work, which Walter Benjamin described as 'the supreme reality in art',[2] appears as a betrayal of those multiple possibilities, or to quote Benjamin again, as the death-mask of the artist's initial conception.[3]

To the extent that a given work is perceived as an aesthetic object of some value, the idea that it exists as a distinct and wholly separate entity became widespread during the early twentieth century. Sobered by this reinforcement of the notion of aesthetic autonomy, the study of a given composition now focused less on the idea of the work as a representation of the composer's struggle to create and more on an imminent analysis of compositional technique. In the influential work of Heinrich Schenker (1867–1935), August Halm (1869–1929) and Ernst Kurth (1886–1946), the essence of a musical work's contents can only be grasped through a minute examination of the procedures used to bring it into existence. In this context the composer's manuscript material enabled a better understanding of the specificity of a given work. In attempting to reconstruct the compositional process, scholars hoped to differentiate between the genesis and the value of a composition. The value of musical relationships was to be precisely and above all 'authentically' determined through a reliable description of how motives, themes and forms are developed and modified within the creative process. The close reading of Ludwig van Beethoven's sketches by Paul Mies (1889–1976) demonstrated how such a thorough examination of this material can lead to a better understanding of the composer's style.[4]

Compositions now acquired their own 'biographies', which sought to underscore their unmistakable individuality. Generic categories were avoided, ignored or simply forgotten. Identifying and understanding the individual and specific aspects of a given work, a task which could no longer be done using traditional compositional categories, became an analytic problem. In the case of the Viennese School, the following questions came to the fore. Is the twelve-tone row developed as a thematic entity or after such an entity has been conceived? Which twelve-tone criteria constitute a given composer's conscious act of composition? How are inconsistencies and discrepancies in row technique to be understood? When dealing with the individualised works of the Viennese School, fundamental questions such as these can only be dealt with by going back to the surviving sketch material.

From the study of Arnold Schoenberg's sketches we know that thematic inspiration preceded the development of twelve-tone rows. The manuscript material also shows that

Schoenberg subdivided his rows into segments, the significance of which had an important influence on the analysis of his dodecaphonic works. On the contrary, in Alban Berg's twelve-tone works, the development of thematic material follows the establishment of row structures, which constitute a substrate of pitch relationships that are axiomatic for a given work. Berg's sketches also had a stimulating impact on the analysis of his works. Very often he would note the exact number of bars making up a section or a movement. These numbers are then applied to other musical dimensions and can acquire a specific sense within the work's structure. The sketches also contain explanatory notes referring to the fact that Berg related certain musical gestures to extra-musical phenomena. This new information has radically changed our apprehension of compositions such as the *Lyric Suite*. Sketches have thus provided access to levels of meaning which cannot be directly extracted from the published score. In this case, the study of sketch material provided a basis not only for the technical revision of previous analyses, but also for the development of new hermeneutic approaches, some of which led to surprising and unpredictable knowledge. The study of sketches (and not just those of Berg) reveals that almost any musical building-block (melody, harmony, rhythm, etc.) can acquire and contain meaning over and above its purely structural significance, and that this meaning may have nothing to do with the way in which the material was initially conceived.

COMPOSITIONAL TECHNIQUE AND THE STUDY OF THE CREATIVE PROCESS

The study of a composer's compositional techniques is a complex endeavour that cannot be read directly out of the surviving documents. First of all, the comments a composer makes on his own work cannot be taken at face value. In letters to friends, Max Reger made misleading statements on the nature of his compositional technique. Whereas he maintained that his works were completely thought out before he wrote them down, his sketches show that, when he began composing, he often had no clear conception of the work he would finally write. Indeed, his concept of the work usually became manifest as he sketched. Reger's creative process was stimulated less by flashes of thematic inspiration than by suggestions from friends, the methodical study of contemporary and historical models, and was even influenced by such extra-musical considerations as the size and format of his staff paper. Hans Pfitzner also insisted on the primacy of inspiration. His sketches demonstrate that only themes and thematic configurations were the product of spontaneous imagination. Most of his compositional activity was based on the careful working out of freely associated musical ideas. On the contrary, Paul Hindemith described musical inspiration as a kind of 'vision', which he compared to the flash of lightning on a night landscape. His sketches demonstrate that on occasion he actually did write out complete drafts of works as though seized by such a vision.

Increased knowledge of the creative process has greatly stimulated research. Composers themselves have often attempted to better understand their own compositional methods and habits so as not to find themselves at the mercy of their 'mood'. Neither Schoenberg nor Hindemith composed with instruments. However, whereas Hindemith always sketched out a work to the end and only then wrote the fair copy, Schoenberg often wrote out sketched sections in fair copy, which is why the latter left behind so many fragments. Hindemith left almost none. As is well known, Igor Stravinsky, who claimed he preferred composing to the finished composition, developed much of his new material by improvising at the piano. This was then quickly written down on any available scrap of paper. Later, in a second phase, he would organise these spontaneously developed ideas. Though Berg composed at the piano, he simultaneously drafted specific formal plans, developed ideas for movements and structured musical building-blocks. He then formed themes, motives, harmonic progressions and tone configurations from this material and used them to fill out the formal plans. Though the various aspects of Berg's working procedures can be distinguished, they cannot be separated from one another. Béla Bartók also used the piano to put himself in a compositional frame of mind, which was then followed by the sketching of thematic ideas. As a rule, he produced continuity sketches of the planned work and supplemented these with sketches concerning particular compositional problems. Occasionally Pfitzner and Richard Strauss sketched out their ideas of complete compositions in words, without musical notation. These verbalised musical developments should not be confused with the programmes or the content description of symphonic poems.

Over the past half-century, the emergence of new compositional techniques (serial, moment form, aleatory, minimalist, etc.) has led to an increased production of sketches concerned with the preparation of material and general principles. These types of sketches often have little or no direct relationship with the resulting composition. Rather they offer information concerning the musical axioms which govern the development of general structural principles covering any number of musical dimensions (pitch, rhythm, sound-colour, dynamics, phrasing, texture, periodicity and form). More often than not, sketches such as these appear as lists, tables and schemata to which the composer refers during the compositional process. The serial techniques developed by Pierre Boulez and Karlheinz Stockhausen immediately spring to mind. However, one could just as easily refer to John Cage's systematic organisation of his chance operations or to Elliot Carter's Harmony Book in which he presents an exhaustive repertoire of harmonic combinations derived from the chromatic scale.

Over time, the mastering of technique and increased knowledge of the creative process can allow the composer to dispense with 'pre-compositional' sketches and to directly compose large sections of a projected work. Missing in these documents are what the composer does not feel obliged to notate because they constitute part of his taste, style, handiwork: in a word, his compositional routine (tempo indications, instrumentation, voice-leading, phrasing, dynamics, the text setting in vocal music, etc.). This does not mean that these aspects have no aesthetic significance, or that they became part of the creative process at a later date. On the contrary, composers do not normally notate what for them is self-evident. However, as obvious as they may be to the composer, these aspects cannot be divined by those outside of the composer's inner circle. In sketches such as these, structural principles are applied directly to the material of the primary musical dimensions, and to the extent that, say, phrasing, dynamics or tempo indications are or become part of this primary dimension, they will then appear in the sketching process. Accordingly, the study of sketches can allow one to define the primary and secondary aspects of a completed work from the composer's point of view.

The source material for Hans Werner Henze's Symphony No. 6 consists of a short score and a fair copy. The former document contains precisely notated thematic material and numerous verbal descriptions as well as general indications concerning pitch content, register, rhythmic figures and instrumentation. Despite the fragmentary nature of this information, the finished work is unmistakably present. Indeed, Ulrich Mosch has pointed out that the short score provides an exceptionally clear presentation of the overall formal conception of the work.[5] In cases such as this, sketching coincides with the first complete draft, meaning that the work was largely thought through before being written down. Hindemith was of the opinion that, for 'real' composers, such an imagined (but not yet written out) work has the same existential status as a notated composition. In the case of his duo sonatas for melody instrument with piano accompaniment, Hindemith's idea of the work was so secure that he would dispense with a complete draft of the full score and successively write out each of the parts to control their specific effects.

PHILOLOGICAL PROBLEMS

The broadening of the field of sketch studies to include work analysis and the research on the creative process has resulted in opening up a labyrinthine network of philological problems.

1. Whether or to what extent a given corpus of sketch material is complete, or if parts have been lost or destroyed, will necessarily remain an open question. The genesis of a composition can stretch over a number of years, during which the composer's living and working habits can change drastically. Normally, composers do not scrupulously save and conserve every scrap of their working documents as though they were historians of their own work. Also, they will tend to discard the material which refers to what they see as preliminary or out-dated stages of their compositional technique. This is particularly true of those twentieth-century composers who conceived their work as being part of the 'progressive thrust' of history. Thus the loss of at least part of the composer's sketch material should be considered a rule rather than an exception.

2. The problem of dating sketches and their chronology is intimately bound up with the writing habits of composers. Sketches written on loose-leaf sheets can hardly be dated with any precision and even a general chronology is difficult to establish. The philological tools developed for the purpose of establishing chronologies (watermarks, paper types, writing utensils and the deduction of dates with the help of secondary sources) are frequently

inefficient because the useful dating of sketches usually focuses on identifying the day on which a document was written. Even the composer's own dating must be cross-checked whenever possible. Schoenberg accused Webern of falsely dating his works in order to reinforce his claim of paternity for certain compositional techniques.[6] Finally the date appearing on a page of sketches does not necessarily refer to everything written on that page. Undated modifications are sometimes added long after the sketch was initially written.

3. Sketches must be comprehensible for the composer, but not necessarily for anyone else. Consequently, the decoding and interpretation of sketch material is often extraordinarily problematic. The notation of pitch and rhythm is often equivocal and verbal explications are sometimes illegible for those outside of the composer's inner circle. The graphical disposition of sketches as well as the individual signs used to create them can be puzzling and frustrating. On many of Reger's sketches one finds short lines, perpendicular to the staff and disposed unsystematically among sketched music. A careful study of the sketches revealed that they have no musical significance.[7] Rather, they appear to have occurred inadvertently as Reger quickly put his writing utensil aside, suggesting that many of his sketches are transcriptions of improvisation done at the piano.

4. Establishing the extent, chronology and interpretation of a corpus of manuscript material is also problematic because a given sketch cannot necessarily be related to one specific composition. Furthermore, if one sketch can be related to different compositions, it can also be used in different ways, acquiring new and divergent meanings in the process. The recycling of previously written material is in fact widespread and often underestimated because for the past 200 years composers, performers and the public have insisted on viewing works, particularly those of the classical canon, as isolated, self-contained entities. The manuscript material of twentieth-century composers, now being made available for public scrutiny in unprecedented quantities, reveals that this practice is pervasive among composers from Charles Ives to György Kurtág.[8] The latter's third string quartet, *Officium breve in memoriam Andreæ Szervánsky*, Op. 28 (1989) is an interesting case in point. Of the fifteen movements making up the work, only four were composed specifically for the string quartet in 1988–9. The other eleven movements are either quotations of music by Anton Webern and Endre Szervánszky or adaptations of music previously composed by Kurtág himself, some of which can be traced back to sketches and drafts written up to fifteen years before he began work on *Officium breve*.

PUBLISHING SKETCH MATERIAL

The paradigm shift in aesthetics described above contributed to the institutionalisation of sketch studies in the 1920s. Though initially carried out as part of philological research undertaken to prepare the critical edition of complete works, the examination of the composer's manuscript material gradually became a field of study in its own right. This in turn had an impact on the meaning of the term 'complete edition'. As well as establishing an authentic text, presenting a chronological ordering of works within a given genre and providing information concerning the reception of specific works, the 'historic' aspect of these undertakings gradually came to include the 'inner' history of a composition: in other words, the work's biography established through a study of sketch material pertaining to it. In the 1960s, sketches began to be published in critical editions of complete works, notably those of Schoenberg and Hindemith.

The question of whether sketch material should be organised and presented in relation to works or independently as source material in its own right impinges on the decision to publish sketches in facsimile or in transcription, and also on how the published material is to be interpreted. Within the framework of complete critical editions, usually only a selective assortment of surviving sketch material is published. These documents are directly related to identifiable works or work projects because the function of sketch material in this context is to clarify the work's genesis. The publication of sketch material outside of such a work-related context does occur (i.e. the publication of sketchbooks used over a long period of time), however it requires extensive commentaries.

The simplest and most reliable editorial method is the publication of high-quality, multi-coloured facsimiles. However, this method also has its limits. First, it is by far the most expensive and, second, facsimile documents can often be extraordinarily difficult to read. For these reasons, sketches are often published in diplomatic transcription: a decision which imposes a great deal more preparatory work on the editor, who must choose what can or should be made legible. Whereas erasures are clearly visible in facsimile, they cannot be easily reproduced in transcription because an erased text can often not be reliably deciphered. Even clearly visible graphic alterations are difficult if not impossible to transcribe. How should one present a minim which has been transformed into a crotchet by filling-in the note head? Sketches can also contain objectively recognisable errors, which touch on the document's musical content. By what criteria are such errors to be corrected, or should they be corrected at all? Normally all deviations between the original and the transcribed texts as well as all ambiguous situations must be fully accounted for in commentaries. In the complete edition of Schoenberg's works, remarks such as 'the erased text is no longer legible' or 'deciphering all aspects of the documents is not possible' occur frequently.

If, for the sake of objectivity, the editor decides to reproduce errors in transcription, then all errors, no matter how banal, must be reproduced and accompanied by an appropriate commentary. Incorrect rhythms that do not fit a given metric system and missing or absent clef signs are examples of the types of minor errors frequently found in hastily written sketches. They are easily recognised but cumbersome to explain and can quickly lead to an overload of information. Such an approach also puts the editor in the uncomfortable situation of having to comment on marks, the sense of which has not yet been definitively understood. Editorial commentaries are further lengthened by the necessity of having to translate the composer's verbal remarks (which can be extensive) written in languages that are not widely understood – Hungarian (Bartók), Finnish (Jean Sibelius) or Danish (Carl Nielsen).

The following examples taken from Hindemith's sketches illustrate the crucial importance of such editorial commentaries, even in the case of relatively unproblematic facsimile repro- ductions. Plate 1.1 presents the first sketch for the second movement of the Concerto for Woodwinds, Harp and Orchestra (1949). The movement's form can be described as ternary: A (bars 1–23) + bridge passage (bars 23–7); B (bars 27–52); A' (bars 53–70) + Coda (bars 71–8).

On the upper staff Hindemith began a two-voice canon, which is broken off after three bars. In the four successive double staves he reworked the same canon for three voices. On the lower staff of the first double system Hindemith added a fourth voice in pencil. He also numbered the last three bars of this double staff from 1 to 3. These numbers appear again at the end of the third double staff and indicate that the corresponding bars are repeated there. At the bottom of the page, Hindemith wrote out a brief plan for the entire movement. He entitled the A section *Kanon zu 2* (canon in two voices). The number above refers to the length of the section in bars. This is followed by *Überl*, an abbreviation for *Überleitung* (bridge passage), without the number of bars. On the same line Hindemith presented the two parts of the B section – *Aria Soli* and *Aria Orch* – and again indicated their exact length in bars, thirteen each. The second line of the plan presents the A' section labelled *Kanon zu 3 mit Figur* (canon in three voices with figure). The term 'figure' refers to the introduction of a new motive in the accompaniment. This section is fourteen bars long. The last line presents the coda, labelled *Kanon zu 6* (canon in six voices), which would be eight bars in length. According to this plan, Hindemith clearly envisioned a symmetric relationship between the main sections of this movement: A = 22 bars; B = 26 bars (13 + 13); A' + Coda = 22 bars (14 + 8). This relationship is modified in the definitive version of this movement: A = 23 bars; B = 26 bars; A' + Coda = 26 bars. Of course, the bar numbers of the initial plan cannot be understood as errors, requiring correction. Rather they record Hindemith's initial idea of a movement whose form consists of symmetrically disposed sections: an idea which, though modified, remains intact in the final version.

Plate 1.2 is taken from the initial sketches for the final movement of the Sonata for Four French Horns (1952), the form of which is a theme and variations based on the folksong, *Ich schell mein Horn* (I sound my horn).

Hindemith began sketching the theme in four-voice counterpoint (bars 1–5) and finished in three-voice counterpoint (bars 6–15). Beneath the theme, he presented information pertaining to each of the four variations. Above the tonal centres, labelled in capital letters (H[=B], E, F, B[=B♭]), the composer noted characteristic aspects of each variation. For the first, he indicated a rhythmic figure (a dotted quaver followed by a semiquaver and a quaver).

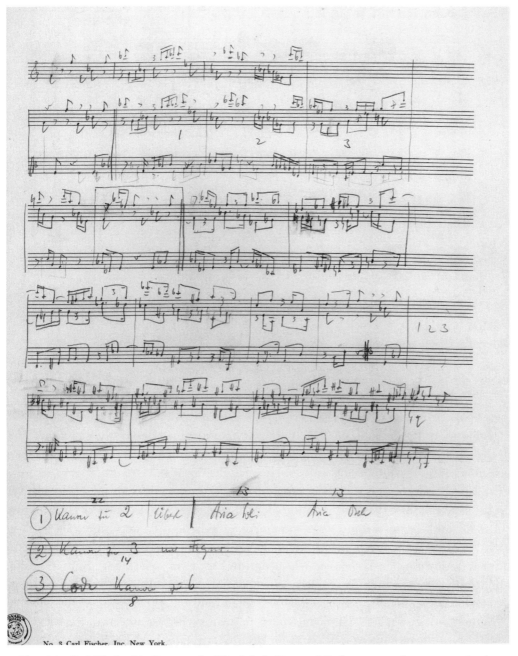

Plate 1.1   Paul Hindemith, Concerto for Woodwinds, Harp and Orchestra, second movement, sketch.
Hindemith Institut, Frankfurt am Main

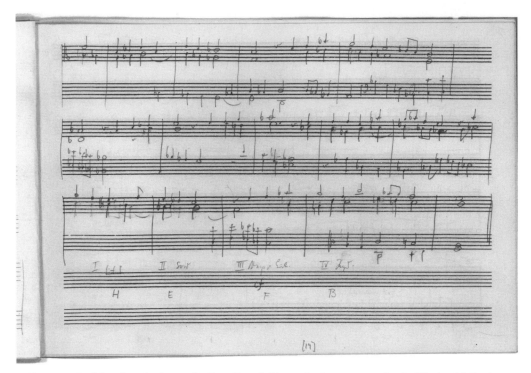

Plate 1.2   Paul Hindemith, Sonata for Four French Horns, final movement, sketch. Hindemith Institut, Frankfurt am Main

This figure is used to separate the sections of the theme, which are presented canonically in diminution. In so doing, one could say that he underlined one of the variation's most negligible aspects. The second variation is based on an ostinato over which the theme is broken up into small groups of motives. Here Hindemith wrote *sord* (= *sordino*), referring to a relatively superficial aspect of this variation (i.e. the use of mutes). He presents a relatively precise description of the third variation's formal structure: Adagio *Einl./* cf (= *Einleitung* [Introduction]/ cantus firmus). The movement is made up of a very slow cantus-firmus variation of the theme, accompanied by secondary voices in free counterpoint and preceded by an introduction. The last variation is qualified by the term *Jagd* (Hunt). In this variation Hindemith composed a character piece using traditional horn calls among which the theme makes one last appearance.

In these written remarks, Hindemith refers to the most diverse aspects of this movement which have little or nothing to do with the decisive attributes of the variations. As a result this rather enigmatic sketch tells us very little about the movement's music and the way it was composed. To understand the document one must bring knowledge of the completed work to the sketch, which reverses the conventional relationship between sketch and work. In this case, the work enables us to read the sketch, rather than the other way around.

THE COMPLETION OF UNFINISHED SKETCH MATERIAL

Attempts to complete works or parts thereof that exist only in the form of sketch material are highly problematic undertakings and raise the question as to whether sketches can claim some kind of independent status. Anton Bruckner died whilst trying to sketch the final movement of his Ninth Symphony. Once he realised that his initial conception could not be completed, he began modifying it. In the surviving sketches, which present a series of short musical fragments, neither the original conception nor the modifications can be clearly distinguished from one another. Consequently, attempting to fill in the empty spaces between these fragments would be a highly speculative undertaking. The same can be said for the completion of Gustav Mahler's Tenth Symphony, though, in this case, the sketch material does provide a more reliable basis. Even in situations in which the resulting composition seems satisfactory from a technical point of view, the results remain problematic. Though Hindemith's lost Sonata for piano, Op. 17, can be reconstructed with great reliability from the surviving sketches, the work will always lack a certain 'Hindemithian' character derived from minor changes the composer habitually made when he produced a fair copy, underlining the stylistic importance of these supposedly superficial additions.

Here again the crux of the problem involves the confrontation of conflicting frames of reference. On the one hand, according to nineteenth-century aesthetics (which are still with us today), the fact that a composition cannot be wholly ascribed to a particular individual can only be understood as a deficiency. On the other hand, Eric Hobsbawm has noted that by the middle of the twentieth century, many of the most influential and widespread forms of Western art (cinema and recorded music for instance) had become essentially cooperative rather than individual because their elaboration tended to be technological rather than manual.[9]

Throughout the twentieth century the recomposition and completion of fragments from the past has produced works that are as successful as they are ambiguous. The third act of Alban Berg's *Lulu*, which Friedrich Čerha completed with extraordinary competence, seems to encapsulate both sides of this problem. *Lulu* went down in music history as a musical fragment and as such acquired a cryptic, almost enigmatic aesthetic quality. Once complete, the opera lost this quality and with it part of its nimbus, and yet the completed work is enormously successful. This apparent paradox can be at least partially resolved if we examine what the arranger or second composer is attempting to achieve. Brian Newbould, Peter Gülke and Luciano Berio all used Franz Schubert's incomplete sketches (Fragment D. 936A) as a basis for writing new works of music. Newbould, a musicologist, boldly claimed to have completed Schubert's Tenth Symphony, as 'Schubert himself might have done'.[10] Gülke, a musicologist and conductor, is far more circumspect about his use of Schubert's sketches. The resulting symphonic fragments are in his opinion hypothetical music of limited authenticity.[11] This depreciatory evaluation did not stop Gülke either from performing or recording the music he produced. Taking an entirely different approach, Berio used the same material to produce *Rendering* for orchestra (1989–90). Rather than attempting a hypothetical reconstruction, he composed what David Osmond-Smith has called, 'conjunctive tissue' around Schubert's fragments.[12] Though his music contains allusions to Schubert's late work (notably the String Trio in B♭ major, D. 898, *Winterreise*, D. 911, and the Sonata in B♭ major, D. 960), Berio is careful to maintain an aesthetic distance between Schubert's fragments and his additions. In the end, Schubert's Tenth Symphony is a figment of Newbould's imagination. As a historical object, it will remain, like Beethoven's Tenth or Edward Elgar's Third, a fictitious work, no matter how much information is obtained from surviving manuscript material. That Newbould and Gülke produced radically different results with the same sketch material (see the first movement) tends to reinforce this point.

Following Stravinsky's death in 1971, the composer's widow invited Charles Wuorinen to write a work based on her husband's last sketches, which could not be related to any known work or work project. Though the sound and style of Stravinsky's late work is unmistakable in *A Reliquary for Igor Stravinsky* (1974–5), it is Wuorinen's composition, not Stravinsky's. Like all other historical documents (completed works, letters, pictures, etc.), the composer's sketches are capable of stimulating both research and creative projects and as such can be seen to have an independent status. They do not allow us to reach back and create objects which never existed in the first place.

Preliminaries before visiting an archive

Ulrich Mosch

The success of any archival research trip stands or falls on the quality of preparation. Yet there are no hard and fast rules as to what good preparation entails, for the conditions are subject to a wide range of factors. First, the type of preparation depends on the chosen subject. A study of conflicting versions of a particular work presupposes a different kind of preparation than is required for an analysis of a composer's creative process during one period in his career, a monograph on a single work, a biography, or a comparative study of different composers working at the same time. Second, the preparation is crucially determined by the amount of information available about source material, and thus invariably depends on the current state of research. Working in relatively well-trodden areas where detailed knowledge is already available is something quite different from tackling largely uncharted fields for which sources first have to be located, and perhaps even sorted and classified. Third, the possibilities of preparation are clearly delimited by whether or not the researcher can obtain working copies of manuscripts in the form of photocopies, microfilms or digital scans. The present chapter takes Luciano Berio's *Requies* for chamber orchestra (1983–5) as a basis for discussing three central aspects of archival research: locating the sources, obtaining and evaluating the information, and purposefully preparing a visit to the archive.

LOCALISING SOURCES AND COLLECTING INFORMATION

As in any other research project, work begins with an evaluation of existing writings on the chosen subject. This includes gathering information on manuscripts and other documents and pinpointing their current whereabouts. Locating sources is not as difficult today as it used to be. Useful aids of widely varying sorts are available. Many entries in large encyclopaedias, such as *The New Grove Dictionary of Music and Musicians* and *Die Musik in Geschichte und Gegenwart*, list the major archives where sources on the composer can be found. Second, the Internet provides a means of finding one's way to the home pages of archives and libraries where manuscripts are preserved. Finally, of course, many references to sources can be found in the published literature on a given composer or period.

Although the twentieth century is well served by bibliographies and reference books (other means of locating sources can be found in the Internet), a sleuth's intuition can still be most useful. When encyclopaedias, bibliographic references or the Internet fail to yield results, a query to a publisher or a colleague working in the same field may clarify where material on a composer or work might be found or who might be able to provide information or assistance. Publishing houses usually preserve only fair copies of scores that served as production masters. They also have documents relating to the production of the printed score (especially corrected proof sheets and correspondence) and to the work's performance history (programme notes, reviews, live recordings, posters and similar items).

The first step is thus to clarify where sources are located and whether any published information exists on the manuscripts for the work or group of works we want to study, for example on the archive's home page, in manuscript inventories and source catalogues, or in standard reference works. If no published information exists, the researcher should contact the institution directly to obtain additional and more accurate information – a step that is in any case never ill-advised. As a rule of thumb, the more precisely you outline the project in your written enquiry, the more accurate will be the information you receive.

In the case of Berio's *Requies*, the results of this first stage might look somewhat as follows: the situation regarding the sources for his music is relatively straightforward, for the bulk of his estate is preserved at the Paul Sacher Foundation in Basle. But sources are also found in many other places, including the music departments of great libraries such as the Library of Congress, private collections, Berio's publishers (Suvini Zerboni and Ricordi in Milan, Universal Edition in Vienna) and the archives of music festivals, broadcasting companies and institutions where Berio worked in various capacities (for example, the Juilliard School of Music in New York, IRCAM in Paris, the Accademia Santa Cecilia in Rome). In contrast, the bibliographical information to be gleaned on *Requies* is hardly worth mentioning. True, the work is occasionally mentioned in writings on Berio,[1] but it has not yet received a separate study, not even within a broader context.

The home page of the Paul Sacher Foundation (see Plate 2.1) can only serve as a rough guide for getting started. It merely reveals whether material on a composer is available at all, and if so what sort, but not whether there is anything specific on a work such as *Requies*. It does at least direct us to a published inventory of musical manuscripts in the Foundation's Luciano Berio Collection.[2] However, though published in 1988, this inventory contains nothing on *Requies*. As no other published information is available, we must inevitably enquire directly at the Foundation in order to learn more.

What does the source information obtainable from printed or electronic media or by direct enquiry usually look like? Sometimes the collection or estate is partly or completely uncatalogued, and the only information we receive is a list of works on which material is available. In such cases, it is always worth trying to find out at least something general about the type of documents involved. Are they mainly fair copies of scores, or are there sketches as well? How much material is available (if only an approximate estimate)? Is it at least roughly sorted or still uncatalogued? Is all the material for a particular composition preserved in one place, or are there documents scattered elsewhere in the collection? Is the material complete or fragmentary? Are there any secondary documents such as letters, verbal texts, programme

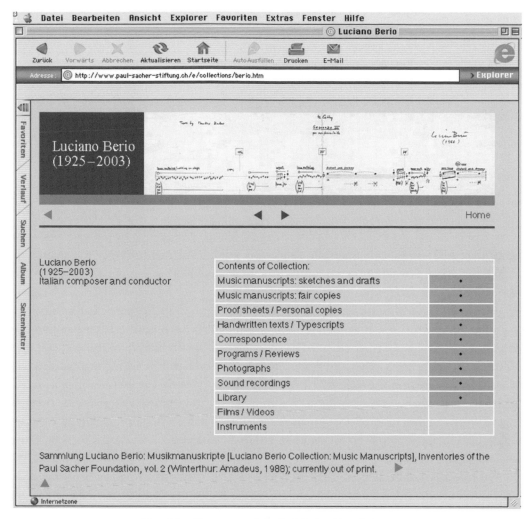

Plate 2.1   Home page of the Paul Sacher Foundation

notes and the like? This sort of information helps us at least to make an estimate of the amount of time we will need for our archival work. The scantier the work previously done in this area, the more time we will have to set aside for such activities as identifying, classifying and describing the materials. If the material is largely uncatalogued, we will need to put more work into the preliminaries – but the likelihood of making unexpected discoveries will be all the greater.

Far more useful than an unspecific list is an inventory that classifies all documents related to a work and gives a complete description of their scope. The above-mentioned inventory of musical manuscripts in the Berio Collection contains, as already noted, nothing on *Requies*,

Requies (klOrch; 1983–1985)

– Skizzen und Entwürfe [28 S., davon 1 S. Fotokopie]
– Particell (Entwurf; unvollständig) [8 S.]
– Partitur (1. Reinschrift; Fragment) [1 verworfene S.]
– Partitur (2. Reinschrift mit Eintragungen) [44 S. + 8 S. Makulatur]

Figure 2.1a   Entry for *Requies* in the second edition of *Luciano Berio: Musikmanuskripte*

Requies (small orch; 1983–5)

– Sketches and drafts [28 pp., including 1 p. photocopy]
– Short score (draft; incomplete) [8 pp.]
– Full score (1st fair copy; fragment) [1 withdrawn p.]
– Full score (2nd fair copy with annotations) [44 pp. + 8 discarded pp.]

Figure 2.1b   Translation of the text in Figure 2.1a

since the collection had no material on this work at the time the inventory was published. A heavily revised new edition is currently in preparation.[3] Here we will find the description shown in Figures 2.1a and b.

In inventories of this sort, terms such as 'sketch' and 'draft' in particular are used to describe documents in a pragmatic sense and may differ in meaning from composer to composer. Still, the information provides clear hints as to the nature of the material. For example, the note on sketches and drafts already suggests that the existing manuscripts will shed light not only on the definitive orchestral score of *Requies* but also on various stages of its genesis. When we are dealing with a complete posthumous estate or a large body of manuscripts, an inventory of this sort also enables us to judge whether the scope and nature of the documents are typical of the work or group of works we are interested in, or whether they form an exception.

As a rule, detailed catalogues of manuscripts only exist after a composer's music has been the subject of extensive research for a long period of time. Where they do exist, depending on how they are designed, they contain information that tells us various things about the work and its genesis even before we have viewed the documents themselves.[4] Unlike an inventory, which classifies all manuscripts connected with a work in summary form, a source catalogue describes each and every manuscript. A catalogue description of part of the manuscript material listed in the above inventory excerpt might look as shown in Figures 2.2a–c.[5]

Depending on the depth of the description, a catalogue entry of this sort does more than simply convey an idea of the nature and size of the manuscript. It also provides information on the paper and writing implements used, the nature of the annotations, the collation of the manuscript, the stages in the compositional process, and the question of whether these stages are completely or only partially documented. It may also provide references to the final score and existing literature. This sort of information already offers an initial glimpse into the composer's creative process: manuscripts such as the second draft in short score

Luciano Berio Collection

Shelf mark: not applicable

Luciano Berio (1925–2003)
[**Requies** (small orch; 1983–5)]
Short score (2nd draft)

[s.l.][1983–5]
8 loose fols., 13 written pp. and 3 blank pp.; 46.9 × 32.3 cm

Fol. 1: beige manuscript paper, 44 lines (G. Ricordi & C. – Milano); loose-leaf; lead pencil, title added later in black felt-tipped pen; fols. 2–8: beige manuscript paper, 32 lines (Scomegna Casa Editrice Musicale L 32.60); loose-leaf; lead pencil

Fols. 1–8 recto: short score (2nd draft; inc.), paginated by Berio, pp. 1–8; from system 2 on p. 4 not used for definitive score
Fols. 1–3 verso: blank
Fol. 4 verso: unidentified sketches with information on orchestral scoring, presumably for an early version of *Requies*, paginated by Berio, p. 3
Fol. 5 verso: short score (1st draft; withdrawn), paginated by Berio, p. 2
Fol. 6 verso: short score (1st draft; withdrawn), paginated by Berio, p. 3
Fol. 7 verso: short score (1st draft; withdrawn), paginated by Berio, p. 6; discontinued on upper half of page
Fol. 8 verso: short score (1st draft; withdrawn), paginated by Berio, p. 1

Figure 2.2a   Catalogue entry for the short score of *Requies* conserved in the Berio Collection

Luciano Berio Collection

Shelf mark: not applicable

Luciano Berio (1925–2003)
[**Requies** (small orch; 1983–5)]
Full score (1st fair copy with corrections; fragment)

[s.l.][1983–5]
1 loose fol.; 2 written pp.; 42.6 × 30.0 cm

Beige manuscript paper, 44 lines (Star Nr. 197, 44 lines); lead pencil; annotations in red pencil

Fol. 1 recto: composition, mm. 1–5
Fol. 1 verso: sketch, opening to 7 mm. after letter J

Scoring (departs from definitive score): small orchestra: fl, pic, ob, eng hn, E♭ cl, B♭ cl, B♭ bass cl, 2 bn – 2 2 1 0 – 2 perc, pf, cel, elec org, harp – 4 4 4 3 2

Figure 2.2b   Catalogue entry for the first fair copy of *Requies* conserved in the Berio Collection

or the first fair copy in full score allow us to draw inferences about the existence of other sources. For example, as we can see from the pagination of the verso pages in the second draft (see Figure 2.2a), pages 4 and 5 are missing in the (withdrawn) first short-score draft, and they have not been handed down separately.[6] Again, although Berio started to write out an

Luciano Berio Collection

Shelf mark: not applicable

Luciano Berio (1925–2003)
[**Requies** (small orch; 1983–5)]
Full score (2nd fair copy with annotations)
'in memoriam Cathy Berberian | REQUIES | per orchestra da camera | Luciano Berio | (1983–85)'

[s.l.] 1983–5
44 loose fols.; 52 written pp. and 36 blank pp.; fol. 1: 64.0 × 43.8 cm; fols. 2–44: 63.8 × 43.4 cm

Fol. 1 = title page; beige manuscript paper, 48 lines with watermark 'Duraflex / C.M. Fabriano'; loose-leaf; lead pencil; all other fols. beige manuscript paper, 48 lines without watermark or name of manufacturer; loose-leaf; lead pencil with annotations in red pencil

Fol. 1 recto: title page
Fols. 2–44 recto: composition, paginated by Luciano Berio, pp. 1–43
Fols. 1–12 verso: blank
Fols. 13–20 verso: pre-ruled with bar lines, no clefs or musical annotations

Scoring: small orchestra: fl, pic, ob, eng hn, E♭ cl, B♭ cl, B♭ bass cl, 2 bn – 2 2 1 0 – mar, cel, harp – 8 8 4 (6) 4 (5) 3

Duration: 13′

Figure 2.2c   Catalogue entry for the second fair copy of *Requies* conserved in the Berio Collection

initial fair copy, only its first page has survived; all the other pages are missing, although it is unclear how many existed in the first place.[7] Moreover, as the first entry in our fragmentary catalogue description reveals, Berio reused the blank versos of pages written on a single side for sketches and drafts. It therefore seems as though some early stages in the compositional process only survived because he reused previously written pages to jot down his sketches or the second short-score draft.

One problem we quickly encounter when studying Berio's musical manuscripts is the incompleteness of the sources. A cursory glance at the published inventory reveals that sketches or drafts exist for only a small fraction of the nearly 100 works listed. A vast majority of the works in the Berio Collection are preserved in fair copies that not infrequently served as production masters for publication purposes and therefore do not convey any information beyond the printed scores unless they happen to contain revisions. Occasionally, as in *Sequenza V* for trombone (1966) and *Gesti* for alto recorder (1966), the fair copies represent preliminary stages of works that only reached their definitive text in the printed edition. Before we can decide whether these gaps can be filled from manuscript material preserved elsewhere, or whether we must learn to live with this state of affairs, we first have to form a picture of why the sources are incomplete. Does the explanation lie in the way they were transmitted, or did the composer (to quote the Swiss writer Hugo Loetscher) have a 'healthy relationship to the waste-paper basket'[8] that led him to discard extraneous materials as soon as they arose? Particularly in Berio's case, we know from his own testimony that he destroyed many sketches and drafts because he was only interested in the finished work – the aesthetic object – and not in its genesis. Thus, unlike Stravinsky or Bartók – or, to remain in Berio's generation, unlike Pierre Boulez, Karlheinz Stockhausen and Bruno Maderna – the documentation of Berio's compositional process is very incomplete. Consequently, the number of works that permit a study of his compositional process is comparatively small. It is only since the early 1990s, when Berio signed a contract with the Paul Sacher Foundation, that we more frequently find large sheaves of sketches and drafts.[9]

Once we have acquired an overview of extant sources on the basis of the available information, we must then clarify whether it is possible to obtain copies of the manuscripts in the form of microfilms, photographic reproductions or digital scans. Not every archive or library is willing to provide reproductions of musical manuscripts or other handwritten documents. The reasons for this are many and varied, and both legal and practical in nature. One of the most important is copyright legislation. Especially when dealing with documents from the twentieth and twenty-first centuries, we frequently discover that many documents are still protected by copyright and will continue to be so for a long time to come, thereby making it impossible for copies to be produced and distributed.[10]

INTERPRETING SOURCE MATERIAL

Let us assume that we have received a microfilm or photocopies of all the musical manuscripts connected with *Requies*. There are now many vantage points from which we can examine the material. In this case, our goal cannot be to retrace the compositional process in detail on the basis of all the extant manuscripts, incomplete as they obviously are. This goal must be set aside for a more extensive study. For the present, we will want to focus on two aspects: the structure of the text, and the chronology of the work's origin. Let us take the first of the eight pages of the second short-score draft as an example (see Plate 2.2). At first glance, this manuscript does not look like a typical short score. Nevertheless, that is how it was classified, for it sets down all the essential elements of the composition: the main melody, instrumentation cues in the form of English abbreviations (STR = strings, WW = woodwinds, TR = trumpet, etc.), the harmony, and the principal roots of the accompaniment parts. Judging from the character of the manuscript, with its sometimes hasty notation, deletions and so forth, we are definitely dealing with a draft rather than a fair copy. Equally obvious is the fact that it represents a preliminary stage *en route* to the fair copy and the resultant printed score. A study of the piece's subsequent history reveals that parts of the preliminary stage did not find their way into the definitive score. This second short-score draft was in turn preceded by an initial draft of which, however, only four pages have survived on the versos of the very manuscript we are looking at.

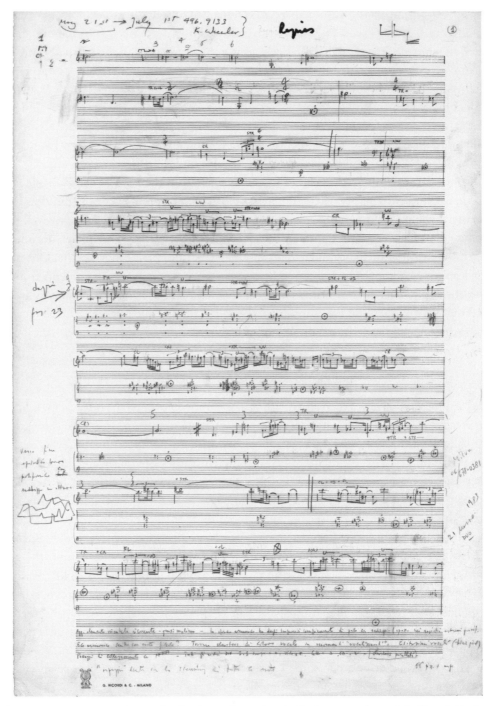

Plate 2.2 Luciano Berio, *Requies* for chamber orchestra (1983–5), short score (second draft), p. 1, Luciano Berio Collection, Paul Sacher Foundation, Basle

Our short score consists of several layers. First, it has a melody line written continuously on a single staff, with two other staves placed beneath it to accommodate the harmony of the texture in which the line is embedded. Second, there is a layer of corrections superimposed on the first draft of the music. At the very opening, for example, we find that the original beginning, with the C♯ in the first staff, has been extended by another bar with a fermata. This bar is notated in front of the staff with the bar number '1' along with a duration, rests and instrument cue (OTT[avino] = piccolo). The new bar numbers are restated up to b. 6 with digits placed above the respective bars. Further, we find such later emendations as the vertical double lines in the third and penultimate system, or the note 'Legni | pag[ina] 23' (woodwinds, page 23) in the left-hand margin, which refers to a lost manuscript rather than the definitive score. Third, the margins and the bottom of the page contain various verbal annotations. Several non-musical annotations in Italian and English relate directly to the context of creation (note the 'May 21st –> July 1st 496.9133 K. Wheeler' in the top margin, or 'Milva | 06/678.0381' and '1983 | 21 marzo | DUO' in the right-hand margin). This layer also includes the title entered in black felt-tipped pen at the top of the page – the only entry not in pencil. By the same token, the bottom page and left-hand margins contain lengthy shorthand verbal annotations directly related to the piece's compositional fabric. At the bottom of the page we read:

> Agg[iungere] elemento orientale ricorrente – quasi melisma – lo sfondo armonico ha degli improvvisi cambiamenti di peso con raddoppi (spesso nei registri estremi gravi). | Eco armonico scritto con note piccole? Trovare clusters di colori vocali su momenti 'vocalizzanti'. Esitazioni vocali (bird girl) | Passaggi di *collegamenti* su 🎵 – Tutti gli archi DIV[isi] I + II sempre a 4, viole a 4, celli a 3, CB a 2 clusters paralleli | 'arpeggi' lenti con lo scanning di tutte le note 🎵 pizz[icati] + arpa

> [add recurrent oriental element – quasi melisma – harmonic background suddenly changes weight with doublings (frequently in extremely low registers). | Write harmonic echo in small notes? Find clusters with vocal colours for the 'vocalising' elements. Vocal hesitations (bird girl) | Passages of *transitions* across 🎵 – All strings divisi I + II always a 4, violas a 4, cellos a 3, double basses a 2 parallel clusters | slow 'arpeggios' with scanning of all notes 🎵 pizzicati and harp]

In the left-hand margin in the bottom half of the page Berio wrote: 'verso fine | episodio tenore [?] | polifonico con | raddoppi in ottava' (towards end of episode polyphonic tenor [?] with doublings at the octave).

Such verbal annotations in Italian are important for an understanding of the music. Though difficult to decipher, they do not present an insurmountable obstacle even if the researcher does not know Italian, which of course would be quite helpful. For one thing, we gradually become familiar with Berio's handwriting and can make a useful translation especially of the shorthand notes by merely consulting a dictionary. For another, we can

Plate 2.3   Luciano Berio, *Requies* for chamber orchestra (1983–5), sketch, Luciano Berio Collection, Paul Sacher Foundation, Basle

always seek the help of native speakers of Italian. Finally, since the annotations relate directly to the music, our understanding of them will be facilitated by a detailed analysis of the score, which often spells out what they are trying to say.

Let us return to the question of chronology. Plate 2.3 shows a page from a sheaf of several leaves. At first glance, it looks like an early sketch of the melody line. What is puzzling, however, are the rehearsal letters, which exactly match those in the definitive score. A comparison with the short-score draft briefly described above leaves no room for doubt that this sketch did not originate until after the definitive score: not only does it present the opening in the definitive form found in the fair full score and the printed edition, it also contains many minor corrections to the melody as the piece progresses. Moreover, a cross-reference to page 19 ('pag[ina] 19') at the bottom of the page leads the reader to exactly the right spot in the fair copy of the orchestral score: the final bar of the sketch appears as the final bar on page 18 of the fair full score (four bars in front of letter K) and is indeed directly followed by page 19. The question therefore arises as to why Berio wrote out the entire melody line once again without instrument cues or harmonic context. One plausible explanation arises only on closer observation: roughly from the middle of the page, after letter E, pedal points and counter-melodies of various degrees of distinctness gradually come into play. This fact is directly related to the above-mentioned annotation in the left-hand margin of the short-score draft, where we can read that a polyphonic tenor with doublings at the octave is to appear towards the end of the 'episode'.[11] In short, Berio used this sketch to work out the definitive form of the principal melody and several passages of counterpoint.

Now let us take a look at a final page from the sketches and drafts (see Plate 2.4). Though the page is unpaginated, a comparison with the full score immediately reveals that it unquestionably belongs to the second short-score draft, albeit from a later stage in the creative process. It contains a large part of the music for the final section, namely, from four bars before letter U to five bars after letter W. Although a detailed discussion is impossible here, hardly any other page grants us such an unimpeded view of the composer's workshop. The first two systems were originally notated consecutively. Then Berio evidently decided, as we can see from his arrows and reference marks, to interpolate another section that he wrote out in the third system. Only then did he resume writing the music of the second system, using a fourth system located to the right of the verbal annotations. The fact that this page was left unpaginated, like the eight contiguous pages of the second short score, is an upshot of its genesis, for it contains music that was meant to replace sections discarded in the latter half of the work in the second short score (pages 4–8).

At this point, let us end our cursory glance at the comparatively complex genesis of *Requies* and turn, at least briefly, to the occasion and context that gave rise to the piece in the second place. The piece is dedicated to the memory of the soprano Cathy Berberian, Berio's second wife, from whom he had been divorced for many years. Berberian, an American soprano of Armenian extraction for whom the composer had written *Folk Songs* (1964)

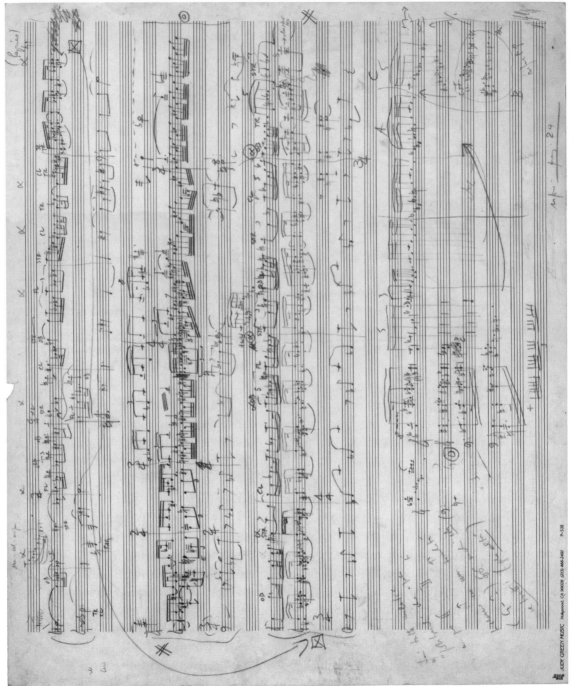

Plate 2.4 Luciano Berio, *Requies* for chamber orchestra (1983–5), short score (second draft), no page number, Luciano Berio Collection,

and *Sequenza III* for voice (1966), among other works, had died on 6 March 1983. As we can see from the date '21 marzo 1983' entered in the bottom right-hand margin in Plate 2.2, Berio obviously worked on the piece shortly after her death, even though it was only destined to be completed two years later. Later he wrote a brief article in the programme booklet for a fragmentary première of this commissioned work on 26 March 1984,[12] when it was performed in Lausanne by the Orchestre de Chambre de Lausanne, conducted by Armin Jordan. Here we read:

> A chamber orchestra plays a melody. More specifically it describes a melody, but only in the sense that a shadow describes an object or an echo describes a sound. The melody constantly unfolds, albeit in a discontinuous manner, through repeats and digressions around a changeable, distant and perhaps indescribable centre. / *Requies* is dedicated to the memory of Cathy Berberian.[13]

This introductory text relates directly to Cathy Berberian, whose voice may be said to be indirectly present in *Requies* as an ineffable but circumscribable midpoint. Moreover, some of Berio's verbal annotations regarding the compositional fabric on page 1 of the second short score (see Plate 2.2) only become fully intelligible in this context: the 'clusters with vocal colours for the "vocalising" elements' and the 'recurrent oriental element' undoubtedly refer to the national origins and the vocal art of the work's dedicatee.

PREPARATION FOR WORK IN ARCHIVES

Having finished our excursion into the study of the sources, let us return to our original question of how to prepare a visit to an archive. Provided the quality of reproduction is sufficient, microfilms, photocopies or digital scans of manuscripts are basically a very good means of conducting essential parts of a research project. However, no matter how we proceed with our work, we will sooner or later encounter two sets of problems: the order of the material on the microfilm or in the sheaf of copies, and the limits of photographic, photomechanical or digital reproduction.

Suppose we are dealing with sheaves of loose leaves rather than bound or at least paginated manuscripts. Here the manuscript itself usually offers no more information than the reproduction regarding the chronology of the work's genesis. Many sketches, unless they occur in a bound sketchbook, consist of unpaginated loose leaves and appear on the microfilm in an order usually set down by the archive during the process of cataloguing. If few or none of the leaves are dated, we first have to reconstruct the chronology from their contents, as exemplified above. The reconstructed order of the work's origin need not match the order in which the documents appear on the film.[14]

But the order of items on the film can also result from completely different factors. The film may have no further aim than to document the state in which the collection was received from the composer or his heirs, or it may function as a security copy without regard to the order of the items. In any event, to avoid drawing the wrong conclusions, the researcher must always ask: how does the sequence of documents in a folder or film relate to the chronology of their origin as reconstructed from the contents?[15]

Thus the same questions of order arise regardless of whether we are examining a microfilm or a sheaf of loose leaves. In contrast, the second set of problems only crops up in connection with reproductions. No matter how high their quality, even the best standard reproductions – apart from rare and expensive colour microfilms or high-resolution colour scans – convey an inadequate impression of many potentially important aspects of a manuscript. Contrasting layers of notation that would be immediately recognisable in a manuscript are often indistinguishable. Entries in coloured pencil or ink, though recognisable in grey tones, must always be verified by consulting the original. In the case of corrections, deletions, erasures or pastings, it is often difficult or impossible to tell from the film or copy with any degree of certainty what the composer has discarded. Questions of paper quality (including watermarks and formats) and the relation between leaves or fragments cannot be answered adequately, if at all, from reproductions. At some point, then, any detailed analysis will require a glance at the original manuscripts. To work with maximum efficiency in the archive, it is useful to keep lists of all questions and uncertainties arising from a study of the microfilms or photocopies in order to clarify or check them against the originals. If well prepared, such lists help to keep the time spent on archival work within convenient bounds.

As already mentioned, some libraries and archives are not willing to provide copies of musical manuscripts or other handwritten sources. In such cases, a visit to the archive is unavoidable in order to view the manuscripts. However, even when no reproductions are available and our preparations are limited entirely to existing descriptions, inventories, catalogues or secondary literature, we still have ways of obtaining a glimpse into an archive's holdings before our visit. Many scholarly publications, exhibition catalogues, sometimes even auction catalogues and programme booklets contain illustrations of musical manuscripts by the composer we are studying. Even when they come from a work outside our field of interest, they can still convey important impressions and discussions of the special characteristics of a composer's manuscripts or working methods. To remain with our example, a fairly large number of Berio's manuscripts are accessible in reproductions, at least in excerpt. Examples can be found in the exhibition catalogues *Komponisten des 20. Jahrhunderts in der Paul Sacher Stiftung* (on various works)[16] and *Settling New Scores: Music Manuscripts from the Paul Sacher Foundation* (on *Sinfonia*).[17] Others are reproduced in *Quellenstudien II: Zwölf Komponisten des 20. Jahrhunderts* (on *Sincronie*)[18] and in David Osmond-Smith's volume of interviews with Berio (on various works).[19] Such publications allow us to become familiar with the composer's handwriting, to confront problems of legibility and to decide whether there are any special prerequisites for a study of the sources, particularly regarding language. These publications, and especially their sections on source criticism, also enable us to situate our own project in the context of source research and to examine the existing research methods.

No less important than a study of source descriptions is a full acquaintance with the work both in score and in performance, assuming that it is available in a printed edition and recording. This preparation will make it much easier to identify creative stages, fragments and points of reference when working with sketches and drafts. If no printed editions or recordings are available in libraries or from retailers, it is always worth while to enquire from the publisher. Publishers are generally more than willing to provide scholars with a printed edition and, if unavailable elsewhere, a recording, even for works that are ordinarily only available on hire.

Knowledge is a crucial prerequisite for understanding the sources. Nevertheless, it is important to avoid being blinded by preconceptions. The key to success lies in engaging with the material and constantly asking whether our hypotheses actually agree with what we see in the manuscript. Previous knowledge is a *sine qua non* for understanding the manuscripts, of course; but to avoid the danger of selective perception, which merely confirms our preconceived notions, it is essential to question, again and again, our own received knowledge on the basis of the sources.

Having thoroughly prepared ourselves, it can still happen when we finally visit the archive that we first have to work from microfilms or some other form of reproduction, such as colour photocopies or photographs. Access to the actual manuscripts may only be granted for a brief period. The reasons here are not legal but curatorial in nature: especially if the documents are fragile, it may be necessary to limit work on autographs to an absolute minimum. When working with reproductions, the above suggestions continue to apply, the only difference being that it is easier in the archive to check problematical readings against the original.

CHAPTER 3

Archival etiquette

Therese Muxeneder

Research source material is always infused with cultural identity, and its historical meaning and value are documented in the way it is conserved. The structure of archives, which function as collections of unique objects bearing witness to a given tradition, reflects the historical, cultural and sociological preferences of specific epochs and prevailing ideological trends. The charisma and seductive power of such institutions are often based on the authenticity and uniqueness of their holdings. A discrepancy does however arise between the promise of preserving these holdings in pristine condition for an unlimited period of time and the fact that all such objects are confined to a finite existence. While it is difficult to stop the aging process of written documents or the material used to produce them, 'preventive conservation'[1] can slow it significantly. Two important preconditions for the preservation of cultural heritage and its transmission to the next generation are: (1) the creation of a procedural guide outlining the ideal conditions for the conservation of archival material, (2) a clearly defined archival etiquette, aimed at both archivists and users. Though the archivist is primarily responsible for the long-term survival of archival material, it is equally important that the user's responsibility be clearly defined. Like all scientific methods, restoration is based on a developing pool of knowledge, skills and techniques, which in the best of cases can slow the aging process. It should however be seen as the last of a series of measures undertaken to guarantee the future scientific usefulness of unique documents and other objects.

The interpretation of art is based largely on a thorough philological study of its source material. Every damage-induced modification diminishes the cultural, aesthetic and scientific value of archival and library material. The knowledge of certain fundamental conservation concepts, such as the physical characteristics of manuscripts, and strict regulations for protecting this material, constitute the basis of archival etiquette.

FUNDAMENTAL CONSERVATION CONCEPTS: THE MATERIAL AND ITS STORAGE

Next to mechanical damage inflicted on documents through improper handling, it is the aging process that is primarily responsible for transforming the flexible and complex substance of paper into a fragile and brittle material. For this reason, user contact with original documents must be reduced to a minimum and often completely eliminated. Furthermore, these documents must be subjected to a conservation process that ensures their long-term survival. The physical make-up of the paper in books and manuscripts produced in the late nineteenth and twentieth centuries explains why these documents are more at risk than a seventeenth-century drawing whose main physical characteristics have remained unaltered for centuries.

Paper, the principal vehicle for twentieth-century compositional source material, is made up of organic and mineral chemical compounds. Fibres and their bonding material represent the organic components of paper. They are what we see and feel, and as such constitute the physical mass of paper. The inorganic components include salts and other minor residues from the production process, such as fillers and pigments. Paper fibre is made of cellulose. Cotton and linen naturally produce an almost pure form of cellulose. The cellulose found in paper from the twentieth century is made mostly from wood pulp derived from resin-impregnated fibres. Containing up to 45 per cent cellulose, this macro-molecular material has a unique ability to build intermolecular hydrogen bonds, a necessary precondition for both the technical and physical aspects of paper production.[2] The higher the wood-pulp content, the less durable and white the paper. Two factors have a considerable influence on the durability of paper with high wood-pulp content: (1) the quantity of added cellulose, (2) the hydrophilic quality and bonding capacity of fibril.[3] Due to its large surface structure, fibril is quickly and strongly affected by cellulose networking reactions and degrades rapidly, setting off an ageing process in which paper becomes brittle and discoloured (yellow and brown), especially if it is of poor quality.[4] For instance, paper made from wood pulp with high lignin content has a short lifespan. Through currently available chemical procedures, the harmful contents of wood pulp in paper can be reduced or transformed in order to increase its durability considerably. These procedures are however both expensive and time-consuming.

Internationally accepted parameters governing the conservation of archival material have been established so as to slow the aging caused by both exogenous (the impact of environmental agents such as acidity, oxidation, the influence of humidity, light, temperature, dust, rust, insects, bacteria and moulds, as well as the degradation of pigments and varnish used in the printing process[5]) and endogenous (deterioration resulting from the paper manufacturing process) factors.[6]

Paper is a hygroscopic material. In other words, it can both absorb and, under certain conditions, release water. Normally, the water content of paper is around 10 per cent, but this percentage increases considerably when paper is exposed to greater humidity. On the one hand, high humidity in a storage space results in damage to all hygroscopic material, caused by micro-organisms and mould. On the other hand, insufficient moisture tends to make both organic and synthetic material more brittle. Under such circumstances, magnetic tape (particularly the older acetate cellulose tape), on which much twentieth-century audio-visual material has been preserved, shrinks. Internationally accepted norms recommend relative humidity values for the following materials: paper, 40–65 per cent; photographs, 50–65 per cent; films, 40–60 per cent; recording tape, 35–40 per cent (the latter constitutes compromise values for all types of recording material).

Plate 3.1   Vault of the Arnold Schoenberg Centre

High temperatures accelerate several chemical processes, which in turn cause organic material to age. Oxygen, humidity and light can cause oxidation and polymerisation. Photochemical reactions brought on by higher temperatures can cause writing materials and pigments to fade. In general, the cooler the storage room, the slower these chemical reactions. This is just as true for reactions due to endogenous causes (for instance, the presence of aluminium sulphate in paper) as it is for those due to exogenous factors (such as SO_2 in the atmosphere). Increased temperatures also encourage the growth of micro-organisms. As a rule, the optimum temperature for paper storage is between $18°$ and $20°$ C. The strict internationally standardised fluctuations in temperature (not more than $\pm 1°$ C.) and humidity (not more than $\pm 2–3$ per cent) on any given day tend to make it difficult to transfer archival material outside of the climate-controlled storage depots. The ideal, according to which the climatic conditions inside the 'vault' (see Plate 3.1) should also prevail in the manuscript viewing room, is of course utopian. The average room temperature in most buildings housing public collections is $22°$ C., and the fluctuation in humidity caused by ventilation and the changing seasons can be quite considerable. Water-absorbing material such as silica gel as well as humidifiers and dehumidifiers are generally not adequate replacements for a high-quality climate-control system. The most important factor to avoid is wide temperature fluctuations, which generate tension in organic material, resulting in damage such as rips and swelling. Thus, original documents start to be at risk long before the researcher comes into contact with these sources.

Another problematic factor for the long-term conservation of source material is light. Ultraviolet rays are a form of energy which generates heat and triggers photochemical processes on the irradiated surface. The shorter their wavelength, the more damage they do. These photochemical processes are influenced in turn by the presence of oxygen, humidity and other airborne contaminants. Almost all organic material is sensitive to light, which will alter both the colour and the consistency of the irradiated object in varying degrees. Paper, dyes and certain pigments, including inks, are among the most sensitive. Light recommended for manuscript material should have a maximum intensity (brightness) of $\lambda 50$ lux; its colour should be limited to a range of 300–400 nm and a power rating of 75μW/lm. Exposure to daylight should be avoided or reduced through the use of light-protecting, agent-bound screens or of glass laminated with a light-protecting film, for instance Plexiglas 201.

Chemical damage to source material takes place through contact with minute quantities of inappropriate substances derived from poor-quality cardboard, adhesive material, the stamping of documents and unsuitable storage procedures. This sort of damage as well as that due to endogenous causes (i.e. the gradual acidification of cellulose brought on by its alteration) can only be reduced through the application of airborne compounds. For packing and storing source material, the use of wood- and acid-free paper is compulsory.[7] Paper can be damaged when placed in poor-quality portfolios containing lignin and acids. The chemical processes started by these agents will damage the paper that is in the portfolio. Manuscript material should never be stacked in piles, and loose-leaf sheets should never be laid directly on top of each other. To prevent damage caused by rubbing and the contamination of healthy paper by previously damaged material, an acid-free sheet of paper should separate each individual document. The use of protective film should be avoided because condensation from this material caused by unfavourable climatic conditions can lead to discoloration and staining of the original document. It is also dangerous to wrap documents in a film because it will prevent the paper from 'breathing' normally, which in turn triggers the displacement of the paper's acidic components.

As well as meeting the above criteria regarding the optimal storage conditions for archival material, it is necessary to have the holdings inspected regularly by qualified restorers. This involves examining the physical status of conserved objects, deciding on changes to storage methods and recommending the restoration of certain items. These inspections also permit the early detection of damage to books, manuscripts and other autographs caused by insects (beetles, amoebas, silverfish, cockroaches) which attack pastes and glues, particularly in book bindings. Insects can also cause irremediable damage to the colours and pigments of manuscripts. In principle, the limits within which temperature and humidity may vary in the storage area also apply to the transportation of documents from that space to the viewing room, as well as to the viewing room itself.

NORMAL PROCEDURES FOR OBTAINING, VIEWING
AND HANDLING MANUSCRIPTS

For those wishing to consult manuscript collections, a written application with a brief description of research objectives and the list of required archival documents is mandatory.[8] Having submitted a complete application, the researcher should expect a written response indicating the availability of the required source material and the visiting hours of the institution. Depending on how the archive is organised, pre-registration is usually followed by recording user-identification data in a visitors' book or on catalogue cards for statistical purposes. In some cases references may be required. For instance, professors may be asked to sign statements on behalf of their students. When ordering up specific documents (be they originals or copies), a complete list of references must be provided. When necessary, correctly and clearly annotated concordant information concerning different sources should also be presented (i.e. work lists, complete works, critical reports, etc.). Normally, the user will only receive a limited number of archival objects at any given time. Secondary literature rarely includes complete information concerning sources. For this reason, curators should routinely carry out enquiries concerning catalogues and other finding aids.

Access to specific items may be restricted for the following reasons:

1. The object is currently being restored or is damaged, and its continued use would mean risking further damage.
2. The original is not needed because high-quality replacement material is available (Xerox copies, facsimiles, microfilms, digital copies).
3. The research project does not justify access to the original object, either because the formulation of the project is too vague or because the user does not appear to be sufficiently qualified.
4. Access may be restricted because of copyright or as a consequence of private ownership; copyright regulations often take time to work out, and access to private correspondence may be restricted for long periods of time.
5. Access to recently acquired collections may be restricted until they have been inventoried. Archives usually establish dates after which the material will be released for use. However, problems may arise prolonging the inventory process and thus pushing back the date. Certain researchers may nevertheless be given access to the material. These users, particularly those intending to publish information gleaned from material that has not been completely inventoried, should be forewarned that all preliminary classification systems (page numbering, the ordering of sketchbooks, etc.) could change significantly.
6. Lenders and donors may also establish specific restrictions.

Filming is of course a particularly effective means of preventing user-related damage. In principle, only secondary media (i.e. copies, microfilm, digital reproduction) should be provided for research involving unique, original documents. From a conservation point of view, the optimum situation would be to have all archival material used via these media. Presently, 90–95 per cent of all archival work can now be done using these media thanks to technological progress. Further progress will be made through the development of scientifically precise and reliable digital cataloguing methods. For economic reasons, however, archives housing large collections will only be able to establish such services over the medium and long term. The transfer of scientifically relevant information to digital formats is not only beneficial from a conservation point of view. Changes such as these are also potentially beneficial for research because they could reduce the need for time-consuming and expensive intercontinental travel and provide researchers with steady access to information outside of the regular opening hours of a given institution. Furthermore, the digitalisation of information contained in archival material and its transmission via the Internet should increase awareness of its cultural importance among a broader public, without diminishing the museological worth of this material. This is particularly true of music manuscripts. As opposed to the visual arts, the interest of these documents is primarily content orientated and less of an aesthetic nature.

Books, fascicles and loose-leaf sheets must always be carefully lifted from their shelves; bound standing objects must never be pulled by the top of the spine. Volumes next to the book should be pushed back so that it can be gripped in the middle. Unbound objects must always be retrieved by gripping the protective envelope, never the object itself. The same rules apply to the extraction of individual fascicles from their holder. Before replacing unbound objects in their holders, the documents must be carefully piled and replaced in the holder as a stack. The rules applying to the storage and removal of archival material must of course also apply to its use. Responsible handling of this material by the researcher is particularly important. The following rules should always be observed when using original sources.

1. Hands must be washed with neutral soap before touching objects (avoid creams and perfumes).
2. Food and drink are absolutely forbidden in archives and libraries.
3. Fingers must never be licked when turning pages. Even when clean, bare hands may transmit acidic substances to paper. To avoid bringing archival material into contact with dust particles and micro-organisms caught in fingerprints, archives should provide users with special gloves made of white cotton. An exception to this rule may be made for particularly fragile documents, which could be damaged by contact with the textile. Laying strips of acid-free paper under individual pages enables users to turn them without actually touching the sheet. Another protective measure to be considered by curators is the reversible encapsulation of frequently used objects in acid-free synthetic material such as Mylar.

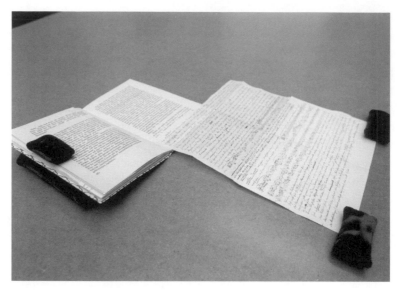

Plate 3.2   Proper viewing of source material

4. Avoid contact between the face and the manuscript via the hands (by rubbing eyes for example). Avoid visiting archives when ill.

5. Making notes or leaving marks on archival objects is of course strictly forbidden. Measuring tools should be supplied by the archive. Always take notes in pencil. Pens and other writing implements, which leave permanent marks, are forbidden because they may cause unintentional damage to original documents.

6. Working surfaces must always be kept clean and smooth. Eraser rubbings should therefore not be allowed to accumulate on working surfaces.

7. Archival material should immediately be replaced in folders and boxes once it is no longer being used to avoid subjecting the material to overly long periods of strong lighting. The user should never pack and unpack source material. This should be the archivist's responsibility.

8. Contact between manuscripts and incompatible material (acidic paper, paste, Post-its, metal clips, etc.) is to be avoided.

9. Never press or lean on archival material with elbows or fingers. Occasionally, small velvet-covered bags of sand are used to support the weight (see Plate 3.2).

10. Manuscripts should only be touched to turn a page.

11. When working with paper, care must be taken not to make marks through careless and unnecessary handling. Manuscript pages should be raised using both hands (see Plate 3.3). The palms should support the sheet from underneath with thumbs holding the edges. Lifting and turning by gripping corners with two fingers can lead to the

Plate 3.3   Proper handling of manuscripts

wrinkling and ripping of the paper. Bound sheets should also be turned with both hands under the page.

12. Oversized sheets must never be allowed to hang over the edge of tables or other work surfaces.
13. When reading, documents should never be held, and the binding must never be leaned against table edges. Bound objects will sometimes be placed on book holders to protect bindings from too much strain (see Plate 3.4).
14. Documents must always be left in the order in which they were received, even when this order contains errors. Archivists are always pleased to be informed of errors in classification.

WORKING EFFICIENTLY IN ARCHIVES: PREPARATION, LEGAL QUESTIONS, CATALOGUES AND COLLABORATION

'Success in consulting primary sources depends upon the cooperation of the researcher and the archivist.'[9] Nonetheless, the user's ability to work efficiently at an archive depends primarily on the degree to which the research project has been properly prepared. The better the preparation and the more specific the questions (whether related to the archival material or to the research project as a whole), the easier and more profitable communication with the archivist or librarian will be. The user must always treat an archivist responsible for collections, whose functions go well beyond the conservation and unpacking of source

Plate 3.4   Proper viewing of bound objects

material, as a scientifically competent colleague. The user should also keep in mind that the successful study of primary source material depends, not on the quantity of archival material examined, but rather on the relevance of its contents for the research goals.

The proper administration of cultural artefacts does not just involve their conservation and protection. It also implies interpreting their contents (in the form of indexes, catalogues and content descriptions), preparing the documents for researchers and the interested public and promoting this material via media such as microfilms, facsimiles and digital means. Attaining these ideal goals can often lead to conflicts of interest, particularly with twentieth-century works still protected by copyright. The interests of the composer, the heirs or the publisher may, when combined with the curator's concern for conservation, create considerable barriers hindering the proper exploitation and promotion of archival material. Libraries and archives do not necessarily own all of the material they conserve. Long-term loans and gifts may be accompanied by restrictive provisions, which may contradict the institution's normal working procedures. All users who need to be aware of them should be informed of such provisions. As well as attempting to establish a minimum of accessibility while respecting provisions such as these, it is incumbent on the archivist to explain clearly any limitations on the use of archival documents, so as to protect the composer, the heirs, the user and the owner.

Whether the methodology is primarily philological or analytical, the acquisition of knowledge is essentially based on the study and interpretation of documents or other objects providing information about a work or its historical context. These sources include not only material concerning the genesis of the work, which refers to compositional technique or to the chronological phases through which the creative process took place, but also a wide range of documents connected to the broader context (texts, published material containing autograph notations, letters, recordings, etc.). It is the responsibility of the archivist to gather knowledge concerning both the range and the content of this source material as well as possible methods for its interpretation. Before the user begins to work at the archive, it is incumbent on the archivist to provide information on the range and dates of existing catalogues, as well as the latest changes made to lists, inventories or other publications concerning the source material. This information should include the location, call number and dates of all finding aids, the enlargement or deterioration of a collection, the absence of specific documents because of restoration, authentication procedures, foliation, corrections and bibliographic data. The user should also be informed about the existence of parts of the collection that are not yet accessible and of any other secondary source material among the archival holdings or elsewhere, which might be useful.

Having researchers fill out clearly formulated questionnaires can improve both the structure and efficiency of their work during a period of study at an archive. However competent and far-sighted an archivist's help may be, it cannot replace the user's own research. This is particularly true because the archivist's viewpoint of the user's object of study is primarily focused on the holdings of which he is in charge, and information available elsewhere will not necessarily be provided. Even in cases where the archivist provides substantial amounts of help and support, the user should never be given the impression that too many questions have been asked. The energy and care which the archivist can devote to a specific problem is dependent not only on his or her willingness to cooperate, but also on the frequency of other users' demands and the archivist's own work (i.e. the preparation of exhibitions and publications, restoration-related work, the interpretation of collections, cataloguing, etc.). The archivist's duty is to inform the researcher of knowledge gaps. On the one hand, overestimation of the archivist's own abilities, or even pretended competence, or underestimation of the user's competence, careless use of finding aids, withholding information and unreasonable restrictions on the use of conserved material should not occur in the day-to-day use of archival documents. On the other hand, there are also limits to the amount of help archivists can provide. It is not up to the archivist to decipher sections of text or even entire documents which the user finds illegible. Also, occasional help with specific problems must not be transformed into general responsibility for solving all problems. The researcher should be informed of problem areas or questions which were not necessarily covered in the initially proposed research programme, as well as of source information of which he or she may not be aware. The archivist should also inform the user of the possible irrelevance of certain documents for the proposed research project as well as of the latest literature and ongoing research projects related to the user's work. All necessary technical means of using conserved material (microfilm reading devices, light tables, audiovisual equipment, etc.) should be put at the user's disposal in the most convenient way possible.

Only when the archivist understands the priorities of scholarly research and the user realises the importance of 'preventive conservation' for the maintenance of the collected objects can both work, each mutually assisting the other in the task of interpreting the sources which bear witness to our culture.

CHAPTER 4

Coming to terms with the composer's working manuscripts

Friedemann Sallis

> On s'éloigne par là des conditions 'naturelles' ou ingénues de la Littérature, et l'on vient insensiblement à confondre la composition d'un ouvrage de l'esprit, qui est chose finie, avec la vie de l'esprit même, lequel est une puissance de transformation toujours en acte.
>
> Paul Valéry, 'Au sujet du Cimetière marin'

> [*We thus move away from the 'natural', guileless conditions of literature, and unconsciously we begin to confound the composition of a work of the spirit, that is a* finite *object, with the life of the spirit, which is a power of transformation always in action.*]

TERMS AND CONCEPTS

The terminology of sketch studies is complex. With regard to music, the vocabulary, which gradually came into place during the nineteenth century, consists of a hodgepodge of terms borrowed from art history and literary criticism that seems to defy clear definition. And yet, a good understanding of both the terms and the concepts we use to classify and qualify the composer's working documents is indispensable if we are to make sense of the enormous quantities of manuscript material now being made available for research. This chapter will examine not just the words used to describe this material but also the concepts underlying them and how these concepts have changed as they passed from the nineteenth to the twentieth century. In this endeavour, reference will be made to parallel developments in literary criticism. To be sure, literary and musical manuscripts are in many ways fundamentally different. Nonetheless, the scholarly examination of these documents appears to have been organised along parallel tracks, with literary criticism often one step ahead of musicology.

Taken together, the terms sketch, draft and fair copy are generally understood as encapsulating the stages through which a work of art comes into existence. They indicate the degree of completion of the content they are purported to contain or transmit. As such they constitute what David Perkins has called an imprinted taxonomy: a classification system based on a hermeneutic circle, requiring names, a concept and a corpus subsumed within the concept. In studying these documents our reasoning moves from one to the other, reinforcing both the validity of the concept and influencing our perception of the corpus.[1]

Taxonomic systems such as these tend to be resistant to change, and in this case the resilience of the system is reinforced by the ubiquity of the terms. They are found in all branches of the fine arts and in all major European languages. And yet, the idea that a musical sketch, draft or fair copy can be defined systematically is an illusion. First, the variety of documents subsumed by these terms is extraordinarily large, mirroring the capacity of composers to imagine novel ways of transmitting their ideas. Also whereas the term fair copy refers to a particular document with a specific function, the term sketch refers to an activity as much as it does to the documents produced by that activity. Though we often assume it to be a preliminary act, composers usually sketch throughout the creative process. The György Kurtág Collection of manuscripts of the Paul Sacher Foundation conserves numerous proofs and printer's copies on which the composer continued to sketch out alternative solutions to compositional problems. Second, the working methods they reflect and the musical thought they transmit differ not only from one composer to the next, but can also vary greatly within the career of a single composer. By comparing the note heads of György Ligeti's working documents spanning the period from 1956 to 2000 (Plates 4.3a, 4.4 and 4.5), one can easily see that they were written by the same hand. However, the compositional style and technique presented in these documents are extraordinarily divergent. Third, the nature of the preliminary working documents also depends on the scope of the compositional project. Sketches for a bagatelle and an opera will appear very different. Fourth, the terms refer not only to the content of documents, but also to the manner in which they were written. Whereas sketches can be so hastily written that they are often impossible to decipher, a fair copy is expected to be clearly legible.

The sheer diversity of these documents is such that attempts to develop abstract definitions always seem woefully inadequate.[2] However, the suggestion that, because a clear distinction between sketches and drafts cannot be rigidly maintained, they should be lumped together in one category containing all preliminary working documents is also unacceptable.[3] Archivists, grappling with the problems of classifying vast quantities of manuscripts, and analysts, attempting to trace the genealogy of a given work among this material, require terms that allow them to differentiate one document from another.

In the following pages we will examine documents chosen from among the Kurtág and Ligeti manuscript collections conserved at the Paul Sacher Foundation. Notwithstanding the fact that these items, like all manuscript material, are highly idiosyncratic, they are also representative of the working documents produced by those composers, who to this day, continue to use pen, pencil and paper to work out their ideas.

SKETCH (FR. *ESQUISSE*; GER. *SKIZZE*; IT. *SCHIZZO*)

The term sketch covers a vast array of diverse types of manuscript documents. Everything from the barest jottings, tracing a thin melodic outline, to pages of densely written, systematic attempts to work out complex compositional problems can be legitimately included under this heading. The material used to conserve these musical ideas is just as varied as their content. Though traditionally written on staff paper of various sizes, sketches can be found on any type or form of paper, from the back side of shopping lists, to notes scribbled in the margins of books. In 1993, Kurtág composed the piano piece *Sorok Sirokay Zsuzsinak* (Lines for Zsuzsa Sirokay), published in *Játékok VI*, on Post-its. The choice of writing material reflects both the mobile form of the piece and, more generally, Kurtág's move towards an open work-concept in the late 1980s.

Sketches are private documents, not normally intended for public scrutiny, and their function is primarily mnemonic.[4] Composers usually write down that which cannot be committed to memory. Consequently, this material is inherently fragmentary and inevitably incomplete. Related to this point is the fact that sketch material usually focuses on difficult problems encountered by the composer. Other less problematic aspects are often written out only in the last stages of the process. Thus, even in those cases where large quantities of dated sketch material have been conserved, the idea that the creative process can be completely reconstructed is a chimera. As Joseph Kerman has pointed out, this material presents evidence of the stages which made up a compositional process rather than the process itself.[5]

Despite their ephemeral nature, sketches can provide considerable amounts of information on a range of subjects related to the creative process. Plate 4.1 presents sketches pertaining to 'Leoparden' (Leopards), the fifth song of the last section of Kurtág's *Kafka-Fragmente*, Op. 24. The page contains three sketches. The first, in the upper left-hand corner, was written in pencil and completed on 13 September 1985. On the following day, Kurtág continued his work with a second sketch at the bottom of the page in blue and orange ink dated '14 IX d.e.'[6] The abbreviation stands for the Hungarian word *délelott*, which means forenoon or morning. Finally, a third sketch was added in the upper right corner on the same day. In this case, d.u. stands for *délutan*, meaning afternoon. Though rare in the sketches of most composers, this precise chronological information became a systematic feature of Kurtág's compositional technique from the 1980s onwards.[7]

The sketch is representative of Kurtág's compositional technique in other ways as well. The antecedent phrase of the song (see the bottom staff of Plate 4.1) emerges out of a simple arpeggio figure written at the top of the page in pencil. The process is intuitive, hesitant and seems worlds away from the systematic, pre-compositional planning undertaken by many composers of the same generation.

Sketch material can also include or be made up entirely of verbal remarks, plans, drawings, scribbling, schemata, charts, lists, inventories, mathematical calculations, algorithms, or anything else the composer might find useful for the elaboration of his or her ideas. Plate 4.2 presents early sketches of schemes for the polyphonic distribution of the texts and the organisation of the voice entries of the Kyrie from György Ligeti's Requiem. Though the text distribution was modified in the final result, the sketches bear witness to the fact that the principles of symmetry and balance are profoundly embedded in Ligeti's musical thought and appear to be operative at the earliest stages of the creative process.

Plate 4.1   György Kurtág, *Kafka-Fragmente*, Op. 24, for soprano and violin (1985–7), sketches for 'Leoparden', György Kurtág Collection, Paul Sacher Foundation, Basle

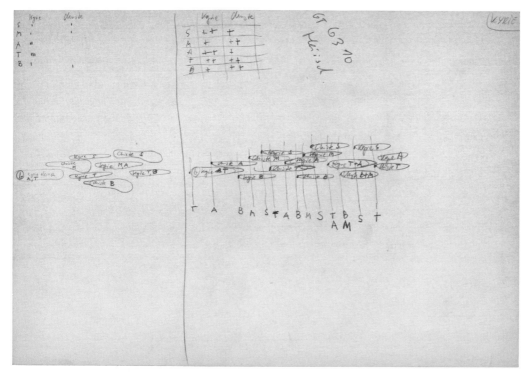

Plate 4.2   György Ligeti, Requiem for soprano, mezzo-soprano, double choir and orchestra (1963–5), sketches for the Kyrie, György Ligeti Collection, Paul Sacher Foundation, Basle

DRAFT (FR. *ÉBAUCHE/BROUILLON*; GER. *ENTWURF/ERSTE NIEDERSCHRIFT*; IT. *ABBOZZO/PRIMA STESURA*)

Whereas sketches are normally incomplete and often extremely fragmentary, drafts present a work project or a section thereof that has achieved some degree of completion. In the continuity draft of Ligeti's 'Tanc Dal' (Dancing Song) from the song cycle *Síppal, dobbal nádihegedüvel* (With Fifes, Drums and Fiddles), the vocal line is written out in full with an incomplete percussion accompaniment. Compared with the fair copy, one notes that the composer modified significant aspects of the song, notably the metric organisation (see Plates 4.3a and b). Nevertheless, the first document gives us the impression that having completed the vocal line, Ligeti was in possession of the piece.

Thus the draft occupies a middle position between the mnemonic sketch on the one hand and the finished fair copy on the other. It marks the point at which the idea of a work takes on some form of written existence. Consequently, of all the composer's preliminary documents, it is the most difficult to identify. Plate 4.4 presents the opening section of Ligeti's *Variations concertantes* for chamber orchestra, one of numerous works left unfinished because of the upheaval brought on by the Hungarian Revolution and the substantial changes his

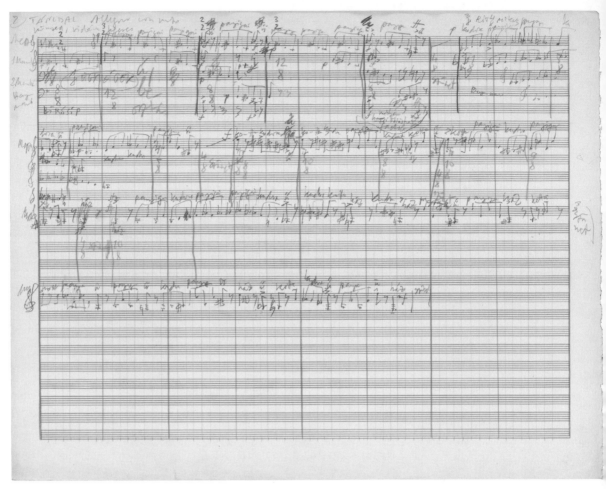

Plate 4.3a   György Ligeti, *Síppal, dobbal nádihegedüvel* (With Fifes, Drums and Fiddles) for soprano and percussion (2000), 'Tanc Dal' (Dancing Song), draft, György Ligeti Collection, Paul Sacher Foundation, Basle

compositional technique was then undergoing. The document is a short score or *particella*.[8] The term refers to manuscripts containing a condensed version of a work for mid- or large-sized ensemble in which the music is compressed on to a few staves, usually two or three. During the years immediately preceding the Hungarian uprising, Ligeti was attempting to integrate aspects of dodecaphonic technique into his work. Each voice is based on the so-called all-interval row. Whereas rhythm, nuance and counterpoint receive a great deal of attention, orchestration is only sporadically indicated (note the abbreviations referring to string instruments at the bottom right of the page, Br = *brácsa* [viola]).

Given the manner in which the document is written and the fact that the work was never completed, we might be inclined to classify this document as a sketch. However,

Plate 4.3b   György Ligeti, *Síppal, dobbal nádihegedüvel* (With Fifes, Drums and Fiddles) for soprano and percussion (2000), 'Tanc Dal' (Dancing Song), fair copy, bars 1–19, György Ligeti Collection, Paul Sacher Foundation, Basle

Plate 4.4   György Ligeti, *Variations concertantes* for chamber orchestra (1956, unfinished), short score, bars 1–26, György Ligeti Collection, Paul Sacher Foundation, Basle

a subsequent unfinished copy of the same music in full score is also conserved at the Sacher Foundation. Though written in pencil, it has all the hallmarks of a fair copy. The fragment is carefully written and it has a degree of completeness that suggests that Ligeti was in fact attempting to set down the definitive version of this section of the work. From a melodic, harmonic and rhythmic point of view, the full score neatly reproduces everything written down in the short score. Indeed, the short score contains a far more complete rendering of Ligeti's idea of the opening of *Variations concertantes* than the draft of 'Tanc dal' does of that song. Thus, the short score can be seen either as a sketch for an unfinished work or a draft of the first section of the work. The decision will depend on what the analyst is looking for and the perspective he or she brings to the documents. This sort of terminological ambivalence will be familiar to all those who have spent time studying sketches and highlights the fact that terms used to classify the composer's working documents cannot be pinned down with specific definitions.

Plate 4.5 is a page from a draft of the Kyrie from Ligeti's Requiem. Written within a decade of the short score of *Variations concertantes*, it shows how far his compositional technique had evolved in a relatively short time. Whereas the former can be understood either as a sketch or a draft, the latter can be placed at the border between draft and fair copy. The two examples allow one to apprehend the range of documents which can be legitimately classified as drafts.

The manner in which a composer consigns musical ideas to paper can be useful because it sheds light on the composer's priorities, underlying assumptions and unconscious givens, which may not be visible in the final version of the score. Though the page corresponds closely with the same bars of the published score, the document also shows that as he wrote it out, he was still refining duration and density of attack. The encircled numbers written on the staves of the four tenor parts indicate the numbers of quavers in a given duration and the numbers without circles above the alto and tenor parts indicate the number of attacks per half-bar. These indicators allowed Ligeti carefully to control the pitch structure of the dense clusters.[9] This aspect of his compositional technique is difficult to grasp from the published score alone. During this period of his career, Ligeti developed procedures which he would apply systematically within a given work. He would however tamper with details, often making the procedure unrecognisable in the end result.[10] Consequently, documents such as this draft can be crucially important for those interested in understanding the structural underpinning of works produced during this period.

FAIR COPY (FR. *MISE AU NET*; GER. *REINSCHRIFT*; IT. *BELLA COPIA*)

Whereas sketches and drafts are private documents, the primary function of the fair copy is to transmit a specific work to the outside world. For this reason, we expect the document to be complete and clearly written (see Plate 4.3b). Normally a fair copy is written in the hand

Plate 4.5   György Ligeti, Requiem for soprano, mezzo-soprano, double choir and orchestra (1963–5), Kyrie, draft, bars 11–15, György Ligeti Collection, Paul Sacher Foundation, Basle

of the composer. This is however not always the case. Two of the movements constituting the fair copy of Ligeti's *Mátraszentimrei dalok* (Songs from Mátraszentimre) for children's or women's choir (1956), were copied by the composer's wife. The terms autograph and holograph are used to specify the authorship of manuscript documents. Whereas the former is defined as a manuscript written in the hand of a known person, the latter is a manuscript written wholly in the composer's hand. In practice, both are used to indicate manuscripts of musical works written in the hand of the composer.

The term fair copy indicates not just a cleanly written score, but more importantly the authoritative source of the musical idea or content of the work. It is often used as the score at the first performances and is the primary point of reference by which we judge success of the first and subsequent interpretations of the work as well as the accuracy of published versions of the score. Given the complex and innovative notation used to transmit much of the last century's new music, many works have been published as facsimiles of the fair copy (see the study scores of Ligeti's *Aventures* and *Nouvelles Aventures*).

During the nineteenth century, German musicology developed numerous terms to designate the various types of final manuscripts, all of which serve as vehicles for more or less complete versions of a given work: *Reinschrift* (fair copy), *Fassung letzter Hand* (the final handwritten version), *Widmungsexemplar* (dedicatee's copy), *Druckvorlage* (printer's score). Traditionally the term *Reinschrift* is used in the singular because, as mentioned above, it is considered to be the authoritative source for a given work. Roman Ingarden has observed that a musical score, including the composer's fair copy, is in fact only a schematic rendering of the composer's ideas and cannot be considered identical with the work itself.[11] As precise as Ligeti's fair copy of 'Tanc dal' is (Plate 4.3b), there remain aspects of the music which are not specifically notated, such as the colour of Hungarian vowel sounds. This discrepancy between the score and the work as a sounding object effectively cancels the notion that one document can definitively represent the composer's idea of the work and undermines the corollary concept of the *Urtext*.

BETWEEN PHILOLOGY AND EPISTEMOLOGY

To this day, the study of the composer's working documents remains influenced by procedures, scholarly habits and modes of thought inherited from the discipline of philology. Defined as a science of language with particular interest in the history of texts, one of its main tasks has been the reconstruction of lost documents. By meticulously comparing the conserved copies of a lost original, philologists construct a stemma, i.e. a chronological ordering of copies creating an arborescent history of the transmission of the text, the purpose being the establishment of an authoritative version of the original.[12]

Before the end of the eighteenth century, interest in the composer's working documents was scant at best and the conservation of such manuscript material that did survive appears in many cases almost accidental. With the rise of Romanticism, which brought with it the cult of the genius, the originality postulate underlying the notion of the great work of art and the gradual introduction of copyright, these documents acquired new value. Starting in the nineteenth century, composers like Robert Schumann, Felix Mendelssohn and Johannes Brahms began acquiring and studying the manuscripts of Johann Sebastian Bach, Wolfgang Amadeus Mozart and Ludwig van Beethoven to uncover or reconstruct the uncorrupted versions of past masterpieces.[13] Philologists and historians interested in music quickly followed suit. Though attention focused mainly on fair copies and final versions, Friedrich Schleiermacher (1768–1834) observed, in his *Lectures on Aesthetics* (published posthumously in 1842), that sketches can provide the scholar privileged access to what he called the artist's *inneres Urbild* (the inner original conception). Before the work becomes manifest as a material object, it exists in the mind of the artist and something of its essence begins to appear in the sketch material once a certain degree of completion has been attained.[14] Of course, this cannot simply be read out of the sketch. According to Carl Dahlhaus, Schleiermacher contributed to establishing the fundamental axiom of historical hermeneutics: that surviving texts remain partially obscure after an initial naive reading and do not disclose their full meaning until their historical preconditions and implications have been thoroughly analysed.[15]

By moving backwards from the work through the autograph fair copy, the drafts and the sketches, nineteenth-century scholars felt they could gain a glimpse of the creative personality of the artist. Evidence for this can be found in the writing of Otto Jahn (1813–69), a trained philologist best known for his biography of Mozart. Jahn was one of the first to make extensive use of manuscript material (both letters and sketches) as an important source of information on the composer. Referring to Beethoven's sketches, Jahn stated that they provided him with a glimpse into what he called the composer's *geistige Werkstätte* (spiritual workshops). In a letter, he wrote, 'I have not only discovered much that is new [about Beethoven], but [I have] made connections between what is known, and so worked myself into the detail of his existence that it is as if I knew him and lived beside him.'[16] Gustav Nottebohm (1817–82), who undertook a ground-breaking study of Beethoven's manuscripts, agreed with Jahn that the composer's sketch material does permit a better understanding of the composer's creative personality and his working methods. However, he also explicitly rejected the idea that sketches can be useful in understanding what he called the spirit of the work:

> They [Beethoven's sketchbooks] show the fragmentary origin and the slow growth of a composition. For us, this type of working causes some puzzlement. The puzzlement lies, in the first and last instance, in Beethoven's battle with his daemon, in the struggle with his genius. . . . The spirit [Geist] that dictated the works does not appear in the sketchbooks. The sketchbooks do not reveal the law by which Beethoven was led in working. They can give us no conception of the idea, which appears only in the artwork itself. They [the sketchbooks] cannot lay the whole process of creation before our eyes, but only single, unconnected events from it.[17]

At the turn of the century, a number of factors contributed to broadening the scope of what could be accomplished through a study of the composer's working documents (cf. chapter 1). Nottebohm's reservations were ignored or simply forgotten as the work of musicologists, such as August Halm (1869–1929) and Heinrich Schenker (1868–1935), focused increasingly on questions of form and structure. As a result, the terms and concepts developed during the nineteenth century were adapted to new purposes as can be seen in László Somfai's work with Béla Bartók's manuscripts. Contradicting Nottebohm, Somfai asserted that the careful examination of Bartók's surviving manuscripts can reveal the composer's 'hidden concepts' and 'the spirit of the work'.[18] In order to access this information, Somfai developed a theoretical model with which he organised Bartók's working documents into 'source chains': chronological sequences of documents leading from that 'exceptional moment of inspiration caught "in the act"',[19] to the definitive version of the composition that would provide the basis for the publication of Bartók's complete works. Though used in ways that could hardly have been imagined 100 years earlier, both Somfai's methodology and his goals call to mind the stemmatics of nineteenth-century philology.

During the second half of the twentieth century this traditional approach began to be questioned and contested. In her study of Arnold Schoenberg's twelve-tone works, Martha Hyde warned against an over-emphasis on chronology.[20] She classified the working documents pertaining to the *Suite*, Op. 25 for piano in four categories: (1) row sketches; (2) row tables; (3) compositional sketches; (4) form tables and charts. Schoenberg used these documents more or less simultaneously, and, according to Hyde, their rigid chronological classification can lead to a distorted picture of the composer's development.[21]

Despite their differences, both Somfai and Hyde implicitly agree that information extracted from sketch material can be useful as supporting evidence for the analysis of music. From this point of view, sketch material is used most efficiently when employed to reinforce previously established analytical hypotheses, developed within a highly defined theoretical framework (i.e. Bartók's style at a given point in his career or Schoenberg's dodecaphonic technique). But what of music created outside of such frameworks? Gianmario Borio has turned the above postulate around, arguing that for much of the new music written during the second half of the twentieth century, sketch studies have become the condition *sine qua non* for the posing of valid analytical hypotheses. In his work with Luigi Nono's sketches, Borio reveals compositional techniques, strategies and concepts which though neither audible in a performance of the work nor visible from an examination of the published score, are nevertheless important if we are to come to a proper understanding of the work.[22]

Problems involved in studying compositions based on open concepts of form provide another case in point. Though this concept has become one of the central categories of much innovative music written since the 1950s, the analytical study of so-called open works has remained problematic. Umberto Eco observed in the early 1960s that the very existence of openness in Western art 'rests on the dialectics between the work itself and openness of the readings it invites. A work of art can be open only insofar as it remains a work; beyond a certain boundary, it becomes mere noise.'[23] In other words we must identify the work as such before we can begin to discuss the degree to which it is open. But how are we to recognise the formal boundary or apprehend the internal coherence of compositions which by their very nature defy formal unity? Eco suggests that the comprehension and interpretation of open works can be best achieved by 'retracing the formative process'.[24]

Going one step further, the proponents of genetic literary criticism in France have suggested that the time has come to abandon the blinkers of traditional philology and move to a broader approach. Rather than focusing on the 'author of a text', we should be looking at the 'writer in the midst of an open-ended creative process'.[25] Laurent Jenny has observed that the practitioners of genetic criticism can be divided into two opposing groups. On the one hand, the geneticist of the text confronts a process and a product in an attempt to establish an interpretation of the latter via an examination of the former. On the other, the geneticist of writing seeks to understand the process of creative thought, using the traces of its wanderings. Such an approach recalls the poetics of Paul Valéry, which appear to be just as interested in mechanisms of the productive literary 'mind' as in the literature which that mind has produced.[26] This sharp division is in fact overstated. Sketches produced as part of a creative process are collected only after a creative artist has actually produced something of interest and the knowledge of that production inevitably acts as a background against which the working documents are studied.

Nevertheless, seen from the perspective of a composer in the midst of an open-ended process, sketch material appears as the vast underside of creative activity out of which individual works emerge rather like the tips of icebergs. This is an apt description of the Kurtág Collection of manuscripts conserved at the Paul Sacher Foundation. In 1999, the collection contained over 15,000 pages of manuscript material directly related to compositional activity.[27] The approximately 50 works, which Kurtág has allowed to be published, are tributary to an enormous network of musical ideas linking the public side of his work with unpublished compositions and unfinished projects. Musical ideas and entire pieces can lie dormant for years before turning up in entirely new works. For example, the last movement of *Hommage à R.Sch.*, Op. 15d for clarinet (also bass drum), viola and piano went through a number of radical transformations before it finally became part of this work, the first performance of which took place in 1990. The music first appears in 1976 as unfinished sketches of a piece for piano and trombone. One of these sketches is entitled *Nagy Sirató* (Great Lament), referring to the Hungarian version of the age-old oral tradition of expressing bereavement through song. In 1979, this same music was adapted for alto flute, trombone, guitar, harp and piano to become the sixth and final movement of an unpublished version of *Grabstein für Stephan*. Kurtág withdrew this work, which exists in the form of a series of six drafts, one for each of the movements. Ten years later, these drafts served as the basis for two different compositions. On the one hand, Kurtág completed a new version of *Grabstein für Stephan* (Op. 15c for guitar and groups of instruments), based on material from the first movement of the rejected version. On the other, the draft of the last movement of the rejected version of *Grabstein für Stephan* became the first eight bars of the last movement of *Hommage à R.Sch.*, entitled 'Abschied (Meister Raro entdeckt Guillaume de Machaut)' (Farewell [Master Raro discovers Guillaume de Machaut]).[28] Rather than discovering teleological source chains, the study of Kurtág's sketch material reveals a complex web of hermeneutic and structural relationships, which may or may not impinge on our apprehension of the completed work. The perspectives gained from the study of this material do however greatly enrich our understanding of the technical and aesthetic contexts out of which it emerged.

Paradoxically, the more knowledge we gain of a composer's failed initiatives, interrupted developments, abandoned fragments, short cuts, dead ends, etc., the more this knowledge seems to undermine the very notion of the musical work as an isolated, self-enclosed aesthetic object. The problem is in fact more imagined than real and, as Dahlhaus has pointed out, results from a shift in perspective:

> That the work of the composer ends where that of the listener begins – with the completed work – is the tangible and banal exterior of the psychological fact that composers not infrequently tend to assign more significance to the process of creation, to the genesis of a work, than to the result, and sometimes in fact so emphatically as to make it seem that the objectification of the compositional process in a structure that outlives it signifies an alienation of art from its true being. The composer conceives of the work, which presents itself to the listener as an unbroken façade, as of a process which in reality is never-ending. And sometimes he is reluctant to come to an end because this also implies renunciation. Some of the possibilities that began to appear as the work progressed remain unrealised. They are sacrificed to the closed nature of the work, which almost always has attached to it an element of violence.[29]

This shift in perspective is the result of a broader understanding of creative activity and undermines the argument that the study of the preliminary working documents of writers or composers has been or will be reinvented *ex nihilo*. On the contrary, the terms and concepts we use to apprehend this material are intimately bound up with the achievements and failures of the past. If we continue to use them, we should remain conscious of the fact that they are tainted by their own historicity. To suggest (as do some proponents of genetic criticism, deconstruction, new musicology and other so-called post-modern perspectives) that this inheritance can be simply abandoned is naïve.

It is perhaps no accident that these new perspectives on old problems have been generated in the late twentieth century. As noted above, the concept of the open work and the perspectives gained from the study of the composer's working documents tend to feed off one another in a kind of reciprocal relationship. Reading the composer's manuscripts is not unlike reading *Finnegans Wake*. In both we find a labyrinthine network reflecting what is actually embedded in the poetics of the composer's work.

CHAPTER 5

The classification of musical sketches exemplified in the catalogue of the Archivio Luigi Nono

Erika Schaller

Scholars undertaking sketch studies of music composed during the second half of the twentieth century often find themselves confronted with vast quantities of source material. Changes in compositional technique as well as the accessibility of inexpensive writing material and photocopiers have led to a proliferation of written documents during the compositional process. Furthermore, awareness of not only the academic but also, in some cases, the financial worth of autographs means that composers and the administrators of their estates carefully conserve all written material. This state of affairs offers great opportunities for the academic study of music because the creative process can be more thoroughly reconstructed. However, the examination, intelligent organisation and interpretation of this abundant source material also pose enormous challenges. For one thing, the musicologist is faced with documents, which, to a large extent, were intended exclusively for private use. For another, depending on the composer's working methods, this material provides no clear information as to why it was created and has neither been dated nor systematically classified.

Such a situation prevails to a large extent in the sketches and music manuscripts of the Archivio Luigi Nono in Venice (hereafter abbreviated as ALN).[1] More than 20,000 sheets of paper are conserved here, referring to both completed and unfinished compositions.[2] So as to provide scholars with access to these sources, a specialised database has been established. The data entry form is presented in Figure 5.1.

The development of a specialised cataloguing system for the holdings of the ALN was motivated by the fact that there are no universally accepted guidelines for classifying musical sketches. Existing procedures for cataloguing music manuscripts are generally based on collections dating from the Middle Ages and early modern periods, and can only be applied to twentieth-century source material with many reservations.[3] Archives housing collections of twentieth-century material usually limit their cataloguing efforts to describing their holdings in detailed inventories. The sheer quantity of material conserved at the ALN rendered such an approach unsatisfactory because it could not provide a clear overview of the documents contained in the collection.

The following description of the database developed for the ALN is intended to make the users of such research tools aware of the various cataloguing categories and their significance. It may also be helpful for colleagues faced with the task of cataloguing an as yet unordered corpus. Given the increasing complexity of compositional procedures, archivists and librarians

1. Call number	2. Location of the original
3. Work- or project title	4. Version

5. Writing material	6. Number of sheets	7. Format	8. Type of paper	9. Condition of the writing material	10. Script and fonts

11. Content

12. References					

13. Comments	14. Archivist
	15. Date of the catalogue entry

16. Detailed description of the contents

Figure 5.1   Data entry form for musical manuscripts conserved at the Archivio Luigi Nono
(simplified version)

often turn to musicologists because the challenges of cataloguing twentieth-century source material can be overwhelming. The categories presented here are also applicable to other types of catalogues and inventories based on lists and card catalogues. However, for organising large quantities of information, databases present advantages which can hardly be overestimated.

THE CLASSIFICATION OF MANUSCRIPTS

In the case of extensive musical estates, the call number is particularly significant. It not only enables the user to find the original document but also establishes a mark of identification providing a reference for a source, which, unlike a book or a signed text, cannot necessarily be identified by author, title, place or year.

Most of the manuscripts conserved at the ALN are preliminary documents created during the course of work on a completed composition or an unfinished project. A completed composition is defined as a work which has either been performed or published in the form of a printed score. Given that musicological research often focuses on a specific work or group of works, the work-concept has been given a major role in the organisation of source material, and this is reflected in the way call numbers are structured. All manuscripts related to a completed composition begin with the same two-digit work number. Work numbers are ordered chronologically. Consequently, the *Variazioni canoniche sulla serie dell'opus 41 di Arnold Schoenberg* for orchestra (1950), Nono's first performed work, bears the number 01 and his last published work, *'Hay que caminar' sognando* for two violins (1989), is numbered 61. All works uncovered since the establishment of the ALN database have been given subsequent numbers. For instance, *I turcs tal Friul*,[4] recently discovered incidental music for the theatre written in the 1970s, has been given the work number 62. The same numbering system has been applied to unfinished works. In this case the letter 'P' prefixes the two-digit work number. Ordering work projects chronologically has however proven to be a far more difficult problem. Most unfinished works remained unknown outside of the composer's immediate circle of friends and colleagues. Sketches pertaining to these unfinished works are scattered throughout the collection, so that previously unknown work projects are continuously being discovered. Consequently, the numbering serves primarily as an unequivocal identification of the material and only reflects the chronological position of these projects in a very limited way.

Work and project numbers are followed by two-digit numbers separated by points. These numbers identify subgroups of sketch material. Sheets within these subgroups are numbered consecutively and are separated from the subgroup number by a slash. Thus 01.01/01 means the first sheet of the subgroup 01 of sketches for the *Variazioni canoniche*.

As noted above, Nono generally did not date his sketches and drafts, making reconstruction of the various stages of his creative process problematic. For this reason, sketches are organised into subgroups based primarily on the content of the documents and only secondarily on chronological criteria. Figure 5.2 shows how varied the sketch material in different subgroups can be.

At the ALN, sketch subgroups with the lowest call number usually contain pre-existent material with which the composer constructed his works. This may consist of texts, works by other composers, songs, scales or rhythms. Often, this material was chosen at the beginning of the compositional process. Notes and underlined sections in books and scores also belong to this type of sketch subgroup. In the case of the *Variazioni canoniche sulla serie dell'opus 41 di Arnold Schoenberg*, this particular subgroup is absent, as the Nono estate contains no copy of Schoenberg's *Ode an Napoleon Buonaparte*. However, for *La fabbrica illuminata*, many

Variazioni canoniche sulla serie dell'opus 41 di Arnold Schoenberg **for orchestra (1950)**	*La fabbrica illuminata* **for soprano und tape (1964)**
01.01/01-13: Sketches: mainly pitch organisation.	27.01.01/01-129: 3 brochures on working conditions of employee of the Italsider steel foundry in Genoa, 1961. Notes on the selection of specific passages for the composition.
01.02/01-02: Sketches: orchestration.	27.01.02/01-106: 2 collections of the journal *Sindacao moderno*, Rome 1963. Isolated comments.
01.03.01/01-10: First and second drafts of the first movement; sketches for the first draft.	27.01.03/01-42: Documents published by the Workers' Union of Italsider, 1963. Notes on the selection of specific passages for the composition.
01.03.02/01-06: Sketches for the second movement.	27.01.04/01-26: Various political texts, most of which concern the steel foundry Italsider. Few comments.
01.03.03/01: Sketches for the third and fourth movements.	27.01.05/01-40: Brochures of the Steel Workers' Union. Few comments.
01.04: Probable first draft of the entire work.	27.01.06/01-11: Divers political texts concerning the situation in steel foundries. Few comments.
01.05/01-05: Attempts at writing a fair copy of the full score.	27.02/01: Cesare Pavese, *Poesie edite e inedite*, Turin 1962, p. 176: *Due poesie a T., Le piante del lago*. Notes on the selection of verses for the composition.
01.06.01/01-155: Parts for the first performance with comments added by the musicians.	27.03/01: Work timetable (27 April 1964 to August 1964) for completion of *Da un diario italiano*. To this point the theme of the factory in Genoa was planned as the second act.
01.06.02/01: Folder which contained the parts.	27.04/01: Undated letter written by Giuliano Scabia and addressed to Nono with suggestions concerning the structure of the work's contents.
01.07.01/01-02: Notes for the reconstruction of the full score from the autograph parts.	27.05/01-14: Drafts of the text by Scabia and Nono for section 1.
01.07.02/01-32: First draft of the reconstructed full score.	27.06/01-27: Drafts of the text by Scabia and Nono for sections 2, 3 and 4.
01.08.01/01: Draft of the title page for the reconstructed full score.	27.07/01-10: General reflections concerning themes and scenic realisation for a new music theatre. The theme "Fabbrica" is mentioned for the first time.
01.08.02/01-15: Fair copy of the reconstructed full score.	27.08/01-07: Sketches concerning form, instrumentation, themes, content, scenic realisation, text declamation, use of tape recorders, amplifiers and the placement of speakers in the performance space.
	27.09.01/01-31: Sketches for the tape: recordings made in the Genoese steel foundry. Elaboration of various types of material.

Figure 5.2   Subgroups of sketch material for *Variazioni canoniche sulla serie dell'opus 41 di Arnold Schoenberg* for orchestra (1950) and *La fabbrica illuminata* for soprano and tape (1964)

	27.09.02/01-25: Sketches for the tape: vocal material.
	27.09.03/01-28: Sketches for the tape: assemblage of the recorded choral music, relationship between the solo voice and tape.
	27.10.01/01-18: Sketches for the choral music of section 1.
	27.10.02/01-04: Sketches for the solo part of section 1 and the beginning of section 2.
	27.11/01-02: Sketches for the solo part of sections 2 and 3.
	27.12/01-03: Sketches for the solo part of section 4.
	27.13/01-03: Various notes of minor importance.
	27.14/01-12.: Parts of a fair copy of the choral music in sections 1 and 2. Attempts at writing this fair copy.
	27.15.01/01-05: First draft of the solo part of section 1. Various attempts at writing this draft.
	27.15.02/01-02: First draft and probably the second half of a second draft of the solo part of section 2.
	27.15.03/01: First draft of the solo part of section 3.
	27.15.04/01-13: Various drafts for the solo part of section 4; sketches and attempts at writing drafts.
	27.16/01-03: Attempts at writing the fair copy of the solo part.
	27.17.01/01-11: Photocopy of the fair copy of the solo part with comments by Nono and the singer Carla Henius, probably concerning the first performance.
	27.17.02/01-15: Photocopy of the fair copy of the solo part with comments by Nono and the singer Carla Henius, probably concerning the first and subsequent performances.
	27.18/01-41: Score for the electronic sound projection and an attempt at writing out this score.
	27.19/01-05: Technical schemes for sound projection in *La fabbrica illuminata* and other works by Nono involving taped music.

Figure 5.2   (*cont.*)

such documents have been conserved, such as union pamphlets and flyers collected by Nono during his visits to steel foundries, as well as a book of poetry by Cesare Pavese from which the composer chose the text for the last part of the work. This material is arranged in seven catalogue entries, as can be seen in Figure 5.2.

The next subgroup of sketches usually contains transcriptions from pre-existent sources, which Nono attempted to integrate into the new composition, through analysis and regrouping. The working documents pertaining to the *Variazioni canoniche* contain a large group of sketches, through which the basic tone row of Schoenberg's Op. 41 is analysed and permutated. The sketch material of *La fabbrica illuminata* contains various drafts of the text involving factory documents and Pavese's poetry (27.04–27.06). Following this are subgroups of sketches, which deal with the work as a whole (i.e. instrumentation, formal outlines and scenic considerations).

An important part of Nono's compositional method, which often preceded the writing out of the full score, was the production of tape-recorded material intended for use during performance. In works from the 1960s and 1970s, this recorded material served on many occasions as a kind of framework, within which the parts presented live by soloists and orchestra were set. As a result, sketches dealing with music, which will ultimately be recorded in an electronic studio, are given lower catalogue numbers than drafts, written on staff paper, of the same music which will be performed live. This ordering was applied to the working documents of *La fabbrica illuminata* even though the chronology of the creative process differed in this case. In three exercise books (27.09.01–03) containing notes on producing taped material, there are also instructions for recording a choir, whose music had already been notated in full score. This choral score was nevertheless given a higher catalogue number (27.14). In the end, cataloguing must be based on clear, systematic criteria because an exact chronological ordering is rarely possible.

For the same reasons, the chronological stages during which the full score was written out (i.e. which movement was written first) are also not reflected in the call numbers. Nono composed most of his works from beginning to end, and his surviving sketch material has thus been systematically organised in this sequence, with sparsely notated material generally preceding longer, more elaborate drafts. For *La fabbrica illuminata*, there exist different sorts of loose-leaf sketches pertaining to the choir and solo parts of the first section (27.10.01–02) and to the solo parts of sections two, three (27.11) and four (27.12), as well as some unidentified and apparently insignificant material (27.13). Following this are various drafts on staff paper of the choral part (27.14) and of the solo parts of sections one to four (27.15.01–04), numerous unsuccessful attempts at writing out a fair copy of the soprano solo part (27.16) and two photocopies of the fair copy of the work (27.17.01–02). A score for the sound projection (27.18) and different schematas for distributing the sound during the concert performance (27.19) are to be found at the end of this omnibus volume.

The genesis of the *Variazioni canoniche* presents far fewer stages of development. All sketches and drafts pertaining to the four movements of this work are catalogued from 01.03.01 to 01.03.03. The entry number 01.04 is an exception in that it refers to a draft of the full score, which is the property of the Paul Sacher Foundation. Thus the catalogue contains extensive information concerning not only the ALN holdings, but also all known manuscripts conserved elsewhere. Incomplete attempts at writing the fair copy can be found under the entry number 01.05. As the original fair copy is lost, the entries 01.06.01–02 contain only the instrumental parts. In 1985, Nono used these parts to reconstruct a new fair copy of the full score. All material used to do this, including the reconstructed score itself, is classified under the numbers 01.07.01–02 and 01.08.01–02.

From these few examples, it should now be clear how varied the sketch material pertaining to specific works by Nono can be. Consequently, the coherent grouping of this material cannot be organised according to a predetermined set of principles. On the contrary, while bearing in mind certain basic rules, this material must be handled flexibly.

CATALOGUING PROBLEMS AND SPECIAL CASES

A work-centred cataloguing system such as the one developed at the ALN offers many advantages, the foremost of which is that it places sources at the user's disposal, based on their content. Such a system is however inherently problematic because in the act of structuring the catalogue, the archivist will inevitably have to interpret material that cannot be unambiguously classified. Users must therefore be constantly aware of the fact that the sources they are working with have not been placed in some kind of definitive, organic order. Other interpretative criteria would justify different classifications of the same material. Extensive cross-referencing within the catalogue, as well as the multiple cataloguing of material related to more than one work, should remind the user of this problem.

The sketches pertaining to *La fabbrica illuminata* present a good example of this type of problem. This work was originally conceived as part of a music theatre project entitled *Da un diario italiano*. Consequently, it would seem logical to give one work number to all material related to this project. In the end, however, *La fabbrica illuminata* became a work in its own right. The rest of the surviving documents related to *Da un diario italiano* refer mainly to three large-scale choral pieces, of which only one was completed. It received its first performance only after Nono's death. Given the vastly different performance histories of these works and the heterogeneity of the material, specific call numbers have been allocated to both *La fabbrica illuminata* and *Da un diario italiano*. Certain sketches are, however, pertinent to both compositions, notably the time plan presented in Plate 5.1. On the one hand, the Roman numerals refer to the four choral pieces originally planned for *Da un diario italiano*. On the other, the indication *per Genova* (for Genoa) refers explicitly to *La fabbrica illuminata* because it was to have been first performed there, as a fragment of the new composition for music theatre.[5] This page, numbered 26.22/01, was placed in the collection of documents related to *Da un diario italiano* because it was originally written with this work in mind. However, a photocopy of the same page, numbered 27.03/01, can also be found in the material related to *La fabbrica illuminata*.

A further cataloguing problem is posed by sketchbooks and notepads containing references to more than one work or work project. With individual pages, copies can be made and

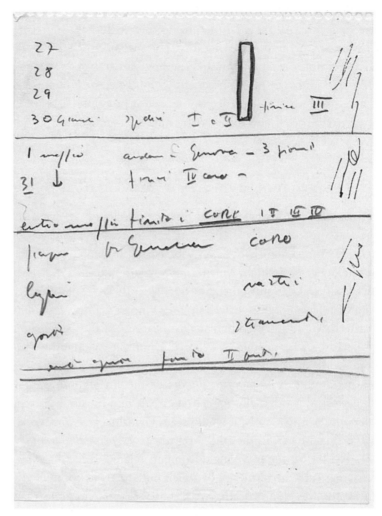

Plate 5.1   Luigi Nono, *Da un diario italiano*, work timetable, Archivio Luigi Nono © Eredi Luigi Nono

placed in different omnibus volumes, as is the case with sketches referring to more than one work. However, given the large number of sketchbooks and notepads conserved in Nono's estate, this solution was neither practical nor reasonable.

In order to deal adequately with this problem, a secondary database was developed which permits sketch material in sketchbooks and notepads to be precisely differentiated and easily located. Each sketchbook and notepad is given a specific call number and catalogue entry: B.01, B.02, etc., for *blocco* (notepad) and Q.01, Q.02, etc., for *quaderno* (sketchbook). Individual sheets from notepads and sketchbooks are then divided into various subgroups

Call number

08.03/01-23

Work title

La victoire de Guernica

Source	Number of sheets	Format (in mm.)	Type of paper
Single sheets	1	235 × 146	Blspqu
Notepad	1	270 × 220	Blqunote, B.02; f.01v
Single sheets	21	270 × 220	Blqunote, B.02

Contents

Sketches dealing with pitch organisation

Reference

B.02

Figure 5.3   Extract from the catalogue entry 08.03

and given appropriate call numbers according to the work or work project to which they refer. Users of ALN holdings normally consult high-quality colour photocopies of the original document. The copied sheets of sketchbooks and notepads can thus be divided among the various works and work projects to which they refer. The physical description of the manuscript and the double numbering of the copied sheets allow the user to recognise the sketchbooks and notepads from which the photocopies have been made. Should the user wish to know more about the contents of the entire sketchbook or notepad, this information is available via the call number provided for each sketchbook and notepad. For instance, under the number 08.03/02, the verso of page 01 from the notepad numbered B.02 contains sketches for the pitch organisation of *La victoire de Guernica* for choir and orchestra (1954) (see Figures 5.3 and 5.4). This notepad also contains sketches for the ballet *Der rote Mantel* for choir and orchestra and *Canti per 13* for chamber ensemble, written respectively before and after the completion of *La victoire de Guernica*.

It is undoubtedly good, user-friendly practice to include the work title with the call number in every entry. Long-standing catalogues of musical manuscripts list not only the definitive title of a given work but also provisional titles found among the preliminary working documents. The ALN catalogue has dispensed with titles of this sort, because most of Nono's sketch material conserved here is untitled. Descriptive titles which differ significantly from the definitive title will occasionally be mentioned in the content description of the sketch material.

Call number

B.02

Document description

Notepad 02

Source	Number of sheets	Format	Type of paper
Notepad	45	270 × 220	Blqunote, B.02

Content

B.01v: Sketches dealing with pitch organisation for *La victoire de Guernica* (08.03/01);
b.02r–40r: Row tables for *Der rote Mantel* (10.03/10-48);
b.41r–43r: Row tables for *Canti per 13* (12.01/17-19);
b.44v–45: Row tables, presumably for the third act of *Der rote Mantel* (10.03/49-50).

Reference

08.03	10.03	12.01

Figure 5.4   Extract from the specific database for notepads and sketchbooks, entry B.02

Whenever possible, sketches for incomplete projects are listed under the title appearing in these documents, even when it was clearly provisional. When more than one title occurs in the sketch material, the title chosen will be either the one occurring at the latest compositional stage, or, in the absence of chronological data, the most frequently occurring title. As opposed to definitive work titles, provisional titles always appear in quotation marks.

Chronological data are generally not used in the ALN catalogue because only about one-tenth of the sketch material conserved here is dated to a specific year. The chronological information which does occur is normally mentioned in the description of the contents of a given manuscript.

As a rule, sketches of different versions of a work can be clearly differentiated. Nono often modified scores after the first performance. For example, *Diario polacco '58*, initially composed for orchestra in 1959, was revised in 1965 for orchestra and tape. This later composition bears the same title and corresponds in large part to the original. Consequently, the field entitled 'version' (see Figure 5.1) has been introduced so as to differentiate sketches for the later version from those pertaining to the original. Sketches pertaining to the first version of *Diario polacco '58* are identified as the 1959 version, indicating the year of the first performance. Sketches pertaining to the revised version are marked '1965'.

THE PHYSICAL APPEARANCE OF MANUSCRIPTS

Compositional sketches can be found on the most varied types of writing material: in books, scores, individual sheets of staff paper, writing paper, etc. As mentioned above, users at the ALN normally consult high-quality colour photocopies of the original documents. Knowledge of the physical appearance of the original manuscripts allows the user to develop a precise idea of their condition. This information can in turn be used to draw conclusions concerning both the dating and the content of the manuscripts. For instance, notes found in the books of Nono's personal library usually belong to an early stage of his compositional process. As he read texts, which he felt he might set to music, he often notated general ideas concerning instrumentation, expressive characteristics and form in the margins of the book. The description of writing material should be limited to a standardised list. This is particularly important when establishing a database, because it allows search engines to seek out specific types.

When cataloguing manuscripts, one usually counts sheets of paper rather than pages. As mentioned above, this standard has been adopted by the ALN because counting by pages suggests an organised sequence of written documents, which, even in the case of Nono's sketchbooks, is generally not the case. Empty sheets are not counted. Their presence is simply indicated in the general comments concerning the condition of the writing material.

The format of writing material provides hints not only about the quantity of information on a given document, but also, under certain circumstances, about the contents of the document. For example, when Nono sketched orchestral works on small-format staff paper, his treatment of the orchestra was normally conventional. However, in his late work he often used large-format staff paper because the instruments were treated as soloists.

The precise description of the type of paper used by the composer has proven to be a relevant factor in the identification and dating of sketch material. Nono used different sorts of paper in the various phases of his compositional career. A specific call number is ascribed to each paper type, creating a database of all paper types contained in the composer's estate (see Figure 5.5).

As well as measurements, this database contains precise descriptions of the physical documents. These descriptions are made up of information concerning paper type (staff paper, unlined letter paper, etc.), the number of staves, lines or squares per sheet, watermarks, inscriptions and the surface condition of the sheet. In the case of manuscripts, whose contents cannot be identified, this type of information may indicate to which group of documents the sheet probably belongs. A careful description of the paper type can also help to establish the authorship of unidentified typescripts.

The physical description of the paper can provide information as to where the work was written. For example, most of the sketch material pertaining to the incidental music for a production of William Shakespeare's *As You Like It*, which Nono wrote in 1954, is written

Call number	Lines/staves	Watermarks
Blqunote, B.02	63 × 55	

Type of Sheet
Medium-sized, individual sheets, squared paper, in a bound notepad

Measurements	Surface conditions
27 × 22	Squares slightly tilted on a greyish surface

Inscription page one	Inscription page two

Used for
La victoire de Guernica, Der rote Mantel, Canti per 13, Liebeslied

Comments

Figure 5.5   Extract from the database of paper types contained in the holdings of the ALN (simplified presentation): entry for Notepad 02

on paper used for no other work. This suggests that the music was written in Berlin on paper purchased there, where the play was staged, rather than in Venice where the composer then resided.

As is the case with types of paper, the writing implements used by Nono also changed during the course of his career. The majority of his sketches and drafts are written in colour. Whereas the use of coloured pencils predominates in material from the 1950s, felt-tipped markers began to be used in the 1960s. Sketches from the 1980s, written predominantly with markers, display a far broader palette of colours. It would no doubt be helpful to create a database with a specific call number for each type of writing implement. Such a database has not yet been integrated into the ALN catalogue because the categories already contained in the existing database have provided a satisfactory solution to classification problems. However, the systematic identification of writing implements would allow for a more detailed analysis of the archive's holdings.

As well as noting the presence of empty pages in sketchbooks and notepads, the field marked 'Condition of the writing material' (see Figure 5.1) also contains comments on the physical condition of the writing material. Here we find information such as the presence of holes made by drawing pins, damage caused by clips and staples, and paper fragments pasted on to the sheet. This information can reveal much about the composer's working methods and give an idea of the importance of certain documents. Nono habitually pinned particularly important sketches to his study walls so that they would be constantly present during the compositional process. As a result, documents containing drawing-pin holes can be assumed to have been very important for the composer as he worked out the composition.

The field marked 'Script and fonts' (see Figure 5.1) provides information concerning the authorship of given documents. When preparing the texts or scenic drafts for theatrical works, Nono often worked intensively with writers, stage directors and designers. It is thus important to distinguish between the various types of handwriting one encounters in sketch material. As was the case with paper types, it is also useful to create a standardised list of handwriting types, which can be expanded as needed.

CONTENT DESCRIPTION AND DATABASE MANAGEMENT SYSTEMS

Each catalogue entry should present a summary description of a given document's content. As was the case with paper and handwriting types, this information should be standardised so that it can be retrieved by automatic search engines. For instance, the names of authors whose texts were used by the composer should be systematically listed. Many researchers at the ALN examine the settings Nono made of texts and are naturally interested in any reference to a specific author made in the conserved documents. Another keyword which has proven particularly useful for dealing with the manuscripts of the ALN is the term 'scenic realisation'. Even though Nono produced only two works for musical theatre in the strict sense of the term, he was continually engaged with plans for various projects involving some kind of theatrical production. Indeed a significant number of his completed compositions were initially conceived as works for the stage. In the case of *La fabbrica illuminata*, for example, considerations concerning the eventual staging of the work also play an important role in the early phases of the compositional process. The drafts for such scenic productions can be particularly important for researchers interested in twentieth-century theatre studies.

Keywords should of course refer as specifically as possible to the material being described. Sketches made for the preparation of magnetic tapes or for the use of electronic instruments in real time should be identified as such. It is also useful to indicate the instrument for which the sketch was intended. In the case of Nono's sketches, this would require a great deal of work and consequently has not yet been undertaken.

The ALN catalogue provides additional space for detailed descriptions of the contents of manuscripts. This field has been established for visiting scholars who wish to contribute supplementary comments under their own signature. Tentative transcriptions of illegible manuscript passages can be listed under this rubric. Such fields are normally not completed by the archivist, whose role should be limited to exact description rather than detailed interpretation of source material.

Cross-references allow the archivist to clarify the close connections, both in terms of chronology and content, which can often be established between different works and work projects. Chronological connections occur where two independent sketches for different works are found on the same sheet. In the ALN catalogue, short comments on connections such as these are to be found in the field marked 'Comments'. Crucially important connections concerning content are indicated in the field marked 'Content'. The call numbers of sketch material for which connections have been established are to be found under the heading 'References'. This procedure gives the user an efficient overview of the relationships linking the documents at hand with other ALN holdings.

No catalogue should be without a field in which the archivist can make miscellaneous comments which do not belong in any other field. For instance, this field may contain information concerning the unusual places where sketches have been found (i.e. sheets laid between the pages of a book or a score), the relationships with other manuscript collections or the provenance of sketches which have been given to the archive.

Knowing the author (archivist) and date of a given catalogue entry can be useful when ambiguous or contradictory information turns up. Not only does the user know to whom to turn when faced with a problem, but he or she can also reconstruct the state of research, when a given document was initially catalogued. Research always brings forth results requiring the revision of earlier catalogue entries. Database management systems, which provide automatic dating for all entries, are particularly useful in this regard.

Libraries, archives, businesses and, lately, even individuals now use databases to catalogue their possessions. The market currently offers a growing number of programs, which are constantly evolving. Consequently, only certain basic functions common to most databases, and which underscore the relative advantage of this technology over traditional lists and card catalogues, will be presented here.

1. Each category contained in a database must be separately retrievable by a search function. For example, in a database containing the categories 'author' and 'title', the program should be able to locate all the works by a given author without listing all titles in which the author's name happens to be mentioned.

2. The search function should allow for a simultaneous search within different categories. This means that the program should find all entries referring to a specific work by a given author, even though author and title appear in different categories.

3. A sorting function is especially important when working with databases of information from sketch material. One should be able to consult entries classified either by call number or chronologically.

4. Database management systems should enable complete entries as well as the information contained in specific fields to be copied so that repetitive data need not be rewritten every time.

5. The database should allow for the transfer of selected information to other databases. Expanded or simplified databases can thus be established for a specific task or shared with other researchers. In the case of databases created or maintained by a team of individuals, the possibility of importing information is also a worthwhile consideration.

6. Working from prepared lists of standardised information saves time when entering information in the database. It also guarantees the uniformity of the database and enlarges the program's search capacity. The same applies to the automatic entry of information.

The basic functions presented above greatly simplify the work of the archivist, while providing the user with quick, direct access to stored information. This technology is particularly useful for scholars dealing with questions that go beyond a specific work. The linking of databases from different collections would open up new perspectives on contextual issues and historic relationships. For instance, by connecting the databases of all archives that conserve sketch material, one could obtain an overview of compositional activity during a given period of time. Projects such as this are now within reach, given the fact that many database systems now commercially available can be sent and received over the Internet. In the future, musicologists should be able to prepare their research projects efficiently at their personal computers, which will make their work in archives and libraries less time-consuming and more efficient.

CHAPTER 6

Digital preservation of archival material

William Koseluk

The process of digital preservation, that is, the creation of computer-based images of actual source material, is now well established, and the equipment and methods associated with it are widely known. Its usefulness should be clearly evident to the scholar, though development in the arts, particularly music, has been slow. This chapter will examine various approaches to digital archiving, with a brief summary of the basic techniques involved, and an overview of how all this may be of use. It should encourage scholars to learn that this area is not overly complex, and to inspire further exploration. Few specific products, brand names or manufacturers need to be mentioned, as these particulars are subject to constant change and are consequently irrelevant in an extended perspective. This discussion will also touch upon the basic strategy of material distribution, and offer a perspective on its ultimate usefulness, in both a broad and narrow context.

Before proceeding a caveat is in order. While those who promulgate technology are quick to embrace its utility and excitement, it is important to understand its limitations and shortcomings. Digital archiving allows for wider dissemination of original source material since access to distant archives can be problematic, and digital data are surely one type of permanent record, but it is never a replacement for the genuine source. The limitations of image resolution – the amount of an original item that can be 'sampled' (copied) and stored for later retrieval – are such that in most situations the reproduction is a mere shadow of the original. A digital copy constitutes a type of bias, which must be seen as a utility and not a replacement. However, it must also be recognised that source material is deteriorating and in many situations damage or loss is irreversible. It may not always be possible to prevent the accidental disintegration of some treasures, but it is possible to record, however inadequately, a representation of the original – a present-day snapshot – that can exist indefinitely. That asset alone renders this technology both necessary and valuable. One should keep this factor in mind throughout the following discussion of digitisation.

Over the past decade, technology capable of creating a digital record of source material has become both affordable and accessible to scholars. Usage is fairly simple and the various procedures involved should become a standard in the field. The basic process underlying the technology can be summarised in the following six steps that describe the process of sampling (i.e. scanning/digitisation) and suggest potential uses for resulting digital data.

I Identifying source material and preparing it for sampling in a manner appropriate to the material
II Sampling source material to create a digital file
III Processing the digital file into multiple formats
IV Placing the digital file into a storage/retrieval context
V Establishing a database utilising the digital files
VI Disseminating the digital record for a number of media

I IDENTIFYING SOURCE MATERIAL AND PREPARING IT FOR SAMPLING IN A MANNER APPROPRIATE TO THE MATERIAL

The nature of the source material will determine the manner of sampling. Methods may include photography (involving different photo processes, depending on the task), traditional photocopying, tracing, or direct scanning utilising any number of scanning devices. The obvious goal is to produce a sample that is as close to the original as possible, though access may clearly pose problems. If a leaf lies in a bound edition and an archive will not allow it to be dismantled, the resulting image will show problematic folds and exclusions. If the source image is a page in a tightly bound book, the same situation exists. Therefore, it is important to manipulate the source into its most advantageous position, and if this cannot be done, then the technology must accommodate.

Flat material may best be scanned directly utilising any one of a number of flatbed scanners. These machines are operated in a manner similar to a photocopying machine. Unlike most standard copiers, however, scanners are usually linked to a computer, which in turn contains or controls the device that will store the data (a standard hard drive or large-capacity removable storage system). Intricate graphics and colour may require more sophisticated sampling devices, particularly if high-resolution prints may be desired at a later time. For this type of work, drum scanners offer high levels of accuracy, yet they may be expensive and difficult to manipulate. The quality of output from basic flatbed scanners, though, is constantly improving, and today even basic devices provide output of sufficient quality for most tasks.

In many cases source material is fragile and cannot be subjected to any manipulation. In such cases the material must first be photographed and then the photo (or slide) can be digitised. A standard 35 mm camera will suffice, with or without flash. Again, some material may be so delicate that even photoflashes may constitute undue stress. This is not necessarily an obstacle since natural light may provide the best and most realistic illumination for photographing source material. Care must be taken, however, to achieve consistent lighting throughout a project or else differences in colour and lighting may suggest anomalies that do not actually exist in the original.

Some material such as simple drawings or figures may profit from a traced duplication, one in which a special tracing pen is connected to a computer or/and tracing tablet. With this system a user traces the graphic elements of a source image and, with a bit of practice, can produce a digital image of some utility. However, since most sampling involves larger accumulations of data than can easily be acquired via tracing devices there are few situations where this method would be valuable.

Once the appropriate sampling method is chosen one then needs to prepare the materials needed for a specific project and these are detailed in the following step.

II SAMPLING SOURCE MATERIAL TO CREATE A DIGITAL FILE

Some terms should be clarified. 'Digitisation', 'sampling' and 'scanning' are related terms in the sense that they all refer to the process of copying an analogue source and generating digital data, i.e. a representation of the source which may be stored, copied, transferred and repeatedly reproduced through various output media. The product of a digitisation/sampling/scanning may be referred to as an 'image', 'scan', 'file', 'sample' or 'digitisation'. When considering this process, the degree of image accuracy, i.e. the clarity of the copy, is also important. 'Resolution' is the term that refers to the amount of information copied/sampled per unit of area. It is usually expressed in 'dots per inch' (dpi). The higher the dpi, the higher the resolution, and hence, such samples/images with higher dpi are more accurate. The higher the resolution, the larger the resulting digital file, since higher resolutions sample more data and require more storage space. These terms, though perhaps confusing and duplicative, are seen throughout technical literature and are often used interchangeably. Therefore, it is essential to know their meanings.

Sampling devices may include flatbed, drum and roll-type scanners as mentioned above; even photography is a type of sampling process (though the output of a camera – a slide or print – is an analogue result and not a digital representation). A computer is required, both to operate the scanning device and to store and manipulate the resulting digital data. Almost any standard system on the market will be acceptable as, again, this technology is well established. The components of a digitisation system are: a standard computing system, a scanner, hard disk storage (most drives sold with computers at the present time are of sufficient capacity to support the storage of hundreds of high-resolution images), a removable storage system, a compact disk recorder (burner), and software for scanning (usually included in the price of a scanner) and for photo/image manipulation (sold separately, usually expensive, but a necessary investment).

Photography (and photocopying) is an intermediary analogue step when source material is too fragile to manipulate or when there are three-dimensional considerations (for example, when there are folds, bumps, tears or other types of markings which require analysis). Either print or slide film may be used, though the latter is generally preferable as it avoids some of the graininess of print film. Resolution is higher in slide film and the ultimate digital representation will be more accurate than a scanned print. Note that a special slide scanner is required when digitising slides; prints may be scanned on standard flatbed systems.

As source material is sampled (either original material or a photographic copy), software will guide the user in the process ultimately leading to the creation of a digital file. This process is straightforward. When a digital image is created, one should determine if the sampling is acceptable. If it is not acceptable, or if image manipulation is desired (for example, changing contrast, brightness, sharpness, etc.), the user should repeat the scanning process until an acceptable scan is produced. It may be wise to produce multiple scanned images from which to choose the best representation of the source.

III PROCESSING THE DIGITAL FILE INTO MULTIPLE FORMATS

Scanning software creates digital files and offers the user many options for saving the material. 'File format' refers to the type of file that is created by the software. Such formats include 'joint photographic experts group' (jpeg, named after the committee which devised the graphic standard), 'encapsulated postscript' (eps), 'tag image file format' (tiff) and others. Most scanning software products also allow for saving a file in the product's own proprietary format. This is only useful if future manipulation of the file will be accomplished with the original scanning software. Since this is not typically the case, and other users may not have access to specific scanning software, it is best to choose a more widely utilised format. 'Format' may also allude to the size and resolution of a file (its dpi), with implications for storage and distribution.

The choice of format with respect to size is somewhat dependent on the intended purpose of the digital data. In general, since access to source material may be limited, it is best to acquire first the largest possible image, one containing the highest feasible resolution with the highest dpi. A researcher may have only one chance to access a source, so it is best to acquire as much information as possible. Large image files can be difficult to manage (they can stress the processing power of lesser computers when manipulated, and they occupy a large amount of disk space), but they are ultimately useful: large files can always be used to create smaller, more manageable versions (for example, for distribution), but small files can never be expanded to include data which were not a part of the original file itself. Therefore, a good scanning practice is to initially establish an image archive consisting of 'first samples/scans', i.e. those high-resolution files from which any number of smaller versions will be spawned, in differing formats depending on the usage application.

For the 'first scan', a good file format choice is either the 'tiff' or 'eps'. A compressed format, 'jpeg', is also a possibility. While technical discussion of the underpinnings of these formats is beyond the scope of this chapter, it suffices to say that either format will provide a strong archive image. Although new formats will likely be developed in the future, it is expected that these options should remain viable indefinitely. New compression strategies (i.e. ways of making large files smaller without degrading data) may emerge as well, but again, this should not invalidate older data stored in either of the above file formats.

Once the 'first scan' file is produced it may be simply stored away, or it may be manipulated and changed in some way. Users should always first ensure that an unaltered copy of an acceptable first scan is saved separately before any modifications are considered. It is very easy to accidentally destroy or damage a file while trying to change it, thus it is imperative that a good, consistent file backup and storage regimen is in place. There is never a question of *if* one will have file damage; it is only a matter of *when*.

From first scans a multitude of processing possibilities exist. Photo manipulation software allows for extensive revision of an image. At this writing, the product 'Photoshop' (published by Adobe Systems) is the pre-eminent choice in this area, which is always evolving. With this type of software the user can crop images, adjust (or correct) colour, adjust contrast and brightness, create more sharpness or blurriness, and provide any number of modifications beyond the scope of the original scan. Most useful is this software's ability to clean up distorted images. Moreover, advanced users may learn how to work with photonegative images (easily created and viewed on a computer) in order to uncover seemingly hidden visual relationships embedded in difficult images. A measure of forensic work may be accomplished in this way. Similarly, skilled users may also superimpose one image upon another in order to create a comparison between two similar images. Many possibilities exist. Of course, while basic scanning and image storage is a process easily mastered by almost anyone, digital image manipulation requires patience and practice. It is impossible to overstate the importance of creating solid backups of original first scan files to allow for probable mistakes.

Before saving or processing/changing an image file, the user will need to assess a first scan and pose several questions. Is the scan acceptable? Does it adequately represent the original source? This involves considerations of several factors, notably colour, lighting and clarity.

Colour

One cannot discount the importance of colour. It nearly defines the image. However, it can be a difficult matter for image archivists, and care must be taken to ensure that a representation is as consistent as possible with its source. Unfortunately, depending on lighting and a multitude of scanning (or photographic) scenarios, the same source may appear very different in different scans. This is not a trivial matter since a computer image will be a static and unchanging view: no matter where the image is shown it will always be the same. (Of course, computer monitors do vary, and there are also a number of 'colour profiles' affecting display properties; sometimes, colours may appear different from one system to another. These, however, are artificial distinctions due to mechanical variance.) The image will always reflect the singular bias of the particular lighting available and scanning/photographic choice chosen when the source image was scanned and that view likely reflects only one of a myriad of other possibilities. Thus it is always a good idea to have a photographic copy to verify original colours (unless repeated access to the source is unproblematic). A guide with digital colour-codes and accompanying colour samples (there are many available) may also prove to be a useful utility if a specific match between a source colour and a digital colour code is desired. In addition, as with the digital file, care must be taken to ensure that the photo copy (or slide) is adequately representing colour as well.

With a good conception of the real colours of the source material, a skilled user can utilise software to alter colours in first scans to match a source, if the colour of the first scan is unacceptable. However, photo software should not be stretched too far. If the colours of the first scan are substantially different from the source, the material should be scanned again. As a rule, the best scans require the least amounts of post-scan manipulation.

Lighting

The importance of adequate and proper lighting of the source cannot be overstressed. Inadequate lighting is essentially equivalent to data loss. Insufficient illumination mars distinction. Similarly, too much brightness washes out detail, and again, data loss occurs. Compounding these difficulties are problems with precious source materials that cannot be subjected to special, bright or artificial light (for example, photo flashes). If it is possible to scan a source directly, the scanner itself will provide a strong and controlled lighting environment. This approach is usually not feasible, however, and source material must first be photographed, and the photo (or slide) subsequently scanned. Thus, natural lighting is useful as it usually provides the best, most realistic illumination for an image. It may be a tedious process to ensure that lighting remains consistent (choosing only sunny days or cloudy days, etc.), but the results will be noticeably improved.

As with colour, lighting can be adjusted with post-scan software. While manipulating colour can present some challenges, adjusting lighting is usually easier. Some scanners tend to produce darkened images, and some images photographed in natural light reveal faint textures, difficult to distinguish with the naked eye, which translate into dark patches on a scan. In such cases, the brightness-altering capability of photo software is very useful. However, as with colour, if the brightness of a first scan differs too substantially from the source, the scanning process should be repeated.

Clarity

The focus of an image is subject to several variables. Was the source in motion when the scan or photograph was made (hopefully not)? Was the camera (or scanner) steady during the copying process? Was the camera or scanner in focus? These questions obviously pertain to basic technique, which may need attention. Less clear, however, are natural focus problems developing out of image angle, with or without three-dimensional considerations. If a camera is held at an odd angle, perspectives may be distorted and a resulting scan can show this as a slight blur – one that cannot be easily focused after the scan (since only a small part of the scan is out of focus). Similarly, if bumps, folds, tears, smudges, ink blots, etc. – three-dimensional features – are seen in a source, some photographs may not accurately capture the perspectives and, again, blurs may appear in some areas. Thus, it is always best to attempt to place the source material in the best possible position, properly squared on a dull background with the camera strategically placed at an angle allowing for the best possible view of the photographic subject.

Photo software can sharpen dull or blurred images quite effectively. It is also possible to sharpen only small areas if desired, for clarifying certain areas or for special study. Sometimes a strong focus will allow faint text to be legible, or it may reveal hidden properties in smudges, handwriting, etc. Too much focus, however, can make an image grainy and valuable faint information may actually disappear! As always, it is best to keep an unaltered first scan stored away in case the post-scan process unduly distorts the image.

IV PLACING THE DIGITAL FILE INTO A STORAGE/RETRIEVAL CONTEXT

In most cases, first scans will be created on a hard disk drive included in the computer system. However, many scans are large files and moderate numbers of them may quickly overwhelm the storage capacity of a standard hard disk. Since backup and archiving of image files is an important part of this technology, the user must acquire some type of storage media. There are many options. Of course, the 'floppy diskettes' of the early computer years are by now old technology and are essentially useless for storage of large files. There are large removable media available (at this writing the Iomega 'zip' drive is one example) that provide floppy-like utility, but these may not provide the security or capacity needed. Auxiliary (externally connected) hard disk systems may be useful (for example, one might allocate an entire external hard drive system for a particular set of images), but these are subject to the same potential errors as a main hard disk contained within a computer.

A good storage system to consider is twofold: first scans should be initially stored on large-capacity removable storage systems. When a number of images are created they should be archived on a compact disk (a 'CD ROM'). All this requires the acquisition of the removable storage device and reusable media, a CD ROM 'burner' (the device which allows for the creation of CD ROM storage) and blank compact disks, which are intended for permanent storage. While blank compact disks may be found in either 'write once' ('CDR') or 'write many times' ('CDRW') formats, it is best to choose the former option for permanent storage. (If desired, rewritable compact disks can be utilised for initial storage, but removable storage media are usually easier and faster for routine work.)

Regardless of the storage choice, it is always best to choose high-quality media. Inferior storage will be prone to error (and loss), and data on lesser media could disintegrate if exposed to direct sunlight! In general, the higher-priced media are less apt to be corrupted, but there is no such thing as 'perfect storage'. Thus, it is never a bad idea to possess more than one backup copy of data, though assembling a second backup copy might best be left for the final stage of a project.

V ESTABLISHING A DATABASE UTILISING THE DIGITAL FILES

When all the first scans are completed it is then time to consider how the images might be used. It is easy to pick several out of the collection and display or distribute them, but a collection is usually most useful as a complete unit. The use of the images is somewhat dictated by the overall size. If only a handful of files are involved, a simple storage medium containing the files may be sufficient. A descriptive text file should be included with the collection to describe the contents. This is not a good solution for larger collections, how-ever, which need to be put into a type of 'digital archive' in order to be of maximum utility.

Collections of data – in this case a collection of individual image files – usually suggest a 'database', that is, a set of many items ('records'), each sharing common characteris-tics ('fields'), all guided by a controlling mechanism (the 'database program'). The sim-plest analogue database is the common telephone book: each entry ('record') consists of a name, with some type of address and telephone number (the 'fields' for each record/name). The 'controlling mechanism' is the book itself and the handy indexes on each page. Com-puter databases are similar. Image archives may be set up such that each 'record' consists of fields which include the image file and a number of descriptive parameters, all con-trolled by a database application which allows for searching, sorting, analysis and general query.

'Database management' is a wide area that may range from the relatively simple to the extremely complex. It would be quite possible to place graphic imagery into the latter context, but this would serve no useful purpose to scholars. Such systems are prohibitively expensive, very difficult to use, and they present serious distribution and access problems (and they are more than is needed for most applications). Besides, there are many lower-end, widely available, and easily learned and distributed applications that provide all the functionality and utility required. Virtually any computer catalogue contains extensive advertisements for all the products one requires, and there are ample reviews available for consideration by the wary consumer.

A complete discussion of database architecture and options is too involved for this chap-ter, but an image archivist should consider two types of applications: the simple database and the graphic library (also a type of database, but arguably more appropriate for image collections). The former pertains to a series of general software products widely available. These applications are not necessarily intended to organise graphic images, but they can be used for this purpose. (Such applications are typically employed for small data collections, financial records, personal collections, etc.) All the basic information can be presented, and it is even possible to examine various arithmetic relationships between records. However, these products do not always serve graphics well. Larger images may cause the database to perform erratically; sorting can sometimes be tedious and image redraw (i.e. the time taken to display each image as it appears on the screen) can be very slow. This model can be improved with the inclusion of 'thumbnail' images (much smaller versions of an image) that can be created to serve as visual placeholders within a database record, serving as a kind of 'visual index'.

'Graphic libraries' are more suitable for image archives. These products have the same functionality as simple databases and their use is nearly identical, but they cater more to the storage, retrieval and display of graphic imagery. Such products – in versions intended for individual use – are inexpensive, and it is not difficult to create effective graphic collections with them. (There are 'multi-user' versions intended for shared access and corporate use; these are much more costly.) Each record in a graphic library consists of the graphic image, which can be viewed in various sizes to show detail, and a number of user-defined parameters that describe the image. Parameters may include dimensions of the source, type of paper, colour of paper and ink, the title of the source, composer information, etc. There are many possibilities for listing descriptive detail. Graphic libraries also allow for other types of media in addition to image files. For example, it is possible to insert digital video or/and audio clips if one wishes to present a 'tour' of a museum or archive. Such clips can be catalogued in the same manner as graphic images, in the same database.

The graphic library has distinct advantages. It is easy to use and it is made specifically for cataloguing media. Most products provide 'runtime' versions, i.e. small utilities that users may freely include with their graphics collections that allow other users to access the images (and the database/library) without having to purchase the main database application itself. This is especially useful if the database is to be a commercial product, since runtime versions do not typically require any type of license fee. Of course, runtime versions cannot be used to create databases, but they allow others to perform all the functions typically required of existing databases, such as searching, sorting, gathering statistics, making comparisons, printing, etc. Standard databases also provide runtime versions that may be freely distributed, but they are generally more costly and do not serve graphic collections as well.

Either type of database will occupy space on some type of storage media. As with the images themselves, the graphic database will need to be archived for security. Usually, the database itself is a relatively small file on a disk or CD controlling the many images, also on the same media. This is not the case with standard databases that include the graphics within the database file. This is another detail discouraging the use of standard databases in favour of the graphic library. In either case, the database and its images are best preserved on compact disk for future examination and distribution.

VI DISSEMINATING THE DIGITAL RECORD FOR A NUMBER OF MEDIA

The database is completed when all the images are deemed satisfactory and have been properly situated within an established database structure. The distribution set should include the images (if separate from the controlling database file), the database file, the runtime version of the database software, and any number of text files describing the database (perhaps a user manual or other supporting material). Before copies are made a 'master' CD should be created and tested extensively.

Testing is extremely important for a successful database. Besides examining the product on one's own computer, the master CD should be tested on multiple machines, preferably on different platforms if the database is intended to run on different types of computers. In addition, although it is tedious, one must also examine each and every record for parameter accuracy. Lists should be run; searches performed. Other individuals should be enlisted in the testing process. There is probably no such thing as too much examination because no matter how thorough the database appears to be, errors always emerge at later times. The concept of testing is similarly pertinent if one is distributing images without a database. One must have an idea in advance of how users may react to material in order to correct misconceptions in the product before mass distribution.

Once the database master is complete there are some basic considerations. Assuming the scholar has received permission to distribute material, or has negotiated the rights to sell representations (this discussion is a volume itself), the question of access arises. The most straightforward mode of access is to simply make copies of the master CD for distribution or sale. This allows the author some measure of direct control over who has access to the material and it may generate some monetary remuneration. If the database is to be given away freely and the widest access is desired, the database could be placed on a web site for access over the Internet. This would necessitate the creation of another database, however, since the foundations of net-based products are substantially different from single computer-based systems. Internet databases are, at the present time, difficult and time-consuming to construct and well beyond the skill set of most untrained individuals.

To be sure, the Internet is an exciting space in which to present one's work. It reaches the entire world and it is easy to access. However, Internet content is essentially a free gift. It is possible to restrict access via subscriptions, fees, passwords, etc., but this introduces an additional level of complexity, which presents more challenges. The aforementioned computer-based databases, however, are far more easily mastered. In addition, the products of such systems are more easily marketed and controlled, if that is the intention of the database project.

IN CONCLUSION

Music, the arts, and graphics, have always been harmoniously intertwined. It was no coincidence that the creative aspects of computing technology would serve all these fields well. It is curious that so few scholars studying sketches and various artefacts have thus far availed themselves of this technology, but given its reasonable cost and its relative ease-of-use, there will likely be a noted increase in the number of graphic collections serving the field in the years to come. This is quite fortunate since precious collections are fading and it is our responsibility to make every effort to preserve what we can, in whatever manner, for future study and appreciation.

CHAPTER 7

Transcribing sketches

Regina Busch

GENERAL CONSIDERATIONS

> Some Frenchman – possibly Montaigne – says: 'People talk about thinking, but for
> my part I never think, except when I sit down to write.' . . . How very commonly
> we hear it remarked that such and such thoughts are beyond the compass of words!
> I do not believe that any thought, properly so called, is out of the reach of language.
> I fancy, rather, that where difficulty in expression is experienced, there is, in the
> intellect which experiences it, a want either of deliberateness or of method. For
> my own part, I have never had a thought which I could not set down in words,
> with even more distinctness than that with which I conceived it: – as I have before
> observed, the thought is logicalized by the effort at (written) expression.[1]

The present chapter is concerned with the transcription of sketches, that is with the creation of 'diplomatic transcriptions', whose purpose is to assist with the deciphering of notes of all kinds (musical, verbal or other), usually in manuscript, and to make possible a deeper understanding, as well as classification and interpretation of the deciphered material. Transcriptions open up the material for specific questions posed by individual researchers. Indeed, in many cases it is only through transcription that the notated content of this material becomes universally accessible and capable of being worked on.

Anyone undertaking a transcription or working with transcribed texts should always maintain a clear understanding of certain basic conditions. Every reproduction, every duplication, every manuscript copy of any source is a transcription. In German, because of the ambiguity of the word *Transkription*, one would have to add that every transcription is an adaptation. Regardless of the method used and the precision of the work carried out, the result is always different from the source. A transcription does not present the original document and cannot be understood as identical to it. The facsimile of a manuscript, the print of a fair copy, and the reproduction of a printed text in any medium are all adaptations, regardless of the degree to which they 'faithfully reproduce' the source.[2] Transcriptions may be compared with translations: they convert what has been notated in the source into another 'language'; they present it anew in another form.[3] Modifications necessarily take place when this happens.

Whether and in what sense source material (i.e. sketches and drafts usually created with a view to establishing a written composition) can be designated 'texts' is an important question, which cannot be dealt with here. Usually written in musical notation, letters and graphic symbols on paper or other writing material, sketches can be arranged in lines, organised in tables, or simply scattered at random throughout the document. These notations may possess the status of text from the start, or alternatively they may only acquire it in the process of being transcribed.

> Paradoxically, the [poetic] text concept, which is tied to oral speech, has not been dissolved by the printing of books. The contrary is true: . . . anything that is mediated through the printing process already lays claim in an external manner to text status. At the same time the preparation of the text by machine, its mode of appearance in a technical medium, makes apparent the fact that the text is indeed tied to a notational medium, but not to a specific, individually characterised one. Text is *structurally*, so to speak, bound up with copying, apographic.[4]

The verbal notations contained in sketches consist of letters, numbers, punctuation marks and other signs, which determine priorities and establish hierarchies (dots, arrows, parentheses, strokes of different lengths and directions, symbols for corrections, deletions, insertions, abbreviations). Numerous other signs are used to write music, including signs for notes (note heads, stems, beams, etc.) and signs for rests, for dynamic, rhythmic and agogic modifications and for performance directions. Some of these have fixed meanings that are immediately evident and remain uninfluenced by changes to their visual appearance (many letters, fermatas, accidentals). Others are sensitive to minute changes, for instance in their length (hyphen v. dash; *diminuendo* v. accent), and only achieve their meaning in conjunction with other signs. Signs such as these can produce different results depending on their context (*tenuto* dash v. dash signifying the continuation of a *ritardando* or *crescendo*; slur v. tie). Much the same applies to successions and groups of signs, the meanings of which result from the sequence and assembly of their elements, their mutual relationship to each other and their positioning on the page. In a word, it is only possible to identify the signs and recognise what they signify when the context and the particular position in which they are located are taken into consideration.

Both in principle and for technical reasons, a transcription can never be a complete reproduction of the original. Indeed, even without invoking the reasons mentioned above, all that is visible in a given source cannot be reproduced in the transcription, and especially not in the way it appears in the original. During the preliminary stages of work, tacit decisions about foreground and background, principal and subsidiary ideas will already have been taken as a matter of course or based on conventions. Also, the printed lines or grids on ruled or squared paper will not be reproduced unless they provide indispensable aids for the interpretation and representation of written material. Verbal indications written on staff paper are often rendered without the staff lines. In the case of musical sketches written in notes, staff lines are usually assumed. In transcription, no optical distinction is made between pre-printed and hand-drawn lines. This type of information is normally included in the critical commentary. Special characteristics resulting from the process of printing music, such as type irregularities, are not preserved at all.

The individual imperfections of handwritten script and the distinctive features and errors of machine-printed texts are usually not transcribed, unless of course the graphic image is to be rendered as an end in itself. The differences between carefully and hastily written texts are also not reproduced in transcription.[5] As long as the essential aspects for the signification of a given document have been preserved, other inconsequential elements can be ignored: the length of note stems, the exact way in which round or square note heads are written, the thickness of beams, etc. Sometimes even the placing of signs before, after, above or below notes (braces, arpeggio indications, accents) and the relative size of signs can be seen as irrelevant. The idiosyncrasies and personal variants of handwriting are also normally not transcribed. The fact that a crotchet rest, a clef or an accidental was written and where it appears in the document are far more significant than how they were written. Signs may be written in ways that allow for more than one interpretation (the letters 'a' and 'e' or semibreve and minim rests, for instance). Here, the transcriber must decide if a definitive interpretation can be established by studying the source, tradition and writing habits, or whether the sign should be reproduced in its ambiguous form. It would be senseless and misleading to 'transcribe' undecipherable and inexplicable signs; in such cases, one can only work with facsimiles and, at most, suggest interpretations in the commentary.

In the situations described above, the realm of self-evident presuppositions has been definitively left behind. The boundaries are, however, fluid. Every 'author' of a transcription takes both unconscious and deliberate preliminary decisions. He determines the extent of the material to be transcribed; that is, he decides what is to be ignored and what cannot under any circumstances be left out. His selection and mode of presentation are bound up with the purpose of the transcription. The intentions of the transcriber leave visible traces in his work even when a source is reproduced in its original format and with its full contents. In other words, the transcription not only reproduces the source (as 'faithfully to the original' as possible), but also always presents something of the adaptor's ideas.

In addition to omitting the self-evident and superfluous, it is usual to supplement transcriptions with additions and commentaries that serve to complete the transcribed text, to make reading easier and to help identify and put in order what was notated (clefs, key signatures, staves and bar numbering may be added; notes, rests, letters, syllables and abbreviations may be completed). These additions bring the content of the transcription closer to that of the original: no transcription can do without them. Decisions concerning the nature and extent of this supplementary information again depend on the purpose of the transcription and are left to the discretion of the adaptor, who must then explain and justify these procedures, especially in ambiguous or doubtful cases. Anything that is added to the original text within the area on the page occupied by the transcription and anything written in the margins of the source must be identified as such by means of colour or typography (different fonts and point-sizes, etc.). Additions to the original text may be distinguished graphically (smaller print) or by means of special signs (parentheses for instance). This also applies to the reporting of omissions. Anything that cannot be reproduced, but which the editor considers worth mentioning (such as erasures, cuts, overwriting, strips of paper pasted over the original text, writing materials, spatial layout, anything written upside down, obliquely or vertically, or the successive stages of work recorded in the original document) should be described in verbal commentaries accompanying the transcription. Commentaries should also contain information about the physical condition of the source (spots, tears, holes), insofar as this affects the deciphering and interpretation of the notated material.

Conventions do exist for all of this, but no firm, universally valid rules. The mode of transcription, the kinds of additions and the amount of information included in the commentaries depend, as stated above, on the function that the transcription is to fulfil, while the detailed procedure will be adapted to the special characteristics of each source as well as to the possibilities and limitations of the reproduction method. If a handwritten transcription is intended to record information that is unavailable in other forms (print, film and photocopy) and which would otherwise remain inaccessible, then the transcription should be kept as close as possible to the source in every respect. Everything, even apparently incidental or unintelligible aspects, must be notated in a form that is 'true to the source', while adding only what is absolutely necessary. In complete or partial editions of a source or group of sources in diplomatic transcription, the bibliographic units must be left in their original order and transcribed as a whole. The breakdown and classification of units according to their content should be left to the accompanying texts. If, on the other hand, the main purpose of the transcription is to reproduce all sketch material pertaining to a particular work in chronological order or in a sequence reflecting the work's form, then many sketches will necessarily be taken out of context and reproduced in isolation. In such cases, it becomes almost impossible to reconstruct the original situation through commentaries and description, and as a result, the sketches can no longer be adequately assessed. Transcription also includes the reproduction of fragments extracted from a single coherent sketch, i.e. groups of signs or a subset of elements representing stages of a compositional process. Such compilations of excerpts are normally used to elucidate a thesis or to present a work's evolution; they are in no sense complete reproductions of the original. The less that is communicated concerning the context from which excerpts have been taken, the weaker their power of demonstration.

Transcriptions, including those that are to be printed, are usually prepared by hand. Only when the graphic image is to be reproduced as such can the original be thought of as a 'printer's copy'. Clearly and unambiguously legible sources, especially fair copies, are best reproduced in facsimile. However, even carefully written fair copies contain ambiguous signs and contradictory indications. Consequently, fair copies reproduced in facsimile are usually more suitable as study scores than as performance material. Careful editing and thorough commentaries are always essential.

Concerning the 'reproduction of the visual findings',[6] the problems arising in the transcription (either by hand or in print) of an original are essentially the same as those which occur when printing any manuscript document. Handwritten and printed transcriptions are subject to the nature of the handwriting and the rules of typography. Thus, in transcriptions, unlike photographic reproductions, the relationships of size and the topographical proportions of the original can only be reproduced approximately. Even a handwritten reproduction cannot and need not duplicate the original in all respects.[7] The size and spacing of signs, as well as the density with which notes fill out bars usually vary in handwritten documents. These changes need not be copied exactly, particularly in the case of monophonic music. With polyphonic music, the vertical alignment of notes, which affects spacing and density in all staves, is of course critically important for a proper understanding of the work.[8] Similarly, the tacit omission of empty staves and the failure to indicate the exact location of a single sketch on an otherwise empty page are problematic.

> Now it has . . . long been known . . . that no deeper insight into the context within which a text is transmitted can be achieved without detailed knowledge of the layout of the manuscript. A judgement as to whether the contents of a page of manuscript belong to one, two or three texts – whether they represent one, two or three texts – is virtually impossible without an understanding of the individual place on the page where something has been written. At the same time there is no sufficiently intelligible (one might say simple) descriptive language which could make all the spatial relationships of the writings on a page explicitly clear – at any rate none that would not seem ridiculous when compared with a simple photocopy of the page. Once the logical conclusion has been drawn . . . nothing will suffice but the facsimile and, in order to understand and interpret the graphic and chronological relationships within the manuscript, a diplomatic transcription, for these are the only means of gaining a clear and adequate understanding of the transmission of the text.[9]

The 'reproduction of the visible findings', indispensable for a transcription that is 'as true to the original as possible', thus runs up against its limits everywhere, a situation that the new methods of reproduction available today, which are continually being expanded and improved, have not changed. By offering greater differentiation, precision and completeness, these new methods broaden our experience, raise our expectations and make imperfections and errors clearer. Also, transcriptions are in no way made superfluous by easier access to the holdings of libraries and private collections and their publication in facsimile editions. Conversely, transcriptions unaccompanied by facsimiles remain at best a stopgap, suitable for a provisional examination, but useless for responsible work with the material, since they are in significant respects unreliable and not infrequently misleading. In the end, facsimiles and transcriptions, however well supplemented with commentaries, do not make the examination of the original redundant, but continually call for it anew.

ANTON WEBERN'S SKETCHES: *FIVE CANONS ON LATIN TEXTS*, OP. 16, AND *KINDERSTÜCK* (CHILDREN'S PIECE)

Most transcription problems that can be discussed with reference to Anton Webern's sketches occur in the same or similar ways when transcribing the work of any composer who has written music in conventional notation. Nonetheless, the conclusions drawn from the study of these problems in this context apply specifically to Webern's music and to the situation of a particular sketch. They are never self-evident. Individual compositional methods will shape the manner in which a composer thinks, conceives, drafts and sketches. The characteristics of these working procedures – those features that remain constant from one work to another, those that change and those that distinguish one composer's work from another's – are manifest in the way a composer sets down ideas.

The great majority of Webern's known sketches, drafts and first continuity drafts are written mainly on manuscript paper in landscape format.[10] His fair copies, on the other hand, are written on paper in portrait format, and generally correspond with how these pieces later appeared in print.[11] Sketches in other formats may have existed, but practically none have survived. This situation is very different from that of Arnold Schoenberg or Alban Berg, who, in addition to working on the most varied types of manuscript paper, used plain paper, notebooks, pages of calendars and envelopes as well as preformed small-format sketchbooks for their copious notes. Webern's sketch sheets consist of various paper types. A few sketches are found on individual sheets and were probably never part of complete sheets or quires.[12] Webern often cut sections of large-sized manuscript paper to fit the format of the paper on which he happened to be working, and at times used only parts of the pages. The row tables of the twelve-tone works from the *Zwei Lieder* (Two Songs), Op. 19, for mixed choir onwards were also written on sheets in landscape format, clipped together in groups of up to three pages.[13] For reasons including those mentioned above, this format, or at least its proportions, should be adopted in the transcription.

We shall now examine one page of Webern's sketches for the *Fünf Canons nach lateinischen Texten* (Five Canons on Latin Texts), Op. 16, for high soprano, clarinet and bass clarinet (see Plates 7.1 and 7.3). This page has occasionally been mentioned in literature on the *Kinderstücke* (Children's Pieces). Felix Meyer has described the page and published a colour facsimile. Certain parts of the document have also been discussed in accounts of the beginnings of twelve-tone composition.[14] Aspects of the compositional histories of both Op. 16 and the *Kinderstücke* have been documented. Consequently, we are not dealing with completely unknown material, and, as we shall see, this supplementary information will be useful in making the transcription.

Op.16 No.2 *(Dormi Jesu)*	summer 1923, finished before 21.7.1923
Op.16 No.3 *(Crux fidelis)*	finished 8.8.1923
Op.16 No.4 *(Asperges me)*	finished 21.8.1923
Op.16 No.5 *(Crucem tuam)*	begun August 1924; finished 29.10.1924
Op.16 No.1 *(Christus factus est)*	finished 12.11.1924

Figure 7.1   Completion dates of each of the five songs of Op. 16

We now know that, from the time he began to feel at home with twelve-tone composition (from Op. 17 onwards), Webern assembled his sketches in bound collections or wrote directly into sketchbooks. Work in the earliest surviving sketchbook was begun in June 1925.[15] All earlier sketches known to date are on loose leaves or sheets. Though the page is in many respects typical of Webern's sketches, it does display certain special features. It belongs to those few pages on which two different pieces were drafted. Moreover, the two pieces were not written in continuous succession, but rather in opposing directions. The two drafts are identified by their headings ('*1. Kanon*, Op. 16', and '*Lieblich*' [lovely]) and are situated end to end. The sheet belongs to a sheaf that also contains sketches for the canons Op. 16 No. 1 and Nos. 3–5 (sketches for No. 2 have apparently not survived). These canons were composed immediately before the works in the first sketchbook, from the summer of 1923 to the end of 1924. The sketches for Nos. 1 and 5 are written on different paper from those for Nos. 3 and 4, which broadly corresponds with the order in which the pieces were written (see Figure 7.1).

The paper used for Op. 16 Nos. 2 and 3 is similar to that used somewhat later for the row tables of Op. 19. Consequently, paper-type identification is not a reliable means of dating these sketches.

Webern used both sides of some leaves contained in the Op. 16 sheaf; page [6] presented in Plate 7.1 is one of these.[16] For the purely technical process of transcription, it is not absolutely necessary to know what is on the 'reverse' side (p. [5]) or on preceding and succeeding pages. In certain places, we find coloured markings or cross-reference signs [♮, o] which recur on other pages in the same sheaf, facilitating identification and creating direct links with the other sketches. Together with other evidence, they provide arguments for addressing the question of which of the two drafts was written first, the piano fragment entitled '*Lieblich*' or the passage from Op. 16 No. 1.

The sketches, written right side up (staves 1–3 and 5–7 Plate 7.1), refer unambiguously to the middle section (bars 8–11) of Op. 16 No. 1. At top left, bars 8–9 are sketched twice in succession on the first three staves and then a third time underneath. Finally, on the right-hand half of the page, bars 8–11 are sketched (staves 1–3), surrounded by cross-reference signs. Except for a few pitches and the positioning of the bar-lines, all four attempts are quite close to the final version.[17] In addition, the autograph title is written at top right. The titles found on Webern's sketches and row tables are usually correct. Often they were added later in coloured pencil together with an opus number and dates relating to the period of

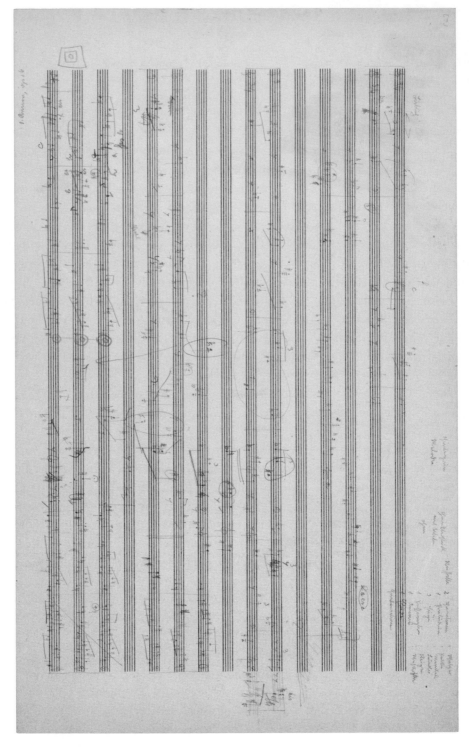

Plate 7.1   Anton Webern, top: *Fünf Canons nach lateinischen Texten*, Op. 16 No. 1, sketches; bottom (upside down): *Kinderstück* (M. 266), sketches, Anton Webern Collection (folder 49, page [6]), Paul Sacher Foundation, Basle

composition, including the date of completion, which could not have been known as the sketches were being written. This applies to the title '*1. Kanon*, Op. 16'. The canon was composed towards the end of 1924, after the other canons had already been completed.[18] The year before, Webern appears to have made fair copies of the middle three canons, which he entitled *Lateinische Lieder* (Latin Songs) for voice, clarinet and bass clarinet.[19] At the time, he wrote, 'the whole closes itself musically . . . in form and expression', though he held open the possibility of adding further canons.[20] We do not know when the order of the five canons and the opus number of the work were finally determined.

Although only a few bars of Op. 16 No. 1 are sketched on page [6] and occupy just over a quarter of the side, Webern assigned the sheet to the canons and not to the fragmentary piano piece, which occupies a far bigger portion of the page.[21] Though the latter does carry a heading, *Lieblich* cannot be considered a work title. It may be either a movement title or an indication of the character of the piece. It is placed immediately above the notes of the first staff and, like the sketch itself, is written in pencil as though it were part of the notated music. The title for the canon sketches, on the other hand, is placed outside the area of the staff lines, at the extreme edge of the page. The reproduction (Plate 7.1) does not reveal that this title was written in coloured pencil, though one can see that it was written more heavily. In any case, its position clearly distinguishes it from the heading of the piano piece. This difference must be reproduced in the transcription.

The above information concerning the title, the heading and Webern's classification of the sketch still does not tell us which of the two sketch complexes was written first. In the transcription of the whole page, this question should remain open, particularly with regard to those sections of the document where the sketches are adjacent to each other. The two sketch complexes can be transcribed separately, which may be appropriate depending on how the transcriptions are to be used. However, this eliminates any possibility of discovering something about the document's chronology. Examination of the remaining Op. 16 No. 1 sketches would certainly help to clarify this question. The 'reverse' side of our sheet alone is still not much help until all the pages have been placed in a plausible sequence that corresponds to the presumed compositional history of the piece. Four of the six pages carry titles such as *1. Kanon op. 16* or *Canons N° 1 |nach lateinischen Texten*. Webern numbered two pages '1' and '2' ([1] and [3] according to the Paul Sacher Foundation's pagination). Taken together, they contain all thirteen bars of the canon. Page '1' contains a draft of the whole piece. After the closing date on page '2', located in the middle of the last system (see Plate 7.2) further sketches for earlier bars follow.

On the remaining, untitled, obverse and reverse sides, Webern continued to work on the same passages as those found on pages '1' and '2'. The order of these documents and consequently the chronology of page [6] cannot be established from the sketches alone. At this point, we cannot even decide which side was the obverse – that is, which side (if any)

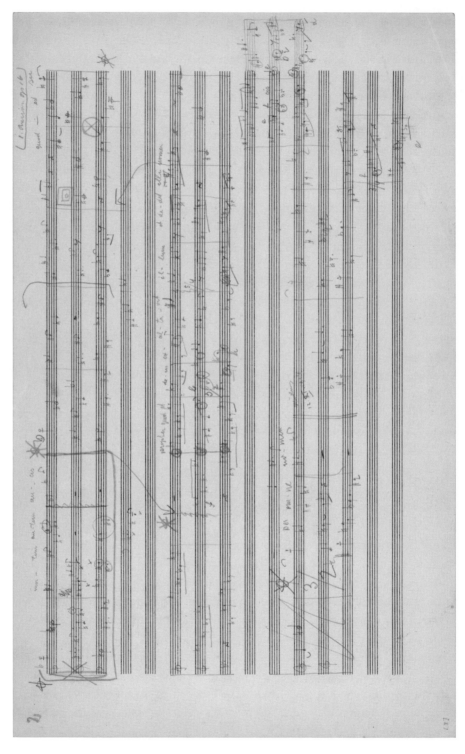

Plate 7.2   Anton Webern, *Fünf Canons nach lateinischen Texten*, Op. 16 No. 1, sketches (identified as page '2' by the composer), Anton Webern Collection (folder 49, page [3]), Paul Sacher Foundation, Basle

should be associated with Webern's pages '1' and '2'. The cross-reference signs provide no unambiguous clues.[22]

Examined out of context, both chronological interpretations of page [6] initially seem plausible. Either the piano piece was drafted first with the canon sketches being written in the parts of the page left blank,[23] or Webern, having used only a small amount of space for the canon, used the rest of the page for the piano piece. No matter which way the page is read, the sketches notated upside down seem secondary. Each sketch complex displays special features that lend it more weight in comparison with the other. The Op. 16 bars, endowed with an official title, are written more strongly and concisely throughout. In this passage, a clearly established idea, which had already been sketched several times elsewhere, is further refined and fully developed, and one version is marked and singled out as the valid one. In contrast, the sketches of the piano piece represent the first stage of drafting and are thoroughly different.

Webern begins by writing a two-bar basic idea, in which the character, dynamics and articulation of individual motives have already been determined. The pitch and rhythmic formulations are immediately modified (staves 1–2 and 3–4, left half of the page, Plate 7.3). Further right, two tone-rows of eleven and twelve notes respectively are notated (the first five notes are identical in both). Apart from a few doubtful places, both may be related to this first draft. On staves 6–7, Webern starts again with the opening motive, this time without indications concerning dynamics, articulation and character, and notates nine bars in succession (staves 6–7 and 10–11 respectively) containing six statements of the eleven-note row *ohne a* (without A) from the fourth staff.[24] Here again, interruptions and alterations are apparent (cf. the variants for the first system on staves 8–9 and the changes to the second system on staves 9 and 12–15).

As mentioned above, the sketches for the piano piece are untitled. The upper margin on the right-hand half of the page is filled with a series of concepts that could be considered as possible titles (see Plate 7.4 and Figure 7.2). However, in order to substantiate the connection between the sketches and the words, more information is required. The mere presence of words and music on the same page is not sufficient. In a letter to his publisher, Emil Hertzka, dated 3 January 1925, Webern mentions his interest in the *Kinderstücke*, which he had begun to write in response to Hertzka's suggestion. However, Webern adds, 'I had . . . to interrupt work on these, because for a long time now I have been very preoccupied with something else, which I . . . must write before the "Children's Pieces". I am working on a cycle of Latin songs and on songs to German texts.'[25] This statement establishes a temporal connection between Op. 16 and the *Drei Volkstexte* (Three Folk Texts), Op. 17. Among the compositions of the composer's estate, there is a piano piece dating from autumn 1924, entitled *Kinderstück*, and like our fragment, it is marked *Lieblich*.[26] The simple piano texture and the manner in which Webern juxtaposes new row forms are both very similar to the procedure in our sketch, reinforcing the idea that the piano fragment on page [6] may well have been part

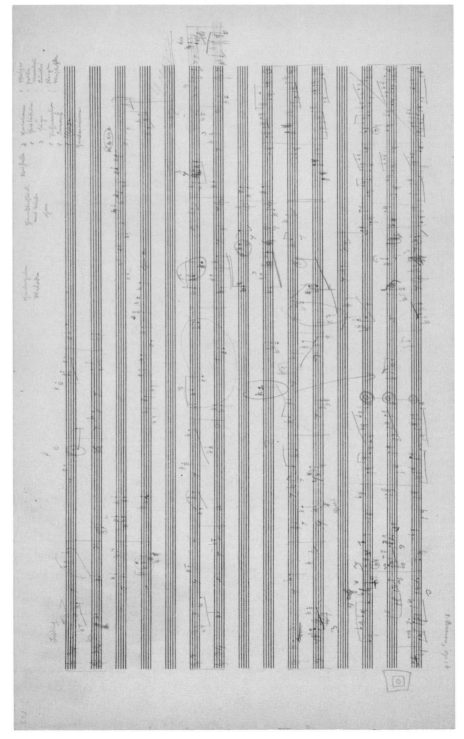

Plate 7.3 Anton Webern, top: *Kinderstück* (M. 266), sketches, bottom (upside down): *Fünf Canons nach lateinischen Texten*, Op. 16 No. 1, sketches, Anton Webern Collection (folder 49, page [6]), Paul Sacher Foundation, Basle

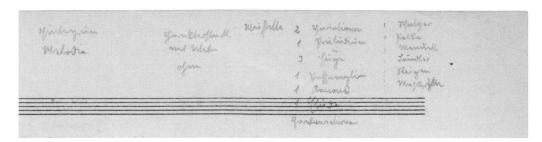

Plate 7.4   Anton Webern, detail from the upper right-hand corner of sketches for *Kinderstück* (M. 266) (see Plate 7.3), Anton Webern Collection (folder 49, page [6]), Paul Sacher Foundation, Basle

		Mussette	2 Variationen	| Walzer
Wintergrün	Charakterstücke		1 Präludium	| Polka
Melodie	mit Titeln		u.	| Menuet
	ohne		3 Fuge	| Ländler
			1 Passacaglia	| Reigen
			1 Kanons	| Mazurka
			1 Etüde	
			Choralvariationen	

Figure 7.2   Transcription of the terms in Plate 7.4

of the planned group of 'Children's Pieces', alluded to in the letter. The jottings in the top margin of the page of sketches could then be interpreted as keywords for a collection of such pieces.

Obviously, more than the two known pieces were planned, but no further sketches have survived, not even for the completed piece.[27] On the other hand, we have no grounds for believing that any of the concepts noted in the margin apply to the two composed *Kinderstücke*. Unambiguous criteria cannot be derived from the lengths of either the completed piece or the unfinished fragment, the 3 time signatures or the markings *Lieblich*. Indeed, the two pieces may even represent two versions of the same type of movement.

Strictly speaking, the list presents a collection of keywords rather than a plan for a cycle of movements. A systematic ordering or grouping according to compositional types or forms (cf. the last two columns in particular) is attempted. It is however impossible to say what *Charakterstücke* | *mit Titeln* | *ohne* (Character Pieces | with Titles | without) means, how *Wintergrün* (Wintergreen) and *Melodie* (Melody) are connected, and what movement types they may represent, or why *Mussette* (Musette) is written by itself between the second and third columns. Perhaps the concepts in the first two columns do not form a group or groups at all and are not intended to be on a par with the rest. They are written somewhat further from the edge and are spaced more widely. One would also like to be able to connect the figures in the penultimate column to a formal scheme, but we do not know if they indicate the order or the number of movements. Whether the figures '2–1–3' next to the terms *Variationen* | *Präludium* | *u.* | *Fuge* (Variations | Prelude | and | Fugue) represent the number of pieces or their order is especially problematic. The significance of the short, vertical strokes before the last column is equally unclear. They certainly should not be read as a column of poorly written figures representing the number 'one'. A more plausible reading would be as a broken dividing line between the last two columns. As long as the significance of these words and signs remains uncertain, and precisely because of this uncertainty, it is essential that the size and position of the words and signs, as well as the distance between them, be reproduced exactly.

Important chronological information is provided in the written material of the example in Plate 7.5, particularly in those places where the two sketch complexes are adjacent to each other: the right-hand side of staves 9–11 and the middle of staves 12–15, from the arrow to the bar-line following the fermata.[28]

As the two sketch complexes are placed upside down in relation to one another, it is easy to distinguish between them: the positions of accidentals, the directions of the quaver tails, clefs, pauses and different handwriting are all indications of this relationship. The bar-lines belong less obviously to one piece or the other, but they can nevertheless be assigned unambiguously according to the number of staves they traverse: three for the three-voiced canon, two for the piano piece. The double bar-line across staves 10–11 (right-hand side) belongs to the *Kinderstück*, as do the two single ones across staves 12–13 and 14–15. Certain bar-lines are touched (staff 14) and cut (staff 13) by quaver tails of the canon sketches, but the number of voices precludes the assignment of these bar-lines to the canon. These points of intersection must not be lost in the transcription, nor should the dislocations in the vertical alignments of notes be straightened, so that the reader can judge which sketch was displaced or constricted by the other, and how.

Between the two systems of the nine-bar sketch of *Kinderstück* (staves 8 and 9), there are alterations, which are not clearly separated from each other. On staff 9, variants for the third bar of the second system (staves 10–11) are found, together with variants for the third and fourth bars of the system above (staves 6–7). By introducing an additional staff into the transcription, one could transcribe these unconnected variants on separate staves, in order to clarify their relationship to different bars. This would however falsify the contiguity of *Kinderstück* and the canon in staves 8–11, as well as rendering Webern's use of the free area between the canon sketches at the bottom of the page implausible.

A new formulation of the third bar of the second system (staves 10–11) begins at the bottom of the page (staves 14–15), immediately to the right of the markings of the

Plate 7.5   Anton Webern, detail from the lower middle section (staves 8–15) of sketches for *Kinderstück* (M. 266) (see Plate 7.3), Anton Webern Collection (folder 49, page [6]), Paul Sacher Foundation, Basle

Op. 16 sketch. This new formulation follows on from the encircled b♮″ on staff 9 and was obviously written *after* the variant of the last bar of the piece had been written in staves 12–13. Contrary to Webern's usual practice, the variant of the last bar (staves 12–13) is not aligned exactly with the bar above. The spacing of the notes is tighter, and the bar ends long before the double bar of the initial version. A similar situation occurs in the variant ending with a fermata on staves 14–15. The arrow indicates the continuation, which begins displaced a little to the right and ends roughly aligned with the variant above it, far to the left of the double bar-line in staves 10–11. A possible explanation for the constrictions and displacements in the vertical alignment is that the Op. 16 sketches had already taken up space. This supposition is supported by a material circumstance: the top and bottom margins of this page are of different widths. In sketching Op. 16 No. 1, Webern always wrote in such a way that the top margin was the narrower one.[29] Consequently, page [6] could well have been used first for Op. 16 No. 1. In addition, it seems more likely for a partly used page of manuscript paper to be filled up with sketches for a new piece than for a problematic passage from the Op. 16 canon to be worked out on a page that was already almost full. If the transcription is to be used to clarify such questions, then one must retain as much information in it as possible, including the scale and format of the staves and, of course, the paper margins.

Assuming that the canon sketches were written on page [6] before the *Kinderstück* sketches, we can no longer say with certainty whether the *Kinderstück* was drafted before or after 12 November 1924, the date Op. 16 No. 1 was completed. We do not even know if the canon sketches on page [6] were written before that date.[30] Webern claimed, possibly retrospectively, that the second, completed, *Kinderstück* (M.267) was composed during the autumn of 1924. The strongest indication that this piece was composed at a later date is the fact that it is based on a twelve-tone row and thus conforms more closely to the familiar rules of twelve-tone technique than does the fragment with its row 'without A'. A completed seventeen-bar piece does perhaps suggest more experience with the new compositional technique than an unfinished draft of half that length.[31] A number of circumstances suggest that the two *Kinderstücke* were written together during the autumn of 1924, before the Op. 16 No. 1 canon had been worked out. However, the sketches on page [6] provide no proof of this.

Plainly, all questions of transcription involve deciphering and are from the outset concerned with compositional problems. Our knowledge and suppositions influence our reading and leave behind traces in the reproduction. Communicating an interpretation of a doubtful passage is meaningful and useful, but in the transcription itself this should be avoided; indeed, the transcription of such passages without the addition of facsimiles should be avoided altogether. In this respect, the fragment of the *Kinderstück* is a borderline case. It belongs to Webern's earliest essays in twelve-tone composition, and therefore it is important to be able to identify what Webern was 'essaying' and in what way. Nothing may be presupposed as certain. The A pitches in a variant of the first draft (staves 1–4) do not mean that Webern here worked only with the twelve-tone row he wrote on the third staff. Some accidentals and one pitch in this row were altered just before the missing A is supplied, which is where the row begins to diverge from the eleven-tone row of the fourth staff. Between staves 2 and 3, letter-names of different pitches are partly crossed out or overwritten, indicating that some things about the row were not yet certain. There are thus uncertain places in the first draft, which should not be determined by means of the row, but should rather be kept open for other interpretations.

Finally, the *Kinderstück* sketches present a further set of problems, making transcription extremely difficult, even if one could exactly reproduce the half-bar with hand-drawn staff lines and notes at the end of staves 6–7, as well as the question mark and the zigzag line (possibly indicating deletion) on the three staves above. The tacked-on bar and the encircled third bar (both on staves 6–7), as well as the variants on the two staves below, beg the question as to whether this draft was in fact written down in one go up to the double bar. When he reached the end of the first system, Webern could have gone on writing in the next one. In other words, was the extended bar introduced later? Are the deletions in the first bar of the second system (staves 10–11) related to the extended bar of the previous system? When were the variants underneath the third and fourth bars notated? Is the encircled third bar the only one that was to be deleted? Why was the penultimate bar of the draft (from the b♮″, staff 9) displaced upwards by one staff? In addition to formal and motivic considerations,[32] the way the sketches 'look' – that is to say, how they were written – now becomes relevant: different thicknesses of pencil, tighter or more widely spaced handwriting, alternate precision and haste.

> What is important is not what sounds, however much it may be the endeavour of the composer to write for the sound, but what has been written: the (geometrical, mathematical or 'architectonic') relationships between pitches and periods of time. If the author thinks of the sound, of the dynamics and the tempo, he himself is here already the interpreter of his thought. That is, he makes use of the means of performance in order to lend his thought the possibility of general comprehensibility. The performing artists are then to a certain degree interpreters of the interpretation. But [the] thought is complete, without any interpretation, as soon as it has been notated.[33]

CHAPTER 8

A tale of two sketchbooks: reconstructing and deciphering Alban Berg's sketchbooks for Wozzeck

Patricia Hall

> I myself went up the mountain very slowly, resting often, and eventu-
> ally, as I was plodding on, without any intention of working, I found
> that the musical expression for one of Wozzeck's entrances, which I
> had been trying to get for ages, had suddenly come to me.
>
> Alban Berg to Helene Berg, 7 August 1918[1]

Reminiscent of Beethoven, who jotted ideas in sketchbooks while strolling in the Vienna woods, this quote also typifies the twentieth-century composer. Sketchbooks are one of the most frequently used formats of this period, often revealing the inception and development of a work in a single document source. And although in their shorter period of existence the leaves of twentieth-century sketchbooks have not suffered as much as Beethoven's from dismemberment and dispersion, we still see the same problems, sometimes even as a result of leaves removed by the composer.[2] This chapter, then, examines techniques of reconstructing sketchbooks, as well as a related topic, deciphering verbal annotations, using two sketchbooks from Alban Berg's opera *Wozzeck*.

THE SOURCES

The protagonists of this chapter are two sketchbooks residing in the Austrian National Library, ÖNB Musiksammlung F 21 Berg 13/I and 13/II. Ernst Hilmar, with the permission of Berg's widow, Helene Berg, examined these sketchbooks briefly in 1975.[3] They became available for general study, along with Berg's other autograph sources, in 1981. In their discussions of these sketchbooks, Peter Peterson and David Fanning have pointed out that what Hilmar described as 'a third sketchbook' (F 21 Berg 13/VII) is actually part of F 21 Berg 13/I.[4] They further note that 13/I dates from the last year of composition (1921), not 'the earliest sketches for the opera', as described by Rosemary Hilmar in her catalogue of Berg's sketches and autographs.[5]

These sketchbooks of 28 and 48 leaves are two of the most important documents among Berg's sketches for *Wozzeck*, showing both ends of the chronological spectrum – the early sketches from the opera's period of inception (1914–18) and some of its final sketches (1921).[6] Thus, it is well worth the effort to analyse these sources for any missing leaves that may appear over time.

ANATOMY OF A SKETCHBOOK

Although paper types among twentieth-century composers are rarely studied to the degree they are with Beethoven, they can be a critical factor in the identification and chronology of a composer's sketches. Berg relied on a music paper still available for sale in Vienna produced by the firm Josef Eberle. The paper most often appearing in his sketchbooks – beginning as early as the Four Songs, Op. 2 – is Protocoll Schutzmarke No. 70, 10-line paper.[7] It consists of a bifolium, often with a shield or the label 10-linig (10-line) appearing on the recto side of the left-hand (A) leaf.[8] (In the following discussion, I will refer to the left-hand leaf of the bifolium as the 'A' leaf and the right-hand leaf of the bifolium as the 'B' leaf.) Since this paper frequently changes format, it is necessary to assess the size of the paper and the layout of the printed image to differentiate different years.[9] For instance, Plates 8.1 and 8.2 show the dimensions for the recto side of the 'A' leaf of our two sketchbooks from 1914–18 and 1921.

Besides differences in size, the musical content or internal evidence also suggests a great gap in time: Plate 8.1 shows a ghost-like trace of Wozzeck's main theme (possibly Berg's first annotation of it). The 1921 sketch (Plate 8.2) in contrast, is a draft of bars 705–12 of Act II, scene 4, nearly obliterated by a doodle included in a draft of a letter (in pen) to Schoenberg from September 1921, in which Berg deferentially begs for more time to compose before returning to Vienna.[10] One can only wonder if this frowning (disapproving?) face is meant to be Schoenberg.

In addition, there is a substantial difference in colour between the two papers. This is because post-World War I inflation resulted both in a paper shortage and in the production of poor-quality paper, recognisable by its discoloration and smell – like that of old, cheap paperback books.

It is a straightforward task to compare dimensions of papers appearing in different archives, even different countries; colour comparison, however, is more subjective. Photographs rarely retain the exact colouring of the original computer screens are even more unreliable. To ascertain the shade of the paper and any coloured pencils used in the sketch, I currently use *Dumont's Farbenatlas*,[11] which lists over 5,500 colours and a formula that gives the per cent of yellow (Y), magenta (M), black (B) and cyan blue (C) needed to create a particular colour. Again, one could never confuse the light off-white of 13/II (given the formula Y10 in *Dumont's Farbenatlas*) with the walnut brown of 13/VII (Y40 M10).

Both sketchbooks are made up of a series of gatherings: four bifolia nested inside one another and stapled in the centre, forming eight leaves or sixteen pages, depending on whether the sketchbook is paginated (page 1, page 2), or foliated (folio 1 recto, folio 1 verso). Since only the 'A' recto leaves of these sketchbooks bear the label 70-linig (70-line) and the outside edges are regular, it is easy to recognise the position of the leaf within a

F21 Berg 13/II p. 59

Berg 13/VII fol. 2

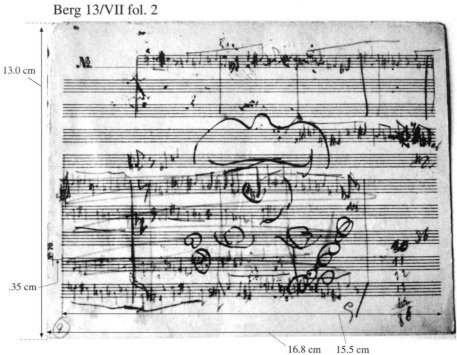

Plates 8.1 and 8.2   Alban Berg, *Wozzeck*, dimensions of the 'A' recto leaf for ÖNB Musiksammlung
F 21 Berg 13/II and 13/VII

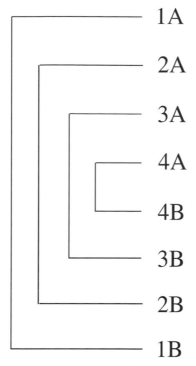

Figure 8.1   Diagram of a gathering structure

gathering. Four bifolia placed inside each other result in the sequence 1A-2A-3A-4A 4B-3B-2B-1B (see Figure 8.1). These gatherings are then stacked one upon the other and stabilised with a binding.

CHANGES TO THE STRUCTURE OF A SKETCHBOOK: DISMEMBERMENT AND ADDITION OF PAGES

Determining the gathering structure of a document is a delicate operation, since any manipulation may cause damage to the manuscript binding. Often the number of gatherings is apparent by looking at the ends of the sketchbook (Plate 8.3). Further, because of the set pattern of each gathering we will see the four 'A' leaves with 70-linig stamped on the recto leaf, two staples appearing between leaves 4A and 4B, followed by the four B leaves. If pages are missing, it is often necessary to gently press down the centre area of the sketchbook between the two leaves to look for evidence of stubs. (As tempting as it may be, prying open sketchbooks or poking one's finger in the binding further adds to their destruction.) Stubs can take

Plate 8.3   Alban Berg, *Wozzeck*, sketchbook ÖNB Musiksammlung F 21 Berg 13/II, showing gatherings

the form of cut edges (in which case, one can the trace the profile of the stub and compare it with that of the missing leaf) or a frayed edge of an 'A' or 'B' leaf. In the case of 13/I, an entire gathering is missing, which, although fortunately still residing in the Austrian National Library, was given a separate call number and incorrect foliation. (The outside bifolium of the gathering, which should have formed the first and fourth leaves, was foliated as 2 and 1.)

This was a fairly simple mystery to solve, and indeed, both Peterson and Fanning reconstructed the sketchbook primarily from internal evidence. More often, however, the leaf is residing in another library or country, which makes immediate comparisons impossible. In this case (and in general) it is safer to play the part of a detective at a crime scene and gather as many types of evidence as possible. For example, Beethoven scholars create the equivalent of a missing poster, listing dimensions, watermark, internal evidence, etc.[12] Using this model, we would expect the missing leaf that constitutes pages 88–9 in sketchbook 13/II to have the following appearance:

1. Its upper right-hand corners (recto and verso) would be stamped with the numbers 38 and 39. This is such a defining piece of evidence that one would hardly need to look further. However, since Berg paginated only one of his sketchbooks, we should also consider more typical types of evidence.
2. The dimensions would conform to the 13/II leaf discussed above. Since this is an 'A' leaf, its recto side would bear the stamp No. 70. The leaf would also be edged in red.

Plate 8.4   Alban Berg, *Wozzeck*, sketchbook ÖNB Musiksammlung F 21 Berg 13/II, showing added leaf

3. The sketch most likely would be in pencil, possibly with additions of lavender indelible pencil.
4. Part of the left-hand edge would be missing, particularly at the bottom left of the recto side. (If a large section is missing, tracing the stub is advisable so that one can match the profile of the stub with that of the missing leaf.)
5. The content of the sketch (the internal evidence) would most certainly be Act II, scene 2, and more specifically, the section that Berg labels in his outline as VII, that is, the fugue that begins in bar 286.
6. The recto side of the leaf would probably show a concave fold running diagonally from 11.3 cm (measuring from the top, left-hand edge of the leaf) to 9.4 cm bottom (measuring from the bottom, left-hand edge of the leaf). This measurement is based on the position of the same fold in previous leaves, since folds tend gradually to migrate to the left or right during the course of a sketchbook.

Page 54 of the same sketchbook, in contrast, is a leaf actually added by the composer (Plate 8.4). Berg has not stamped the leaf with a page number, thus, it was added after Berg had organised the second half of this sketchbook by stamping each leaf with a *numerator*. Moreover, it is a 'B' leaf between two 'A' leaves, a physical impossibility in the normal gathering structure. Note that the ripped edge of the leaf appears as the outside edge. The musical content of the leaf is completely in line with the sketches of previous and later leaves, and Berg has written a small 'W' in the upper left-hand corner to remind himself that the leaf contains sketches for *Wozzeck*. So however this leaf became detached, Berg has placed it in a location logical for the musical content of the sketchbook.

SUMMARY DIAGRAMS OF SKETCHBOOKS

Another useful tool in sketchbook research for which we can thank Beethoven scholars is a summary diagram of the entire sketchbook, indicating pagination/foliation, gathering structure and missing leaves. Figure 8.2 is a diagram of 13/I, assessing missing leaves, as well as the proper placement of the missing gathering, 13/VII.

Although this sketchbook appears hopelessly mutilated, it has only four leaves missing, as well as the flyleaf for the back cover. Detached leaves of sketchbooks, or 'cuttings', often exist because the composer, or relatives of the composer, presented them as gifts. In this case, we are lucky; only Berg and his wife owned the sketches, in contrast to the many hands through which Beethoven sketches have passed. Still, sketchbook leaves are easily removed, but successfully restored only after a great deal of effort and research.

DECIPHERING VERBAL ANNOTATIONS

One of the curses of studying sketchbooks, besides dismemberment, is messy, often illegible handwriting – in Berg's case the result of composing while riding in cars, trains, on walks, etc. And this also applies to the verbal annotations that frequently appear in twentieth-century sketches. Visit any manuscript table and you will see scholars sounding out words and furiously debating whether a scribble in the left-hand corner of a sketch is an 'a' or an 'e'. There are, however, established methods for deciphering handwriting.

Scholars who study a composer's handwriting over an extended period of time often construct an alphabet chart identifying typical shapes of letters. A starting point might be one of the texts that display handwriting from different eras of the twentieth century.[13] It is also possible, of course, to construct a chart from a clearer source of the composer's handwriting, for instance, formal correspondence in which the composer was at least attempting to write legibly. To truly learn to decipher a composer's handwriting, one often needs to practise by imitating how the composer wrote both letters and words. This may seem like a tedious process, but in fact, it saves the researcher untold time in the long run. Moreover, the intimate knowledge one gains of the composer's handwriting allows one to more easily recognise other hands – in Berg's case, his wife's, or even a student's. Once a chart is compiled, one can list typical variants. For instance, Berg regularly writes the following versions of capital T:

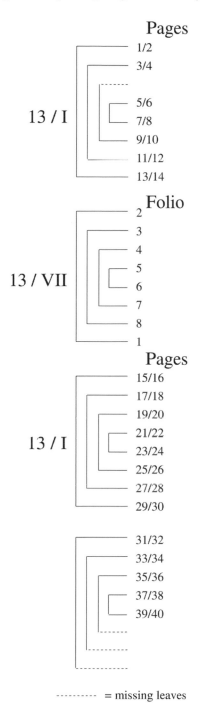

Pages

13 / I

1/2
3/4
5/6
7/8
9/10
11/12
13/14

Folio

13 / VII

2
3
4
5
6
7
8
1

Pages

13 / I

15/16
17/18
19/20
21/22
23/24
25/26
27/28
29/30

31/32
33/34
35/36
37/38
39/40

--------- = missing leaves

Figure 8.2   Summary diagram of ÖNB Musiksammlung F 21 Berg 13/I and 13/VII

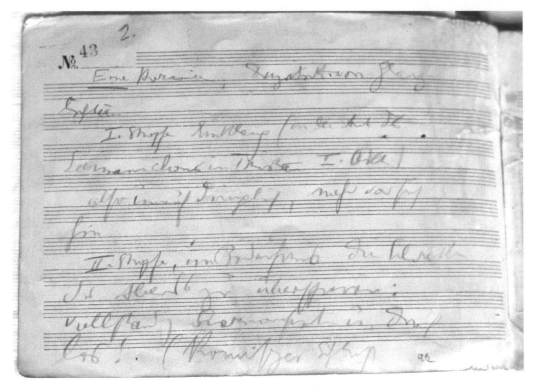

Plate 8.5   Alban Berg, *Wozzeck*, concept sketch for Act I, scene 2, ÖNB Musiksammlung F 21 Berg 13/II p. 92

Attempting to decipher words without a strong knowledge of the language in question is almost hopeless. Even a native speaker would be wise to share their transcription with other scholars doing similar work; it is too easy to make embarrassing errors. Fortunately one usually becomes acquainted over the years with other scholars doing the same kind of deciphering.

It would be comforting if computer images, selected for colour, manipulated by magnification, brightness and other factors solved some if not all of these problems. While computer scans of sketches are invaluable for study away from the archive (minimising the time one spends deciphering the original document), without a thorough knowledge of the composer's handwriting, a magnified word will be just as unclear as in the original manuscript. In truth, the worst handwriting nightmares are usually solved when sitting in front of the original manuscript with a magnifying glass and good natural light – often as the team effort of several scholars.[14]

A single leaf, F 21 Berg 13/II p. 92, can teach us a great deal about Berg's handwriting (Plate 8.5, transcribed in Figure 8.3). I have previously cited this sketch of Act I, scene 2, in

No

Eine Harmonie   Dazutritt von Glanz -

lichtern.

I. Strophe Einklang (in der Art des

Seemannchores in Tristan   I. Akt /

also unauf dringlich, mehr vor sich

hin

II. Strophe, im Bedürfnis die Schrecken

des Abends zu   überschreien:

vollständig harmonisiert u. drauf

los!   (Komischer Schluß

Figure 8.3   Transcription of ÖNB Musiksammlung F21 Berg 13/II p. 92

relation to the inception of the opera. Here, in contrast, I will focus on Berg's formation of letters. The sketch reads:

> One harmony, along with luminous lights. First strophe, unison, in the style of the Sailor's choir in *Tristan*, Act I. That is, unobtrusive, more to oneself. Second Strophe: The need to scream above the horror of the evening. Completely harmonised, and then off! Comical ending.

Probably completed in 1918, this concept sketch is one of a number of Berg's analyses of dramatic action and psychological tone of the Büchner text that he hoped to portray musically. The writing implement for almost the entire sketch is indelible pencil, and the paper itself is highly distressed. (We need to remind ourselves that twentieth-century sketches are frequently in worse condition than those of earlier eras, often having experienced two world wars and various natural disasters before being placed in an archive.)

The handwriting suggests haste or even creative frenzy that matches the expressionistic tone of the scene. As a result, the letters are fairly widely spaced and details like the dot of an 'i' or the cross of a 't' often appear slightly to the right of the actual letter. However, we can still see patterns in Berg's formation of letters, some of which are characteristic of Austrian handwriting during this era, and others specific to Berg. These patterns include: the relatively large clockwise loops in the s's which complete the words *des, Seemannschors, Bedürfnis, Abends, los*; the horizontal counter-clockwise loops of Berg's d's (*Dazutritt, des,*

Plate 8.6   Alban Berg, *Wozzeck*, concept sketch for Act I, scene 2, ÖNB Musiksammlung F 21 Berg 13/II p. 93

dringlich, *die*, *drauf*); the very strong K's, in which the second stroke extends out beyond the first stroke and forms an approximately 30° angle, similar to Berg's v's; the figure eight shape of Berg's capital S (*Strophe*) which allows us to recognise the similar gestalt of his 'S' for '*Schrecken*'; the tail of Berg's t's which form a 30° angle from the perpendicular base of the letter, the loop appearing above u's.

And even in this single sketch we see variants of letters. Berg makes the standard, triangular shaped A which he also uses in his signature for '*Art*' and '*Abends*'. '*Akt*', however, is formed with a counter-clockwise loop.

Of course, logical patterns of vowels and consonants, expected syntax, and the general content and context of the sketch help us as well. As with any transcription, deciphering annotations requires constant analysis of the passage in order to understand the logic of the composer's comments. Does the first strophe of Andres' song in Act I, scene 2, remind us of the sailors' choir in *Tristan*, Act I? Do the successive statements of the song suggest a heightening of the anxiety level of both characters? Is the sketch based on the text or musical directions for the opera?

Mercifully, this is the case with the next page of the sketchbook, which exhibits the same frenetic handwriting as the previous leaf (Plate 8.6). Moreover, as one of the last leaves of the sketchbook, it is stained and bent nearly beyond recognition.

This is one of those sketches in which words in the top and bottom margins are simply too light to read, even when the original document is magnified. Selecting magenta in Photoshop does allow us to read most of the words, but unfortunately, this sketch does not contain the marvellous insights of the previous page. Given the amount of time required, we need to ask ourselves if deciphering this particular leaf is worth the effort, or if time would be better spent elsewhere. And if any doubt exists about the identity of a word, one should spare future scholars a great deal of frustration by placing the word in brackets with a question mark.

Deciphering verbal annotations is a very time-consuming endeavour that requires an optimistic frame of mind and an almost obsessive will to succeed. At the very least, such sketches show the development of the composer's ideas over time, and in special instances, give us a view of a composition's potential not yet realised. And although the sketchbooks from which these annotations arise will not always give us a complete, or even ordered, image of a work's development, they do give us valuable glimpses into the creative process and psychology of the composer.

CHAPTER 9

'Written between the desk and the piano': dating Béla Bartók's sketches

László Somfai

> Q.: How do you work? Regularly? – *Bartók*: I would say that I don't like mixing my work. When I undertake something, then, I only live for it, until it is finished. – Q.: [Do you compose] At a desk? At the piano? – *Bartók*: Between the desk and the piano.
>
> (1925)[1]

Béla Bartók (1881–1945) was close in age to Anton Webern (1883–1945) yet very different in his attitude to the inception of composition and to the use of a sketchbook. Webern is, of course, only one of the suitable subjects for comparison. To simplify a much more complex case, for Webern the large-format sketchbook was a kind of diary of the search for ideas in which he often dated sketches and occasionally formulated even verbal commentaries about the character or the inspiration of a planned composition.[2] In the case of Bartók, first of all, the time-periods dedicated to composition were rare but extremely intensive (his regular days were filled with ethnomusicological studies, concert tours, practising and teaching piano, etc.). Dating sketches or making verbal notes about compositional plans was not at all his habit; a sketchbook was a seldom adopted aid. Bartók noted down compositional sketches in a sketchbook only when he was away from his home and piano, and thus could not improvise and work on ideas at the instrument, which was his typical routine when beginning a major composition.[3]

The physical appearance as well as the function of sketches is so diverse in the workshop of different composers that the applied terminology seems to be a key issue. I personally doubt, however, that the compatibility of definitions in sketch studies is crucial for us to understand each other. Our goal must be first and foremost the reliable reconstruction of the compositional process, which goes beyond the sketches anyway. The process, the typical routine as well as the working method in an irregular situation may be considerably different in each composer's case; accordingly the function of sketches varies. For a reliable reconstruction of the compositional process years-long extensive studies are needed. Preconditions are the thorough investigation of the full source chain of several individual works from different genres and periods (taking the original manuscripts in hand) and access to the complete source material of the whole oeuvre during these investigations (at least in copies). The sketch terminology ought to be the result, not the preliminary, of such studies.

In Bartók's working process the *draft* is the key source. Under normal conditions this was preceded and partly accompanied by intensive *improvisation* at the piano. Varied types of sketches surround these two acts, i.e. the virtual source (improvisation) and the physically existing main autograph source (draft):

- *Preliminary memo:* notation of mostly short musical ideas during the preparation for a new work, typically before the intensive improvisation.
- *Side sketch:* notation of related ideas, typically on the margin of a draft, either for the continuation of the same work or for another composition, which came to Bartók's mind when he revised the draft again, prepared the orchestration or copied the manuscript; these are valuable 'sketches in context'.
- *Partial sketch:* quick elaboration of contrapuntal, harmonic, textural, and most typically scoring problems on a separate piece of paper in the course of the writing of a draft or an orchestration.

The 'between the desk and the piano' compositional routine produced several intermediary types. A first quick notation (at the desk, on normal music paper) of what has already been crystallised during the improvisation/maturation (at the piano), hence a 'sketch', usually does not look sketchy at all. Many such fragmentary notations then submerged: they became the first block of the draft proper. Others, Bartók put aside. If he did not destroy them, we could call them a 'sketch'.[4] There is no doubt, as I have discussed elsewhere,[5] that in the first decades of his life, up to the end of World War I, from time to time Bartók checked his manuscripts and destroyed unnecessary autographs, sketches and also drafts, if the work had already been copied or printed. Due to such losses, the very beginning of the source chain of earlier compositions (including *Duke Bluebeard's Castle* and String Quartet No. 2) is at least provisionally incomplete; the reconstruction of the vitally important first steps in the creation of a work is hardly possible.

A *sketchbook*, as already mentioned, is a relatively rare phenomenon in Bartók's compositional routine. There are all together three such pocket-sized books (with ten printed staves,[6] typically used during folk-music collecting trips),[7] which Bartók took with him to write down shorter or longer sketches when he was far from his fully isolated studio housing his piano. Between 1907 and 1922, Bartók repeatedly used the first sketchbook (the so-called *Black Pocket-book*, published in facsimile) for sketching a number of compositions: among others, sections for the Violin Concerto op. posth., pieces for *Fourteen Bagatelles*, the whole of the second half of *The Miraculous Mandarin*. The First and Second Violin Sonatas were also outlined in this sketchbook. The second and the third pocket-sized books, his Arab and Turkish field-books (containing Bartók's folk-music notations from 1913 and 1936, respectively), were used in the American years in 1942–4 and contain the memo sketches as well as the major part of the elaboration of the Concerto for Orchestra and the Sonata for solo violin.

In these sketchbooks occasionally a *memo*, a longer sketch (*continuity sketch*), and what could be called a *continuity draft*, are subsequent steps of the same process on the same page. The first idea developed gradually; the music was drafted at length in a next step or later. Here the improvisation at the piano – the 'white hole' in the formation of so many Bartók works – is falling out automatically. The composer was turning ideas over in his mind, yet this could not substitute for playing and chiselling the stuff on his instrument, or simply rejecting it. He missed his piano. Therefore more was written down than under normal conditions. Consequently, sketches in sketchbooks may tell us more about the birth and perhaps even about the 'general spirit' of the work (Bartók's expression)[8] than his other sketches do.

*

I have chosen the Sonata for Violin and Piano No. 1 (1921) to demonstrate the methods we use for dating Béla Bartók's sketches in a sketchbook. The six-page-long sketches occur on folios 24v to 27r in the *Black Pocket-book*; see Plates 9.1–9.6. Bartók's handwriting is surprisingly clear so that a full diplomatic transcription is unnecessary.[9] These sketches, and nothing else, were outlined by the composer before October 1921. Then in October, under normal conditions in his Budapest home ('between the piano and the desk'), he started to work on the full autograph draft on normal music paper.

Dating is very precarious in this case. The intensive period of composition is well documented. Bartók dedicated and dated the Sonata in the printed edition: *A.J.-nek, Budapest, 1921. X.–XII.* (To J[elly] A[rányi], Budapest, October–December 1921). In addition, he noted the date that he completed the first movement (*1921. okt. 26.*) as well as the third movement (*1921. dec. 12.*) in the draft (which is very rare). However, planning and writing down sketches could have begun months, a year, or even more than a year before. Based on the simple fact that Bartók used a sketchbook and not normal music paper, I am convinced that these sketches date prior to the time between 24 September and 4 October 1921 in Budapest when he became familiar with Jelly Arányi's fascinating violin playing.[10]

More confusing is the chronological uncertainty, because it is generally believed that the composition of the First Sonata was directly inspired by Jelly's violin playing, including the concept that throughout the work the violin and the piano present separate, instrument-idiomatic themes. Two documents give us contradictory evidence. According to Bartók's wife Márta (written in a Hungarian letter to the composer's mother), on her birthday (19 October) as a present Béla showed her the violin sonata on which he worked:

> I'm so grateful to Jelly Arányi whose wonderful playing on the violin made this (as he says) long-dormant [*régen szunnyadó*] plan jump out of Béla.[11]

This is a simple and authentic statement. The sketches confirm, as we shall see, the existence of the 'long-dormant' plan. The other document is Bartók's almost-love-letter to Jelly Arányi (9 November 1921, written in Hungarian, only a partial translation is known),[12] in which he confessed that,

Your violin playing has indeed impressed me so much that I decided on that
Tuesday [4 Oct.] when we last played together: I will attempt this, for me, unusual
combination only if both instruments always had separate themes – this notion
has taken definite form so that already next day the plan & the main themes for
all three movements were ready. When we said goodbye on Thursday [6 Oct.] I
could have mentioned it. I wanted very much to do so, but I did not dare, I did
not know whether after such a long silence – 2 years – which had been imposed
on me I could still compose.

Had Bartók indeed written down 'the plan and the main themes for all three movements'
as late as 5 October 1921? It is a nice romantic narrative. Certainly Bartók exaggerated the
two-year-long silence too (he wrote *Improvisations on Hungarian Peasant Songs* for piano, an
important work, in 1920). The truth presumably was what he told his wife Márta.

Let us visit the sketches and discuss the initial written memos in detail. As an aid to
identify the content and the rough chronology of the sketches in Plates 9.1–9.3, Figure 9.1
gives a map-like depiction of the sections (writing units) of the six pages. This division of
the sections is neither a preliminary nor a mechanical one but represents the achievements of
research based on philological observations as well as the analysis of content. The sections are
marked with letters, and with additional numbers if they were written down in subsequent
steps. Here is a concordance of sketches A to K with the final form. (In the Universal Edition
print the bars are not numbered, so we refer to the rehearsal numbers with plus or minus
bars.)[13]

A   Movement I, from the beginning to 2^{+6} plus three bars
B   Movement I, related to the theme from 7 to 7^{+5} in another key
C   Movement III, from the beginning to 7^{-4}
D   Movement II, from the beginning to 3^{-3} plus three bars
E   Movement I, from 5^{+2} to 5^{+6}
F   Movement I, from 21^{-5} to 22^{-1}
G   Movement I, from 24^{-2} to *c.* 24 (violin only)
H   Movement I, from 24 to 24^{+5}
I   Movement I, from 17 to 17^{+7}
J   Movement I, from 25 to 25^{+6}
K   Unused sketch (for Movement I?)[14]

The development of the ideas and the actual sequence of the sketches A–B–C–D did not
necessarily follow the alphabet in every detail. We have already pointed out that, when Bartók
worked with a sketchbook, he initially wrote down relatively short ideas (memo sketches) as a
reminder, leaving ample space for the continuation on the page. In the case of the First Sonata,

Plates 9.1 and 9.2   Béla Bartók, Sonata for Violin and Piano No. 1, sketches in the *Black Pocket-book*

Plates 9.3 and 9.4   Béla Bartók, Sonata for Violin and Piano No. 1, sketches in the *Black Pocket-book*

László Somfai

Plates 9.5 and 9.6   Béla Bartók, Sonata for Violin and Piano No. 1, sketches in the *Black Pocket-book*

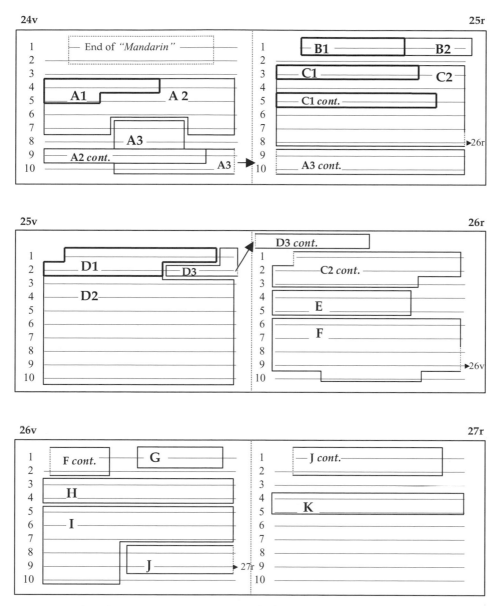

Figure 9.1   A guide to the writing units of the sketches for the Sonata for Violin and Piano No. 1 on six pages in the *Black Pocket-book* (fols. 24v to 27r)

in his initial sketches on three subsequent pages (fols. 24v, 25r, 25v) he fixed the beginning of the three movements plus a contrasting theme to the first movement. In Figure 9.1 these crucially important memo sketches are framed with bold lines.

At first glance the following sequence of notation of the initial memo sketches might be considered self-evident:

A1 On a verso page (following the end of *The Miraculous Mandarin* sketches) in staves 4–5, the first four bars plus one note: beginning of Movement I of the Sonata, written in two staves (but meant for piano and violin), including the opening piano passage (two $\frac{3}{4}$ time bars in C♯) and the head-motive of the violin theme (two bars plus a minim a′ in the third bar).

B1 On the top of the opposite page: a contrasting theme also in $\frac{3}{4}$ time (which may suggest that it belongs to the same movement), at first only the upbeat, two bars and a minim c′ (the last two bars, B2, were added in a next step): unambiguously noted as double stops for violin (but later this became a characteristic piano theme in Movement I at 7, *Vivo, appassionato*).

C1 Also on the opposite page (in the third staff, eight bars only, ending with four semiquaver bs) a contrasting piece or movement as it were, in $\frac{2}{4}$ time, built on the C♯ chords of the piano: the beginning of the rondo theme of Movement III, followed by two further motives of the rondo-theme complex in the fifth staff (four bars corresponding with the motive at 4, and three bars forecasting the closing motive of the rondo-theme complex at 6^{+6-10}), crossed out when in a next step, C2, Bartók sketched the continuation of the opening theme in staves 3 (end), 4, 6–8.

D1 On the top of the next verso page: the beginning of the slow second movement in $\frac{6}{8}$ time, six bars in the first staff, four bars and a dotted minim d′ in the second.

According to this reading, Bartók worked on the beginning of the first and the third movements that were in the same key (C♯) before anything was fixed on paper for a middle movement. This does not mean that originally Bartók planned a two-movement sonata and only later modified the concept to a more traditional three-movement form. Here we face the typical danger of sketch studies: one can place the first written notes under the magnifying glass and interpret them, but one cannot even guess what took place in the composer's head. In Bartók's case, thinking about a new composition in a broader sense and writing down already crystallised musical ideas, he surely worked in parallel channels. We have no reason to doubt that in his first mature sonata, written nearly two decades after the previous attempt in the genre,[15] Bartók planned anything but a normal three-movement composition, assuming of course that at this point he was thinking about a genuine sonata and not just pieces for violin and piano without a fixed concept or title. The *attacca* two-movement form of the Second Sonata, written a year later, must not confuse us. This structure can be understood as a revision of the sonata concept accomplished in the First Sonata, in fact a much-too-long work perhaps not without compositional problems as Bartók could have observed after he played the Sonata in spring 1922 half-a-dozen times.

   Theoretically, one cannot rule out the possibility that the sequence of writing these memo sketches was not the here described A1→B1→C1→D1, but rather A1→B1→D1→C1. That is, first Bartók may have written only one memo per page (as he often did in a sketchbook): the opening theme and a contrasting theme for the first movement, the theme of the second movement, and after this he returned to the second page and sketched the beginning of the finale. Such a return would not be unusual in Bartók's compositional process. Re-reading a theme in his own manuscript sometimes inspired the birth of a similar melody (as the end of movement II of the Violin Concerto No. 2 inspired the *Più mosso* lyric theme in the finale of *Contrasts*);[16] or he outlined the variant form of a theme directly on the opposite page in the sketchbook, as he did in case of the Second Violin Sonata, where sketches to the basic themes of movement II appear opposite the opening theme of movement I (on fols. 27v–28r in the same sketchbook). This was a two-movement concept with not just tonal but close thematic relationships too.[17] Nevertheless, a thorough look at the handwriting, as we shall see, does not support the second supposition.

However, something is wrong with both suggested sequences. The first sketch is written on a page that already had music on it. This was not Bartók's habit in working with a sketchbook. In fact there is a third possibility too, B1→A1→C1→D1, a fascinating sequence, and certain physical evidence of the handwriting speaks for this hypothesis. According to this sequence, Bartók could have noted down the violin double-stop theme B1 first, opposite the end of *The Miraculous Mandarin* sketches on the top of the next blank page, which was his habit. Only after this still-vague idea have the opening themes A1 and C1, and in a next step D1, been crystallised.

For a careful study of physical evidence of the handwriting we must examine the original manuscript, preferably by daylight. Nuances of the strokes of the pen are more ambiguous in any facsimile reproduction than in the original manuscript: distinction between thinner and thicker strokes, or between a slightly darker or lighter colour of the ink are less apparent. For the following discussion I studied Bartók's original sketchbook, and can assure the reader that, for instance, theme B1 is in fact written with a thicker type of writing; A1 and the first line of C1 with considerably thinner writing; the second unit of C1, seven crossed-out bars in the fifth staff, again with thicker writing. To explain this phenomenon we need a short digression.

First digression: writing with fountain pen

In his mature compositions under normal conditions Bartók used a fountain pen, as did several of his contemporaries. This makes the philologist's work difficult. The identification of different pens, as a traditional aid in separating layers in the handwriting, is immediately apparent, albeit the diversity of pens used in a twentieth-century manuscript is seldom as meaningful as, for instance, in Mozart's autograph manuscripts written with quills. Bartók, by nature an economical and pedantic man, used the same fountain pen and for a long time refilled it from the same bottle of fountain-pen ink. Therefore in his typical manuscripts neither the stroke nor the colour of ink shows strong contrast. Fortunately there are at least two areas of the investigation of fountain-pen strokes that might help us in unfolding the chronological layers of the handwriting in a given manuscript.

One is the study of the stroke of the pen. The same fountain-pen nib can produce both thinner and thicker lines. Without suggesting an oversimplified theory, at least in the case of Bartók's fountain pen and due to his writing habits, thin lines generally signal the beginning of a new writing act. It tells us that the cap of the fountain pen was screwed in, the just-opened fountain pen's nib was still dry; the stroke is scratchy, the continuous flow of ink follows only after a number of healthy strokes. In other words, a pause in writing preceded such a sketch – of course we do not know whether of some minutes, hours or days. Among the memo sketches of the First Sonata, A1 and the first eight bars of C1 clearly show this dried-out-and-thin stroke. In contrast, thicker lines signal the more or less continuous use of fountain pen, and these make up the major part of the notation.

The other area of investigation, though not limited to fountain-pen writing, and one of particular value here, is the size and angle of certain musical symbols (the average size of notes, stems and accidentals; the angle of stems and beams, etc.). Every interruption in the writing act may slightly change the position of the paper on the composer's desk, or of his hand on the music paper, and consequently affect the inclination of vertical lines (most characteristically that of the stems). There are writing units with regularly vertical lines as well as lines leaning slightly right or left. In addition, after a longer interruption, the lighting may also have been considerably different (daylight, twilight, lamplight), thus the size of the notation may become discernibly larger or smaller. To take examples from the first two pages of our sketches, the facsimile alone reveals that (on the second page) the notation of theme B1 is larger than C1. Or picking up finer nuances (from the first page), the angle of the stems in the first two bars of the opening violin theme (A1, bars 3–4) differs from the following bars (A2), just as the stems of the piano passage in bar 7 differ from the violin theme above it.

There are nuances in the shades of colour too, even if the same bottle (or, at least, the same brand) of fountain-pen ink was used. These mostly originate from the speed of writing, the flow of ink. Writing quickly with a well-used pen nib leaves not only a thicker but also a lighter line: the ink colour is less black, rather dark-brownish (B2, compared with B1, is a good example of this; incidentally, the shade of ink colour of B2 is similar to the beginning of A2 or C2). Such nuances can, however, be studied only in the original manuscript, and the observations may be considered as hypotheses at most.[18]

Returning to the third hypothetical sequence of the memo sketches (B1→A1→ C1→D1), and in all probability the correct one, what do the pen strokes tell us about the micro-chronology?

The additional information provided by the thicker pen stroke is that the notation of the violin-idiomatic theme B1 was not preceded by a pause in the use of the fountain pen;

Bartók was in the middle of writing. Which is of course embarrassing: how, then, could theme B1 be the first sketch written down for the Sonata? But do we know what Bartók was writing at this point? A plausible explanation could be that he was writing something other than sketches: for instance, letters, or he could even have been correcting proofs of another composition when this theme came to his mind. Several of his letters to publishers, friends and family members indicate that Bartók often had the proof sheets of his compositions sent to his temporary address during the summer holidays, a situation where he also used the pocket-sized book for compositional sketches. We also know that on a trip he sometimes orchestrated from the already finished short score, another routine job he could complete while away from his study.

Can external musical evidence – primarily thematic or conceptual correlations between the sketch and a previous composition which the composer was scoring or proof-reading at that time – help us to define the approximate date of undated sketches? It may not be useful for other composers, but it can be attempted with Bartók. There are three good reasons to do so: (1) Bartók noted down compositional sketches in pocket-sized books only when he was away from his home and piano; (2) the dates of his whereabouts (summer holidays, folksong-collecting trips, concert tours, family visits, etc.) are well documented,[19] as is the list of projects on which he worked during the trips (proof-reading, even scoring);[20] (3) a direct or indirect motivic link between the revisited earlier composition and the invention of the next one, even if unintentional, was not rare in Bartók's working process.[21]

Second digression: chronological context of undated sketches

Bartók finished drafting *The Miraculous Mandarin* by July 1919;[22] thus the sketches of the last five bars (written with dark-brown ink on the top of fol. 24v of the sketchbook) had to be fixed in the sketchbook by this time at the latest. The sketches for the Sonata are written with distinctively different black ink: the following five trips can be considered:

- 20 February to 1 April 1920: trip to Germany, staying mostly in Berlin. Documented links: Bartók was reading proofs of *Fifteen Hungarian Peasant Songs* for piano (1914–18), and worked on the German translation of *Five Ady Songs*, Op. 16 (1916).[23]

- 16–20 April 1920: short trip to visit his mother in Pozsony (Bratislava). Documented links: he sent the printer's copy of *Three Studies* for piano, Op. 18 (1918), to Universal Edition, and read the next proofs of *Fifteen Hungarian Peasant Songs*.[24]

- 10 July to 6 September 1920: summer holidays in Kertmeg puszta, Hungary, in his sister's house. Documented links: he read proofs of *Three Studies*, composed six pieces (Nos. 1–2, 4–5, 7–8) of *Improvisations on Hungarian Peasant Songs* for piano, Op. 20 (1920).[25] Special conditions: a piano was available (but not isolated as in Bartók's study at home); *Improvisations* were drafted on normal music paper.

Example 9.1a Béla Bartók, *Three Studies* No. 1, bars 38–41

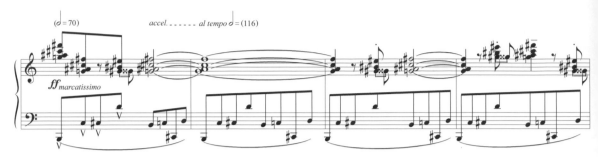

Example 9.1b Béla Bartók, Sonata for Violin and Piano No. 1, sketch B

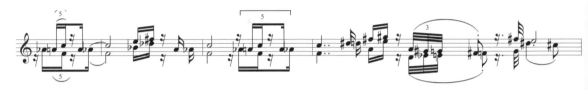

- 19 March to 4 April 1921: a further trip to Pozsony. Documented link: in a letter he discussed *The Miraculous Mandarin*[26] with his publisher.
- 1 to 20 August 1921: summer holidays in Austria. Documented links: he scored Nos. 1–2 of *Four Orchestral Pieces*, and read proofs of the revised edition of *Suite No. 2* for orchestra, Op. 4 (1905–7).[27]

Based on a careful comparison of the Sonata sketches with the seven compositions that were in Bartók's hand during the five trips, *Three Studies* seem to deserve special attention. The *ff marcatissimo* contrast theme of the *Allegro molto* first *Study* (Ex. 9.1a) is closely related to the first written theme B1 of the Sonata sketches (Ex. 9.1b), though more in its gesture and rhythm than in its chord structure.

We assume that the idea of the violin double-stop theme came to Bartók's mind when he made contact with *Three Studies* again. The probable date would be mid-August 1920 when he was reading the proofs of the *Studies* during his summer holiday in Kertmeg puszta. But why would Bartók use the pocket-sized sketchbook? His sister's piano was available; he drafted the new peasant-song arrangements, *Improvisations*, on normal music paper. A psychological rather than philological explanation could be that *Improvisations* was already a work in progress, prepared in the normal way by improvising at the instrument and drafted on normal-sized music paper, whereas the notation of this violin theme was no more than an idea that fitted in the sketchbook.

More cannot be suggested. I see no further convincing link between the listed works and the Sonata sketches.

As a working hypothesis, we may then accept that the first memo sketch (B1) probably dates from August 1920. Yet we do not know whether the further memos (A1 and C1, perhaps also D1), or even their continuation (at least A2 and part of C2), were written down soon after this sketch in Kertmeg puszta or considerably later, in August 1921, during Bartók's summer trip in Austria. External musical evidence can neither prove nor refute one or the other supposition. Therefore we should concentrate on the musical context of the existing sketches to unfold the chronology and the creative process.

In 1920–21, indirect evidence points to Bartók's growing interest in writing a substantial chamber-music work for a string instrument (violin would be his obvious choice) and piano to present himself as a pianist-composer at his best. At the 8 March 1920 Bartók concert in Berlin, organised by Hermann Scherchen's 'Die neue Musikgesellschaft', in addition to blocks of shorter piano pieces, the large-format compositions were not Bartók's own works, but the Violoncello-Piano Sonata by Kodály and Ravel's Trio. Bartók played the Ravel Trio on 16 March 1921 in Budapest again and performed Debussy's Violin Sonata with young Zoltán Székely on 23 April 1921. Neither the two-movement Kodály sonata nor the three-movement Debussy seems to have been Bartók's direct model; rather it was a challenge to create something different of larger format. The 'long-dormant plan', as Márta heard it from her husband, presumably concerned this decision.

With theme B1, conceived for violin, the realisation of this plan had begun. In Bartók's stylistic realm this surely was not an opening theme for a major composition, just a characteristic motive. Now it was time to search for material. After reflecting on appropriate ideas, Bartók could find the opening theme A1: with dried-out-and-thin strokes he wrote the opening theme, as a natural reflex, before theme B1 in the sketchbook (i.e. on to the previous verso page, below the last bars of *Mandarin*), because in the composition it was designed to go before the double-stop theme. Then, again after some time – thus written with dried-out-and-thin strokes – as the opposite pole in the composition, Bartók outlined the primary theme of the finale (C1), an invented pseudo-peasant fiddler dance theme, very modern in sound, wild in motion – a perfect Bartókian novelty for the post-war scene of contemporary music.

Third digression: sketches and the concealed plan of a work

At this point in his plans, even if only a few bars of sketches existed on paper, in all probability Bartók had already conceived the concept ('general spirit') of the sonata. Nowhere in his essays and letters can we find one single word about the plan or the form (or, as we would call it today, the narrative) of the First Sonata. Yet the concept is fairly obvious for a Bartók expert, even if verbalising an abstract concept is a calculated risk.

The fundamental concept of the First Sonata – a Sonata in C♯ – is simple and straightforward. An emphatically art-music-style expressive first *Allegro*, bold in its free tonal treatment, opposes a totally different robust finale, inspired by rural music (in the style of fiddle dances from Transylvania, without actual peasant-music quotations).[28] The dramatic function of the ternary-form slow middle movement is transitory. Themes of the abstract/sublime exposition return, after a bridge of 'transformation', in a lively Hungarian embellished version. The multi-movement form thus leads from the perplexed world of ego towards community; a return to nature, to the unspoiled values of a rural community. This is clearly present in the First Sonata and has a deep Bartókian message.

Scholars working on the music of other composers of the twentieth century may doubt that sketch studies ought to deal with the hypothetical 'concept' or 'narrative' of a work at all. In Bartók studies this approach makes sense. The understanding and critical evaluation of sketches are hazardous enough. An outsider, with a sort of 'tunnel vision', can relate the embryonic form only to its developed version, which is a dangerous oversimplification. We must at least try to recognise the intended characters and contexts beyond the 'sonata form' or another formal surface of an instrumental composition. In fact, sketches often point towards the essence of a piece or a character in a clearer way than the finished score; the elaborated texture with all the notes, the scoring and performance instructions may obscure the essential notes or rhythms.

A close look at the continuation of the first four memo sketches, considering the physical characteristics of the pen strokes as well as the coherence of notation of the music, reveals the to-and-fro jumps in the writing act. Bartók clearly worked on the beginning of the third and the first movements in parallel. According to our reconstruction of the assumed sequence of the sub-sections:

C1 Continuation: Bartók wrote four plus three additional bars in the fifth staff; this is still a memo sketch, crossed out, when in the next step he returned to the elaboration of the beginning of the finale.

C2 Back to the third staff, he began the elaboration of the opening theme up to note g′ in the fifth bar in the eighth staff. Here a 'memo' is developed into 'continuity sketch'. Then Bartók stopped and returned to the opposite page.

A2 Continuation of the violin theme, then, in a next step, of the passages of the piano. (The horizontal {brace with letter *a* in the first bar, a typical Bartókian abbreviation, is connected with the continuation.)

A3 Corrections of the piano passage in the eighth staff and the addition of the syncopated/dotted piano motive in the seventh and eighth staves. We assume that the birth of this piano motive signals Bartók's decision that the two instruments will present independent themes; accordingly the violin double-stop B1 motive could not be used in its original form in the Sonata (the piano version of it appears as the second theme at rehearsal number 7).

A3 Continuation of the waltz-rhythm transitory theme in the last two bars on fol. 24v and in the ninth and tenth staves on fol. 25r. (The piano chords in pencil at the very bottom of the page were probably written down when Bartók started to write the draft and, as preparation, surveyed the existing sketches.) At the end of the page (fol. 25r) Bartók interrupted the sketch; the next page already included material for the second movement, so rather he worked on the continuation of the finale theme.

C2 Continuation of the finale theme in the last four bars in the eighth staff on fol. 25r and in the first three staves on fol. 26r (because on fol. 25v material for the second movement was written: D1, perhaps D2 too).

Sketch D is a special case that perhaps ought not to be discussed in detail. Bartók worked on the continuation of the preliminary memo in at least two stages and finished the correction of the violin melody at the top of the next page when fol. 26r was partly filled.

The rest of the sketches (E to K) on the fourth, fifth and sixth pages represent a new phase in the compositional process of the Sonata and need a less extensive introduction. These were written down piece by piece in the sequence of the alphabet, each in one writing act without any visible hesitation. In this phase, after the crucially important beginning of all three movements was settled, Bartók focused on the continuation of the *Allegro appassionato* first movement. In addition to the opening 30 bars (A1–3), some 43 further bars (E to J) – all-together 73 bars of sketches for the 274-bar sonata form – were produced.

A concordance of sketches E to J with the final form may indeed be very misleading. Using a twofold approach in interpretation we clearly see that danger. In relation to their final position in the sonata form, the sequence of these ideas makes no sense. It does not look like Bartók later needed to put the originally invented form of a theme either into the recapitulation or the development section.

An unprejudiced reading of the same set of ideas makes more sense. According to this inner logic, Bartók first designed variant forms of the opening violin theme that could be part of a long primary theme area. In the final form he maintained the syncopated version (E) in this function, though put it to the end of the section; the subdominant version (F) was then replaced with another variant of the opening theme in other keys and with a different piano part (see from 3^{-2} to 5 in the printed score). Yet this dreamlike version was too good to lose, so Bartók spared it for the *Tranquillo* recapitulation of the violin theme where an appropriate head-motive in the tonic was set before. (Incidentally, Bartók had absolute pitch and seldom changed the key of the first noted form of an idea.) The second group (H–I–J) collects material for the piano. Here Bartók converted his first memo for violin into a theme for piano with ample contrary motion between the two hands, built on a C♯-major/minor chord (H). With this, and the two additional themes that fitted into the closing theme group, the chances of writing a sonata-form head movement were assumed.

	Compared to the final form:[29]	According to the inner logic:
E	Exposition: closing motive of the primary theme area.	A syncopated motive derived from the opening violin theme.
F	Recapitulation: the primary theme (but from the ninth bar only).	A close variant of the opening violin theme (in the subdominant).
G	Recapitulation: a *bariolage* figure.	A sketch for a *bariolage* figure.
H	Recapitulation: the secondary subject.	After transformation of the double-stop violin theme (B), the creation of a piano contrast theme (in C♯).
I	Development section: varied return of the closing theme.	A related dotted-rhythm idea (closing theme?).
J	Recapitulation: new theme in the closing theme group.	A further related idea (another closing theme?).

Finally, we should record what was not sketched; after all, substantial components of the three-movement concept are missing.

Missing from the development section of the first movement are: the magic mirror-motion scenes of the piano (from 11^{-3} and from 13^{-3}); the special *ondeggiando* effects and *quasi-trillo* tremolos (from 10, 11 and 12) that Bartók supposedly borrowed from Szymanowski's *Trois Mythes* and *Notturno e Tarantella*, pieces which he first heard in Jelly's performance;[30] and the *con impeto* outburst of the violin before the recapitulation (from 18) in which the two-note bowing foreshadows the finale.

In the second movement nothing but the 'abstract' exposition was begun; in the third movement only the rondo theme of the sonata-rondo form was sketched. The embellished Hungarian recapitulation of the second, and the not just Romanian but also Ruthenian, Arabic and merged peasant-music background of the continuation of the third movement – vitally important ingredients of Bartók's narrative – are entirely missing from the sketchbook. Were they also missing from the original narrative existing only in Bartók's mind? I would say: definitely not. But here the possibilities of sketch study end.

CHAPTER 10

Defining compositional process: idea and instrumentation in Igor Stravinsky's Ragtime *(1918) and* Pribaoutki *(1915)*

Tomi Mäkelä

> I love the composition of music more than the music itself.[1]
>
> Igor Stravinsky

THE POETICS OF ELABORATION

The genesis of a work of music is an enigmatic and, from the lay person's point of view, even a magical process. Professional analysts are seldom able to decide whether a composition constitutes an ingenious collage of innovation and inspiration, or if it results from careful elaboration and deft organisation. More often than not, it is a successful blend of both fantasy and professionalism, and seldom emerges out of a homogeneous, uninterrupted creative process. In many cases, the parameters of a musical gestalt are conceived neither simultaneously nor within a unified methodological framework. Hardly any wonder, then, that the creative process is viewed by some with awe. This also explains why music tends to be examined in terms of isolated aspects or layers and why some parameters get more attention than others.

Igor Stravinsky was aware of the fact that both elaboration and inspiration were important aspects of his art. In his *Poetics of Music*, he underscored craftsmanship,[2] but he also had a high opinion of spontaneous innovation.[3] Though his published writings and correspondence can provide useful information concerning his compositional process, his manuscripts promise to be an even more reliable source. Most loose-leaf sketches were either retained by the composer or given to friends and admirers who knew the value of such unique documents. Stravinsky himself recognised the historical significance of his sketches by allowing their publication in facsimile.[4] Thanks mainly to the Igor Stravinsky Collection of the Paul Sacher Foundation, most of the unpublished source material is now accessible. Examination of the manuscripts can reveal: (1) how ordered or indecisive the unfolding conception of the work actually was; (2) whether specific musical ideas (melodies, rhythms, instrumental and vocal sounds) first appeared in isolation, or whether and to what extent they are essentially context-related; (3) within which parameters these ideas were first written down.

Since its inception in the nineteenth century, the study of sketch material has tended to focus on pitch. The examination of how pitch structures develop in the sketches of Beethoven and other composers has produced significant results.[5] Pitch structure is however only one of many parameters making up the creative process. Rhythm and sound-colour also constitute essential compositional parameters. The analysis of these parameters is problematic. During the nineteenth century, the grammar and syntax of music were inconceivable outside of the tonal framework. Even a composer as sensitive to colour and texture as Jean Sibelius revealed the 'Riemannian' roots of his musical thought in the following statement written on 9 June 1910 in his diary: 'The sound is mainly dependent on the pure musical *Satz*, its polyphony etc.'[6] At this point in his career, Sibelius clearly believed that good orchestral sound was a consequence of voice-leading and harmony. With the disintegration of tonality, the syntactic organisation of phrase groups and periods outside of a tonal framework became an important locus for the development of innovative techniques and new ways of conceiving music. Magnus Lindberg, for one, developed a method by which structured sound-qualities are used as a replacement for tonal modulation.[7]

If composers such as Lindberg, György Ligeti and Giacinto Scelsi have been remarkably successful with regard to their use of sound-colour, the tools we need to analyse this aspect of their work remain underdeveloped. Joseph Kerman has recently noted that musicologists 'are slow to discuss musical texture because this is notoriously hard to do and the results are usually unhappy'.[8] Be that as it may, the following analysis of Stravinsky's *Ragtime* and *Pribaoutki* will demonstrate that sound-colour is a crucially important structural element in his music and that it can be examined systematically if the necessary source material is available.

Stravinsky's syntax has been compared with the 'hard cuts' of Sergei Eisenstein's films.[9] Though the building-blocks and layers in works of both the composer[10] and the film-maker do not appear to be put together organically, this does not mean that their relationship is arbitrary. Such readings are in fact a consequence of overly romantic concepts of narration many of us bring to bear when listening to music or following a film. Comparison of various published versions of Stravinsky's compositions shows that isolated bars were cut without substitution and that the order in which formal sections came into existence is often very different from the final version;[11] and yet the composer maintained a rather conventional concept of the work of art throughout his career. The idea of the 'work in progress' (which is in fact Romantic in origin[12]) or the post-modern concept of the open work can only be related to Stravinsky's creative processes and not to their end results. Although he did modify many of his previously published compositions, these modifications are for the most part marginal and were motivated first and foremost by problems arising from twentieth-century copyright regulations. The key to a better understanding of Stravinsky's creative process in general and the organisational logic of phrases and sections in particular is to be found in the *poietic* detail of the earliest conceptual phases of this process rather than in the changes made in later versions of the published score.

SKETCH STUDIES AND CONFLICTING CONCEPTS OF THE WORK OF ART

In art there is always a reciprocal relationship between the end result and the process which brought it into existence (a relationship contained within the definition of the term 'art'). Music can be composed in self-contained stages or in a continuous process; composition can be goal-orientated or it can take an extraordinary number of obscure detours; it may be spontaneous or carefully thought-out; driven by emotion or rational; fast or slow; laborious or playfully easy. The creative process can be inspired by a commission or some other 'non-musical' occurrence, but it can also be entirely subjective.[13] More than one person may be involved in the process (opera being the prime example), though we normally associate it with master individualists like Stravinsky.[14] Any rules that may govern the compositional process as such can only be understood through comparative analysis of the works and work habits of a number of composers. Given the broad range of Stravinsky's work, it would seem particularly appropriate to use it as a point of departure for such a comparative study. Stravinsky's sketches are remarkable in that they reveal so many different facets of this process, from the ingenious isolated act and emotionally motivated gestures to the rational application of technique. Though his published works have been successfully analysed without reference to his sketches, many relevant questions concerning the composer's style and technique presume some knowledge of his working documents and early versions.

The growing importance of the so-called *poietic* perspective (as opposed to an 'aesthetics of published documents') among scholars, students and the general public may well lead to a demythologised vision of art and to a decentring of the completed work as the authoritative object of study. The lessening of respectful interest in the works of the great masters will however be counterbalanced by increased respect for creative activity *per se*. The 'great works of music history' will be understood less as museum pieces and more as artefactual experiments with sound, undertaken as solutions were being sought to specific compositional problems or subjectively inspired on the whim of a moment. Furthermore, these experiments will not necessarily be read as being fundamentally goal-orientated, and sometimes will be seen as having no goal at all.[15]

Increased interest in the composer's sketches also raises an ethical problem. For many artists, their handwritten notes and preparatory work are confidential documents and should not be available for public scrutiny. For instance, Max Reger never exhibited his unfinished works and sketch material, even to his closest friends.[16] He wanted to maintain the illusion that for him, composing was playfully easy, involving little or no preparatory work, as it was supposed to have been for Mozart. In fact, Reger was a master elaborator. He knew this, and yet he valued pure innovation and inspiration more than the careful working out of compositional problems, which was indubitably his strength.

The fragment is now increasingly seen as an aesthetically and philosophically significant document of much twentieth-century experimentation.[17] What used to be considered compositional dead ends have now become objects of interest in their own right.[18]

INSTRUMENTATION AND THE CREATIVE PROCESS IN *RAGTIME* AND *PRIBAOUTKI*

Approximately two decades ago, Arnold Whittall astutely raised the question of the status of music analysis as an academic discipline: should it maintain its traditional place as part of the human sciences or should it be situated among the pure and applied sciences as some in the American theory establishment had proposed? Avoiding extreme positions on all sides of this issue, he responded by saying yes to both alternatives. Whereas music is always a deeply contextualised phenomenon and must be interpreted as such, the pure sciences, and notably biology, do provide models for the rigorous study of how individual objects are structured.[19] Notwithstanding the fact that compositions are rarely homogeneous and linear in their development, they can be understood as having an organic structure, whose form can only be fully comprehended through insight into how it came into existence. The composer's manuscript material is particularly important when dealing with the complex parametrical relationships in new music. Among the manuscripts one finds the usual sketches and preliminary versions, but also tables and drawings, often without conventional notation. These latter documents can provide information on the various strategies used by the composer to prepare and produce the work. The general broadening of musical thought, technical innovation and the questioning of traditionally accepted fundamentals (tonality, metre, sound-quality, etc.) do not normally take place during the writing out of the fair copy, but rather as ideas are initially conceived and shaped. In line with Whittall's argument, the original moment of creation can thus be understood as a genetic key for all that follows, rather like the seed of a flower.

Whereas the notation of pitch and duration has been carefully 'rationalised' (in Max Weber's modernist sense of the term[20]), the same has not generally occurred with the so-called secondary parameters, and conventional notation is limited in its ability to symbolise these aspects of music. Though new notational systems could easily be developed, composers have generally shirked this task and continue to sketch the secondary parameters more or less 'by rote'. On the whole, experiments undertaken over the past century to modify conventional notation have not been standardised. The traditional system of musical typographics is by no means neutral and actively contributes to maintaining conventional paradigms. Rather than being standardised, unusual signs and symbols are often eliminated, at the latest during the publication process, and much valuable information is lost.[21] During the years between 1910 and 1920, for instance, Anton Webern's manuscripts show that he notated phrasing, intonation and dynamics with much more precision than that which is present in the published scores.[22] Nonetheless, the scores of the Viennese School are in general relatively rich in unusual signs and symbols. This is exemplified in the lengthy verbal instructions and footnotes that Alban Berg added to his scores and the H- and N-signs introduced by Arnold Schoenberg to clarify polyphonic relationships. Also, even though some signs and symbols referring to the agogic aspects of Webern's music may have no structural significance, it is important for performers to know whether they were part of the composer's initial idea or were added or altered later. In Stravinsky's case too, agogic indications occur frequently at a very early stage of his work. In the following, attention will be focused on the earliest notated evidence of secondary parameters such as sound-colour and instrumentation. Stravinsky's style does indeed justify the common division of parameters into secondary (i.e. ornamental) and primary (essential) categories. Using the sketch material, these categories can be re-evaluated on a work-by-work basis, and hierarchies can be established chronologically as defined by the creative process rather than on paradigmatic grounds.

The context of Stravinsky's compositional technique is first and foremost dominated by a fascination for orchestration and sound-construction, omnipresent in modern Russian music of the late nineteenth century. The maxim that musical thought is not orchestrated after the fact but is, rather, generated out of an imagined 'sounding' reality, stems from Stravinsky's teacher Nikolai Rimsky-Korsakov.[23] In the magnificent scores from the early part of his career, from *Scherzo fantastique* (1908) and *Feu d'artifice* (1909) to *Le rossignol* (1914), Stravinsky continued this tradition, in which orchestral sound-construction takes pride of place. Largely influenced by Rimsky-Korsakov and Stravinsky, the art of orchestration became one of the essential characteristics of twentieth-century European art music. Around 1910, Stravinsky was one of the first to begin experimenting with unconventional instrumentation and voice-leading, which over time led to the rejection of the conventional orchestra.[24] *Pribaoutki*, *Berceuses du chat* for three clarinets, *Ragtime* for eleven instruments, *L'histoire du soldat* and *Les noces* all bear witness (though each in its own way) to Stravinsky's search for new types of ensembles as vehicles for innovative sound-configurations, and the various facets of this endeavour are richly documented in his sketches. However, the elaboration of these projects is complex, experimental and often difficult to follow.

Surviving sketch material clearly shows how important the problem of the 'new sound' was for Stravinsky and how much time he spent looking for solutions. Boris Asaf'yev spoke of the composer's knowledge of functional relationships and of the mutually dependent elements making up a sound-texture, as well as pointing out how significant this was for the development of his new style.[25] During the second decade of the last century, Stravinsky carefully formed a functionally connected web of elements, and the solutions he envisioned among the possibilities and necessities of this soloist-orientated new sound were all original. Rimsky-Korsakov's maxim that sound-colour is not orchestrated afterwards, but rather occurs simultaneously with the working-out of pitch and rhythmic structures, applies only partially to Stravinsky's new compositions. His sketch material demonstrates that, though instrumentation is often set down at the beginning of the composition process, it can change many times before publication of the full score. In *Ragtime*, for instance, the introduction of the Hungarian cimbalom in place of the piano occurred late in the creative process even though this change has a decisive impact on the sound-quality and texture of the end result. In the fair copy of the full score, Stravinsky still included the piano as a possible alternative for the cimbalom, and it was only during revision of the final proofs that the piano was eliminated from the score. This is borne out in Plate 10.2 (see below). This fragment of the score, written on the back of a draft for a letter with interesting references to the war, dated 9 January 1918, contains only a piano part. Thus, while specific sound-qualities were

Example 10.1   Igor Stravinsky, *Ragtime*, motive for cornet and trombone, transcribed from Sketchbook V,
Igor Stravinsky Collection, Paul Sacher Foundation, Basle

clearly an essential part of the original idea, Stravinsky continued to elaborate this aspect as
he composed, and this process can be followed through the sketches.

The divergence between the imagined sound and how these ideas were set down on
paper can be illustrated in details from sketches for *Ragtime* and *Pribaoutki*. The questions
to be addressed are: (1) How essential are the early instrumental indications, and to what
degree are they 'marked'? (2) At what point in the compositional process does a complete
sound-structure emerge out of a welter of individually conceived figures, and to what extent
is it definitive? (3) What is the relationship between this sound-structure and the other
'secondary' parameters, such as phrasing and agogic aspects?

1. In the earliest extant draft of *Ragtime*, the major second (Ab–Bb) at bar 81 was originally scored for cornet and trombone and its length is precisely determined by a dotted-
crotchet rest (Example 10.1). In the draft of the short score, the instrumentation is omitted;
however, the dotted-crotchet pause following the interval suggests that Stravinsky's initial sound-colour was retained. In the final version of the work, the interval is scored
for cimbalom. This first appears in the fair copy of the full score. Here the rest is no
longer indicated because the cimbalom's delicate sound fades away rapidly (the end of
notes written for brass instruments would of course have to be clearly marked). There is
an enormous difference between the initial and final sound-colour, and though it appears
in the earliest sketches, Stravinsky changed it radically at the end of the compositional
process.[26]

2. In the earliest sketches for *Ragtime* one finds sound-elements of the work in
their definitive form. The sketch presents a trombone melody, the melodic and sound-
qualities of which remain unchanged in the published score (see bar 73; Plate 10.1 and
Example 10.2).

The melodic line written in pencil was preceded by an erased version which differs from
the later version in just one respect: the characteristic off-beat syncopation of the first
beat, so important for the ragtime character of the piece, is still missing. In Example 10.2,
diplomatic transcription, the erased semibreve is presented in square brackets. Stylistically
important details such as this are often introduced after a first rough draft has been established. The principle of refining relatively simple ideas through extensive elaboration also
applies to other motives found on the first page of the *Ragtime* sketches. For example,
the two-voice motive beginning at bar 52 in the published score was at first partially con-
sonant. In its initial form, the motive (A/F♯–Ab/G) was written in a square box at the

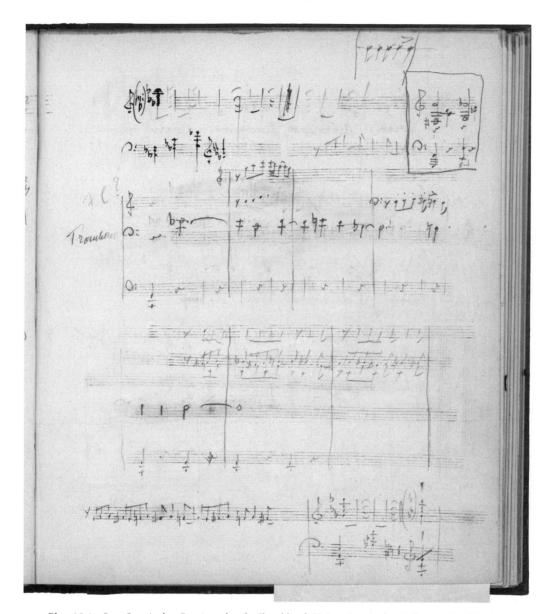

Plate 10.1   Igor Stravinsky, *Ragtime*, sketch, Sketchbook V, Igor Stravinsky Collection, Paul Sacher Foundation, Basle

Example 10.2   Igor Stravinsky, the original trombone melody transcribed from Plate 10.1

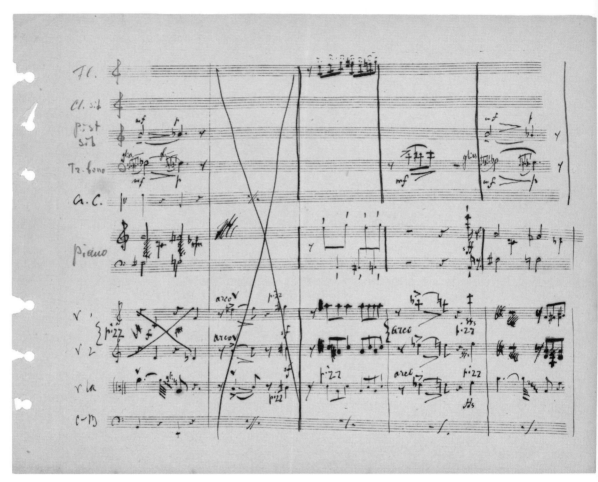

Plate 10.2   Igor Stravinsky, draft of the full score, notated on the back side of a draft for a letter written to
Edwin Evans and dated 9 January 1918, Igor Stravinsky Collection, Paul Sacher Foundation, Basle

upper right-hand corner of Plate 10.1. It was only while the sketches were being written
out in short score that the idea was given its final form (A/A♭–A♭/G) (see bars 1 and 5 of
Plate 10.2). The elaboration of this motive, leading from simple, preliminary gestures to
complex composition, shows that Stravinsky's surprisingly dislocated passages often have
very tender, even banal roots.

The score fragment presented in Plate 10.2 was written before Stravinsky completed the first draft of the full score, and the fact that this particular passage (bars 52–5) was orchestrated in full score at this early stage is puzzling. As noted above, the two-voice chromatic movement between the cornet and trombone (see bars 1 and 5 of Plate 10.2) is clearly present in the earliest-known sketch of *Ragtime* (Plate 10.1). Within the context of the published score, this motive may appear to be relatively insignificant, at least melodically. The sketch material clearly suggests that the early orchestration of this motive was important for the beginning of the compositional process. Thus a careful study of these documents enables hidden structures and motive hierarchies to be traced, showing that an analysis based on the melodic characteristics of the published score must be revised in light of its genesis.

3. The *Pribaoutki* song cycle is stylistically very different from *Ragtime*. Nevertheless, its unusual instrumentation can be seen as leading up to *Ragtime* as well as to *L'histoire du soldat*. In preliminary work on 'Natashka', which was initially to have been the first song of a three-part cycle, the vocal line of bars 1–15 was written out in pencil. Following this the composer reflected on instrumentation and then wrote out a flexible four- to six-voice short-score sketch in ink (bars 1–10). For bars 11–14, Stravinsky produced a nine-voice full score in pencil, over which he wrote *Pribaoutka* in ink (Plate 10.3).

Details were then added in ink. More important than these details is the barely legible, erased sketch underneath. Ensuing work on these bars included the division of the original flute part between the clarinet and the flute and the reduction of the original ornamentation. Especially intriguing, however, is the fact that the erased version of the string parts is closer to the published score than intermediate versions. In Stravinsky's manuscripts one often finds that earlier sketches written carefully in pencil are closer to the end result than later drafts written confidently in ink.

The above-mentioned principle of refining relatively simple ideas through extensive elaboration also applies to Stravinsky's text settings. In the earliest sketches for the third song, 'Polkovnik', the flute part doubles the voice, and the F♯s in both parts are accentuated (Plate 10.4). In the published score, both the accents and the F♯s have been eliminated, reducing the voice to straight declamation on C♯ (see bars 27–32 of the full score). Despite this apparent simplification, the resulting composition is more complex. The independence of the upper winds compensates for the agogic monotony of the voice. The tension originally to have been created by 'false' accentuation of the text in the sketch is reconfigured within the passage by the accents of the woodwinds and the asymmetric rhythms generated through the combination of voice, woodwind and string parts. Changes such as these are indicative of the development of a musical idea, first sketched in only a very raw form. The woodwind parts are not really new. Rather, they reset the original innovation in a more complex form. The core of the idea stems from the earliest sketches and, though it was modified in the course

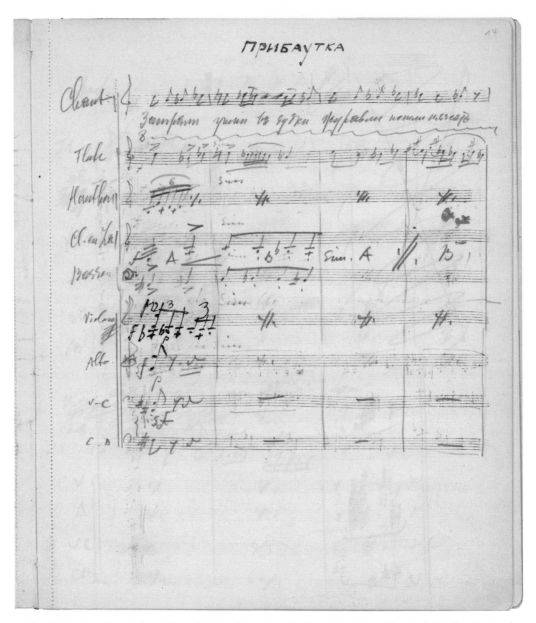

Plate 10.3   Igor Stravinsky, *Pribaoutki*, 'Natashka', sketch of bars 11–14, Igor Stravinsky Collection, Paul Sacher Foundation, Basle

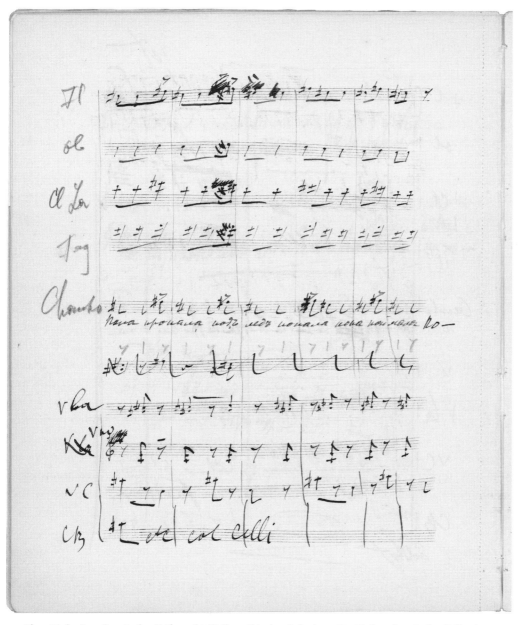

Plate 10.4   Igor Stravinsky, *Pribaoutki*, 'Polkovnik', sketch for bars 27–32, Igor Stravinsky Collection, Paul Sacher Foundation, Basle

of working out the composition, it nevertheless left its original imprint in the published score.

The formal examination of manuscript material depends on the development of a rational approach to the study of the creative process, which must extend beyond the contingencies of documents related to a specific work. Questions to be asked are: (1) How and to what extent are standardised forms transformed as the composer's style evolves? (2) Why did Stravinsky choose certain sketch formats for specific compositional tasks? (3) What is the significance of the composer's hand, which can alternate radically between hesitation and confident energy? In Stravinsky's case, there is no correlation between the certainty with which a sketch is written down in pencil or ink, in short score or in full score, and its possible inclusion in the published work.

Stravinsky's working documents are extraordinarily diverse. Indeed, before the 1920s they are never easy to order in categories, continuously or chronologically. When beginning work on a new composition, he will typically set numerous short motives, whose sound-colour is often precisely indicated (sketch material for *Ragtime* provides a clear example of this). These small, apparently unconnected elements should in no way be understood as musical ideas in a crude state. On the contrary, they are usually formulated with great care and, when considered according to the premises of the composer's syntax, they can be seen as constituting a kind of musical continuity, which may or may not be included in the final score.

The table presented in Figure 10.1 lists the most important sketches for *Ragtime* and presents a summary description of their contents. The documents are ordered according to call numbers attributed by the Sacher Foundation. The material appears to have been written between 10 December 1917 and 5 March 1918. The former date marks the completion of *Berceuse à ma fille Mika*, which was sketched just before Stravinsky began work in earnest on *Ragtime*. The latter date is found at bar 178 of a sketch of the last section of *Ragtime* (see the fourth item from the bottom of the table). Not included are the stylistically related sketches for piano, which were written before 10 December 1917 and contain *Ragtime*'s characteristic dotted rhythms.

Whenever possible, the bar numbers of the published score are indicated in the left-hand column. This is, however, not always easy to establish. Much of the material can be related to the completed work only in terms of general outline or gesture. Indeed, elements planned for a given composition will often turn up later in other unrelated works or are simply abandoned. These inter-textual relationships open up a particularly interesting dimension

Bar numbers in the printed score	Description of sketches	Call number
?	SVE, rh, nK, ag	*–0243/44*
?	PFE, rh-mel	
52	PFE	
73–(79?)	4ISE, Sc (fl/cb, tromb/cor à pist) diff from Print, partly nK, ag	
(56–57?)	SVE, nK	
?	PFE, rh-mel, ag	
(52–54?)	3SSE, Sc (db), figure	*–0245*
52–57	3–4SS, partly nK	
?	2SSE	
61–67, 70–72	3–7PSS, Instr (tromb/cb, fl, cl, cor à pist, hr, vl 1+2, vla, P: gr c) partly diff from Print, partly nK, ag	*–0246*
?	3–4SSE, rh-mel, ag	*–0247*
126–130 (73–?)	3SSE, Sc (cl, db), Instr (fl, tromb/hr, cor à pist)	
	SVE	
(130–131?)	2ISE, Sc (fl)	
(126–132?)	3SSE, Sc (tromb/hr, cl), Instr (cl), partly diff from Print, partly nK, ag	*–0248*
(124?)–130	1–3SSE, Instr (fl, cl, tromb, cor à pist/hr, db) partly diff from Print, partly nK, ag	
(62–63?)	2SSE, Instr (cor à pist, tromb), ag	
77–84	3–7PC, Sc (fl, cl, cor à pist/cb, tromb/cb, vla, db, pf/str), Instr (fl, cl, cor à pist, vla, db, gr c) partly diff from Print, rh-mel, ag, Text, figure	*–0249*
90–93	3–4SSE, Sc (vl 1+2, vla), Instr (tromb, fl/hr, cl/hr, cor à pist) partly diff from Print, nK	*–0250*
?	2SSE, rh-mel, partly nK [3PCE]	
92–93	3SSE (2), Instr (fl/hr, cl/hr, cor à pist) diff from Print, partly nK	
(130–?)	4SSE, rh-mel	
?	4SSE, Sc (db), Instr (fl, cl), ag, figure	*–0251*
84–94	3–4SS, Instr (tromb, P: gr c), partly nK, ag, figure	*–0252*
?	SVE, rh-mel, partly nK	*–0253*
103–104	PFE	
103–104	2SSE, rh-mel	*–0254*
103–(110?)	2–4PSSE, ag	
?	SVE, Sc (cl)	
?	4SSE, partly nK	*–0255*
(16–20?)	2SS, Instr (cl)	
25–34	3SS, ag, figure	*–0256*
35–43	3–4PSS, rh-mel, ag	*–0257*
(44?)–52	3–4SS, Instr (pf/str) diff from Print, ag	*–0258*
1–11	4PSS, Sc (gr c/cb) diff from Print, ag	*–0259*
12–18	3SS, Instr (cor à pist, tromb, P: tam–tam), ag	*–0260*

Figure 10.1   Table of sketches for *Ragtime*, written between 10 December 1917 and 5 March 1918. All documents are conserved in the Igor Stravinsky Collection (Film 123-0242), Paul Sacher Foundation, Basle

?	1SSE, Instr (fl) [3PCE]	
? Forts.	3SS, Sc (fl, cor à pist, hr, tromb, db, cb), partly nK	*–0261*
73–83	3–4PSS, Instr (fl, cl, pf/cb, db/cb, cor à pist, tromb, P: GrC) partly diff from Print, ag, figure	*–0262*
77	2SSE, Instr (vl 1+2, vla)	
(175?)–178	2–3SSE, Instr (fl, cl, cor à pist, hr, tromb, vl 1+2, vla), partly nK	*–0263*
177–178	7SSE, Sc (fl, cl, cor à pist, hr, tromb, vl 1+2, vla, db), Text [dated '5.3.1918']	
(175?)–178	2–4SS, Instr (vl 1+2, fl, cor à pist)	*–0264*
(173–174?)	3SS	
171–176	4SS, Sc (fl, vl 1+2/cb), Instr (db, vla, cl) partly diff from Print	*–0265*

Legend of uncommon abbreviations:
ag: agogics
Instr: instrumentation
ISE: instrumental score element
mel: melody *only*
nK: without key signature
P: percussion
PFE: piano element
Print: printed score
PSS: percussion short score
rh: rhythm *only*
rh–mel: rhythm *and* melody
Sc: scoring
SS: short score
SSE: short score element
SVE: single voice element

Example: '4ISE', instrumental score element with four lines; vl/cb: violin (sketch) instead of cimbalom (print).

Figure 10.1   *(cont.)*

for further work with the composer's sketch material. The table also indicates the number of staves,[27] the type of score (one-staff sketches, piano score, short score, etc.) and the dominant instrumentation. It thus provides information on Stravinsky's methodology. For example, we can observe to what extent agogic indications were developed in conjunction with or separately from instrumental colour.

Stravinsky began work on *Ragtime* with what would become a secondary idea in the published score (see bars 52, 73, etc.). The work's characteristic 'signal motive' of the first bar was written much later. Once this motive was established, however, the speed with which Stravinsky completed the work increased significantly. From the available sketch material, it is not clear if the 'signal motive' was initially conceived to be the beginning of the work. The earliest-known working document (see Plate 10.1) presents a colourful mixture of various types of sketch material. The sketches, which deal exclusively with rhythm, point to a widely held conception of the music's style: in 1918, one often spoke of 'syncopated music' when referring to ragtime and early jazz. Among other elements, the page contains a short sequence written on a four-staved score, one voice of which is a trombone part. Even at this early stage, agogic markings are already present. On the following page, Stravinsky continued this sketch in short score, on which numerous voices are indicated on one reduced staff system. The creative process appears to accelerate on the next page with new material on an enlarged short score. This music fills in the gap between bars 57 and 73 of the published score. The short-score sketch is precisely notated, including numerous agogic indications and even a percussion part. The instrumentation indicated in this document differs to a large extent from the final score. Following this, Stravinsky wrote out motives which would appear only in the recapitulation. This sequence of elements, present in Stravinsky's early sketches, does not differ radically from the formal logic of the definitive version.

Throughout these sketches, the short score dominates as a vehicle for the composer's evolving musical thought. The format's flexibility allows for rapid sketching of melodic elements and permits the composer to easily try out different instrumental combinations. As the creative process continued, Stravinsky produced a significant number of isolated building-blocks which were then inserted into previously composed material. Many of these elements would never be used in this composition. This over-abundance of ideas is typical of the composer's working documents.

Figure 10.1 is a first step towards a formalised apprehension of the creative process. It presents detailed information about written documents in a compact form and it enables the reader to follow many of the detours taken by Stravinsky as he composed. The table does not take into account erased sketches or 'paste-ons'.[28] In any case, it does not tell the whole story. Manuscript material is rarely complete, and even if it were it still would provide no access to the *prae-scriptum* genesis of a given work. The tangible advantages of this type of systematic study will become more apparent once observations about larger collections of sketch material have been brought together and quantified. Applying this method to the sketch material for *Ragtime* has produced interesting results because Stravinsky's compositional technique generated such an unusually rich diversity of working documents, particularly in the experimental years between 1915 and 1920.

CHAPTER II

Floating hierarchies: organisation and composition in works by Pierre Boulez and Karlheinz Stockhausen during the 1950s

Pascal Decroupet
in memoriam Herbert Brün

The present contribution hinges on a double trajectory: primarily that of Pierre Boulez, with supplementary information gleaned from works by Karlheinz Stockhausen. From the high rigour of their early achievements, both evolved towards more subtle forms of musical thought. Thus, one of the fundamental postulates of serial music (i.e. the relationship between form and material in which the elementary characteristics of a given point of departure are carried through to higher levels of formal articulation) underwent a radical modification within a few short years.[1] How do we define serial music in such a rapidly evolving context? During the early 1950s, examples of works based on an integral serial organisation were legion, suggesting a shared perspective. Just five years later, however, differences between composers and even between works by the same composer became so marked that establishing a common denominator seems futile.[2] For the purposes of this document, serial thinking will be summarised as a systematic approach aimed at solving a given compositional problem in which the exhaustive methodology does not necessarily filter through to the end result.

What does the sketch material of serial composers reveal? How can sketches be used to analyse their works? What are the limits of their usefulness? Often, this material reveals the abstract foundations of the composer's work: serial tables notated in pitch or in numbers, with or without instructions for their use; various early elaborations of this elementary material leading progressively and sometimes over different paths towards the final score; verbal ideas circumscribing the project; successive versions of the work, etc. On the one hand, we uncover the raw material in continuous auto-referential deployment, and on the other, a collection of developmental strategies. If the raw material constitutes the focus of the analyst's attention, the developmental strategies can often broaden considerably the conceptual framework within which the analysis takes place, opening up previously unexplored lines of thought.

Sketches are by their very nature incomplete. They are the result of a process and not just evidence of a journey. In and of themselves, sketches are incapable of revealing all of the stages linking the material and the work. However, through careful observation one can extrapolate, generalise and even invent fundamentally important criteria, which may have left no trace in the composer's working documents. The analyst must therefore fill in the blanks and engender coherence, the goal being an understanding of the work in its entirety and not merely of these particular fragments of thought consigned to paper by the composer to structure his manner of working. If the archaeological reconstitution of the composer's thinking is by its very nature an illusion, careful study of sketch material can endow the analyst's hypotheses with a certain degree of probability.

FROM STRICT ORGANISATION . . .

So as to transfer the principle of serialised pitch organisation to other acoustic dimensions, and thus provide the work with a higher level of musical organisation, Boulez borrowed the concept of 'function' from mathematics.[3] In a letter to John Cage dated August 1951, he writes: 'It is possible to consider that a series, *in general*, may be defined as a function of frequency $f(F)$, acting on the functions of duration $f(t)$, of intensity $f(i)$ etc. . . . where only the variable changes, the function remains constant. Overall, a serial structure can be globally defined as $\Psi \{f(F), f(t), f(i), f(a)\}$.'[4] The numerical symbolisation of sound allowed Boulez to achieve the uniform manipulation of pitch, duration, dynamics and articulation, each provided with scales of gradation designated as 'chromatic'. Another ramification of his notion of function can be observed in the serial tables, where the order of transposition reproduces the initial function. In other words, the prime form of the series is used to align the twelve transpositions of the row. Such a table constitutes a 'function of functions' that can be translated directly into the work. Regarding the organisation of pitch and duration in Boulez's *Structure Ia*, dating from the spring of 1951, the function is doubly present: whereas, in piano I, the transpositions of the function follow the order of the inversion, in piano II, the transpositions of the inversion adopt the order of the function. In the second part of the movement (bar 64 ff.) this relationship is inverted. The compositional idea actually consists of projecting the function to different levels of articulation within the work, from specific acoustic dimensions to the form of the work. The principle governing this projection is that of *isomorphism*. As for intensity and articulation, these dimensions modify previously established forms governing pitch and duration. Intensity and articulation are organised as a simple function made up of numbers selected diagonally from the serial table.[5]

In the tables prepared for the *Première étude de musique concrète*, produced during the autumn and winter of 1951–2, a supplementary systematisation of the serial method takes shape. Unlike *Structures*, the numbering does not simply unfold from one to twelve (see Figure 11.1a), but translates the chromatic hierarchy inherent in the series: $C = 1$, $C\sharp = 2$, etc. (see Figure 11.1b). Whereas to understand the logic of the former, one must resort to the note names of the series and its transpositions, the latter can be understood in purely mathematical terms. Henceforth, each series had its own absolute point of reference. This internal hierarchy of the serial numbering system provided an indispensable link between the increasingly complex permutations and the compositional point of departure.

Eb	D	A	Ab	F#	E	C#	C	Bb	G	F	B
1	2	3	4	5	6	7	8	9	10	11	12
2	8	4	5	6	11	1	9	12	3	7	10
3	4	1	2	8	9	10	5	6	7	12	11
4	5	2	8	9	12	3	6	11	1	10	7
5	6	8	9	12	10	4	11	7	2	3	1
6	11	9	12	10	3	5	7	1	8	4	2
7	1	10	3	4	5	11	2	8	12	6	9
8	9	5	6	11	7	2	12	10	4	1	3
9	12	6	11	7	1	8	10	3	5	2	4
10	3	7	1	2	8	12	4	5	11	9	6
11	7	12	10	3	4	6	1	2	9	5	8
12	10	11	7	1	2	9	3	4	6	8	5

Figure 11.1a   Pierre Boulez, *Structures I*, serial table

1	6	3	4	10	11	5	12	7	9	2	8
6	11	8	9	3	4	10	5	12	2	7	1
3	8	5	6	12	1	7	2	9	11	4	10
4	9	6	7	1	2	8	3	10	12	5	11
10	3	12	1	7	8	2	9	4	6	11	5
11	4	1	2	8	9	3	10	5	7	12	6
5	10	7	8	2	3	9	4	11	1	6	12
12	5	2	3	9	10	4	11	6	8	1	7
7	12	9	10	4	5	11	6	1	3	8	2
9	2	11	12	6	7	1	8	3	5	10	4
2	7	4	5	11	12	6	1	8	10	3	9
8	1	10	11	5	6	12	7	2	4	9	3

Figure 11.1b   Pierre Boulez, *Première étude de musique concrète*, serial table

Before undertaking *Le marteau sans maître*, Boulez developed a system of permutations in which intervals between successive terms of the series are used to displace those terms on the table. As with isomorphic transpositions, serial structure intervenes both vertically and horizontally as a modifying factor.[6] The sketches for the 'formant' *Antiphonie* from the Third Piano Sonata exemplify the theoretical principle according to which the size of the

3	4	5	6	1	2	
3	1	6	2	4	5	3
				3		1
			3			6
					3	2
	3					4
		3				5

Figure 11.2a   Procedures for the displacement of values on the serial table

3	1	6	2	4	5
1	–	–	5	3/6	2/4
6/2	5	1	3/4	–	–
5	6/4	–	–	1/2	3
4	3	2/5	–	–	1/6
–	2	3/4	1/6	5	–

Figure 11.2b   Completed table

interval is brought to bear on the order of succession.[7] For example, the relation between the numbers 5 and 9 is +4, which means shifting the 5 four columns to the right (positive results requiring a shift to the right, negative results requiring a shift to the left).

Georg Friedrich Haas formulated an interpretation of this permutation system, in which the horizontal order of the chromatic hierarchy intersects with the vertical displacement of number positions in subsequent lines of the table.[8] Take for instance the six-digit series: 3-1-6-2-4-5 (see Figure 11.2a). To displace the first term (3), two preparatory operations must occur. First, the chromatic order number is aligned with its equivalent serial term. Beginning with this number, the chromatic order is then rotated from that point (3-4-5-6-1-2) and placed above the serial form. Second, the serial form, beginning with this same number, is aligned vertically in the margin. The number to be displaced is then positioned at the intersection between the chromatic order numbers above the table and their equivalents of the serial form in the margin. Accordingly, the number 3 will be placed in the column marked 1 (column five) of the second line, in the column marked 6 of the third line, in the column marked 2 of the fourth line, etc. As a result, each of the numbers of the original six-digit series is present in each line and each column of the table (similar to the situation created by the isomorphic transposition of the twelve-tone row). However, this system also entails a certain irregularity exemplified by empty spaces and by spaces containing more than one term (see Figure 11.2b).

4	2	5	6	9	8	10	7	11	3	12	1
11	–	1	5/9/10	2	–	6/3	8	–	–	4	7/12
1	4	12	7	8	2/6/9	5	10/3		11		
7/12		4/9	1		5		6	2/8		11/3	10
8	7/11		12	6/1	4	9	2/5	10/3			
				4/5/7/12			1	6	2/8/10	9	11/3
6/10/3		7/11				4/2/1	9/12	5		8	
5	8		4/11/3			7	12	9/1	6	2/10	
	10	2/3			1	7/11	4	12	5	6	9/8
	6	8/10		3	11/12				9/7/1	5	4/2
2/9	5/3/1		8		10		11	4/7	12		6
	12/9	6	[2]	10/11	3	8			4	1/7	(2)/5

Figure 11.3   Pierre Boulez, *Le marteau sans maître*, 'Bourreaux de solitude', serial table (1=C)

In the 'Bourreaux de solitude' cycle of *Le marteau sans maître*, Boulez uses a table such as this, based on a twelve-tone row (see Figure 11.3) and its inversion.[9] At the beginning of the sixth movement, the table should be read horizontally, keeping in mind that: (1) the empty squares represent interventions by percussion instruments of indeterminate pitch, so that the duration of each serial form is twelve units (the unit itself may change from one serial form to the next); (2) Boulez chose the succession of serial forms, taking advantage of specific relationships at the intersections of different serial forms.[10]

Aside from the internal hierarchy of the series, Boulez also modified the interpretation of the terms as early as *Structure Ib*. Up to this stage, numbers symbolised discrete values within a scale referring to pitch, duration, dynamics or articulation. Henceforth, the terms could also signify measurements of various kinds. For instance, the numbers 4-5-8 can be used to create the following relation: a duration of eight units is subdivided into sets of four and five notes respectively, each with its own mode of articulation or dynamic level.[11] Techniques such as these gave rise to the notion of 'group', a fundamentally important development for the evolution of serial thinking. Composers now tended to focus on larger, more readily perceptible groups of notes and shaped musical entities, which could become veritable figures or gestalts.[12] As a technical term, a group can be understood as a variable of density: the successive notes in a single rhythmic subdivision (*Structure Ib*, *Klavierstück III*); the sum of notes that constitute a chord or a figure (the second cycle of *Klavierstücke*); the number of partials constituting a synthetic spectrum (*Etüde [Konkrete Musik]*, *Studie I*); a duration or a unit of duration (*Structure Ib*, *Zeitmaße*); etc. This grouping of elements highlights a common trait, conferring a sense of overarching unity on those elements. This explains why Stockhausen refers to superficial characteristics to clarify the meaning of 'group' in his 1955–6 retrospective analysis of *Klavierstück I*, rather than developing a definition based on the technical foundations of the craft of composition as such.[13]

The idea of grouping led Boulez to invent a new technique for the derivation of material, called *multiplication sonore* (translated as 'frequency multiplication' in *Boulez on Music Today*).[14] By virtue of the fact that the concept implies the ramification of partial or local functions, it is a logical consequence of previously developed techniques involving functional deployment. For example, in the 'L'artisanat furieux' cycle of *Le marteau sans maître*, the notes of a twelve-tone row are grouped into different cells, whose harmonic characteristics are transferred to all cells in an exhaustive combinatorial process. The blocks of sound resulting from frequency multiplication are abstract harmonic entities similar to the pc-sets of Allen Forte's theory. Within these blocks, linear succession is subordinate to the 'diagonal dimension', made up of both vertical and horizontal intervals. In the following pages, the pitch content of such blocks or interval networks as harmonic entities will be spelled from the bottom up.

The serial tables resulting from the technique of frequency multiplication possess harmonic characteristics that the composer may or may not choose to underline. The basic principle implies that all terms of a line or a column share a common element. In the third movement of *Le marteau sans maître*, Boulez read his tables in homogeneous lines, so that, at a higher level, five successive sonorities form a group by means of a given constant, which Boulez chose to emphasise on the surface level of the work. For the alto flute solo at the beginning of the movement, all of the sonorities result from multiplications by the cell B♭–B–C♯–D, spelled as C♯–F–D–E (a transposition of B♭–D–D–C♯) in the score (bar 4, Example 11.1). This results in a general prevalence of whole-tone relationships in bars 1–7, giving way to minor-third relationships in bars 8–9. In Example 11.1, this is illustrated by grouping the pitches into their respective whole-tone sets (class 2) or into minor-third sets (class 3).

With regard to the rhythmic treatment in the 'L'artisanat furieux' cycle, Boulez relies on the notion of 'global values', a concept which he presents in his analysis of the opening of *Le sacre du printemps*.[15] In the pencil manuscript of movements I, III and VII, all the rhythmic cells have been identified by the composer (see the upper-case letters above the staff in Example 11.1). How is this treatment of rhythm related to the pitch structure? The series, which groups the twelve-tone row into cells, operates according to five ratios (2–4–2–1–3).[16] To establish the five tables, the series responsible for grouping begins once for each term, constituting a transfer of the notion of function. The five rhythmic cells (labelled A, B, C, D, E) of respectively 2–4–2–1–3 global values act in parallel. In Example 11.1, the 'B' above bar 3 refers to the four crotchets contained within it. Considering that local functions are involved in the concept of frequency multiplication, the relation between pitch and

Example 11.1   Pierre Boulez, *Le marteau sans maître*, 'L'artisanat furieux', bars 1–9. In this example the alto
flute is spelled in sounding pitch, according to the composer's first ink manuscript. The upper staff presents a
reduction of the musical text. The two lower staves present the whole-tone (class 2) and minor-third (class 3)
relationships, which can be extracted from the melody.

rhythmic structures is, metaphorically speaking, the same as the relation between a function
of functions and a simple function. These two dimensions are dealt with independently,
and their automatic counterpoint produces a working context within which the composer's
imagination is able to act. For the beginning of 'L'artisanat furieux', Boulez chose the serial
form D–C–B–A–E (see Example 11.1). Subsequent orderings progress regularly, one line
for each form. Only the durations written in normal-sized note heads are to be considered
part of the rhythmic cells. Grace notes are excluded. For all cells of the same family, the
derivations can be proportional or irregular, symmetrical or asymmetrical. In addition, the
composer can choose to subdivide global values into equal durations. In Example 11.1, cell D
is subdivided into seven semiquavers, and cell E is subdivided into three units of five semiquavers, one crotchet and two quavers respectively. Further latitude for the composer's imagination is obtained through the irregular deployment of embellishing grace notes, which, as
mentioned above, are not part of the rhythmic cell structure.

. . . TO SERIAL COMPOSITION AND FREE WRITING

The system developed by Boulez for the third movement of *Le marteau sans maître* is
rigorously applied within the limits of its specific conditions.[17] If we disregard the various
copy errors appearing in Boulez's successive fair copies and the two published editions,[18]
only one note deviates from a systematic explanation of the entire movement in terms of
harmonic blocks. This deviation can however be justified if we consider it from the point of

view of the harmonic idea that underlies the *principle* of frequency multiplication, that is, the transfer of harmonic characteristics from one cell to another. At bar 8 (see Example 11.1) we find a transposition relationship between the intervals of the two three-note figures in the vocal part. Boulez replaced the C, predetermined by the system, with an F (penultimate note of bar 8). This altered pitch is present in all of the versions of the score, beginning with the first pencil draft dated 23 September 1952. Excluding the unlikely possibility of a copy error, we shall now attempt to reconstruct the train of thought which led the composer to make this specific choice. Initially, the pitch grouping in bar 8 contained two isomorphic sets related by inversion: F–G♯–A and C–C♯–E. The registration required to make the isomorphic relationship between the two sets perceptible would have resulted in a high C, outside of the alto's range. Changing the note from C to F actually reinforced the isomorphic relation between the two sets: rather than being related by inversion, the new set, C♯–E–F is now simply a transposition of F–G♯–A. The change also enabled Boulez to meet requirements of range, register balance (which is symmetrically disposed within the framework of the vocal phrase) and the subtle variation between the figures. The F creates a relationship of a minor third with the D of bar 9, reinforcing the presence of this interval at that part of the vocal line. Rather than being an arbitrary anomaly, the alteration foregrounds the composer's search for not only technical but also stylistic coherence.

The necessity of deriving entire works or sections thereof from a given compositional point of departure is something that both *Antiphonie* and the first insert in Stockhausen's *Zeitmaße* have in common.[19] In *Antiphonie*, the principle of derivation creates specific pitch groupings, which cannot be predicted by examining the initial series. Within this derivation principle, blank spaces, which Boulez interprets as zeros in multiplication, constitute the reverse side of harmonic entities. Thus at a second level of derivation, which generates the pitch material (lines A to L in Example 11.2a), certain pitches or pitch agglomerations are displaced more than once, while others are simply eliminated. The basic idea behind this approach is that of the 'defective series', enabling the composer to dispose of a variable number of pitch classes in accordance with the horizontal or vertical layout adopted for different derived forms.[20] At the beginning of the section entitled 'répons 1', three serial forms (E–L–K) are intertwined, generating high repetition rates for specific pitches. The harmonic emphasis on B and C in the upper register (see Example 11.2b, bars 1–2) results from the simultaneous presence of cells from the E and L forms. From bar 2 onwards, these forms are synchronised by a common pitch: E written as a dotted quaver tied to a quaver. In the lower section of Example 11.2b the piano score has been decomposed. The cells of the E form are placed on lines 1–5, those of the L form on line 6 and those of the K form on line 7. The E, appearing in lines 4 and 6, is derived from the fourth cell of the E form and the first cell of the L form (compare Examples 11.2a and 11.2b). The initial bar of the 'répons 1' begins with the first two cells of the E form (G♯ and B♭). The other pitches are derived from the third cell of the E form and the first cell of the L form. The repetition rate of the

Example 11.2a   Pierre Boulez, the serial table for *Antiphonie*. The first two staves show the basic series and the first derivation from which the serial table (lines A to L) is generated.

Example 11.2b   Pierre Boulez, *Antiphonie*, 'répons 1', bars 1–4. The seven lines appearing at the bottom of this example decompose the piano score into its respective cells: E form (lines 1–5), L form (line 6) and K form (line 7). The cells of the E and L forms are presented in normal order. The order of the K form is rotated, beginning with F♯.

notes is increased further by doubling the pitches almost systematically, signalling both the start and the end of a structural duration. The value of these pitches can vary from a grace note of no measurable length to a complete structural duration.

A structural duration is thus usually obtained by combining the duration values of at least two pitches. In bar 1 (see Example 11.2b), the structural duration of five semiquavers is obtained by adding the three semiquavers of the B♭ (upper staff) to the two semiquavers of the G (lower staff). The end of this duration is indicated by a new occurrence of the B♭, expressed as a grace note following the G (lower staff). A structural duration can also occur by superposing different durations within a single melodic line. For instance, a pitch of eight and another of nine units can be combined to form a structural duration of nine units. The first will last eight units, and the second, one unit, completing the structural duration. Thus the melodic line implies a kind of 'hidden' rhythmic polyphony, not unlike the polyphonic structures implicit in Johann Sebastian Bach's suites for violoncello. Boulez described this procedure as a 'static illusion, where polyphony . . . can take on the aspect of homophony or even monody, by a sort of projection of these elements onto an even plane.'[21]

The link between the completed work and the compositional point of departure in *Antiphonie* results from a second interpretation of the initial series. The form of *Antiphonie* is: 'verset 1' // 'répons 1' // 'répons 2 – verset 2 – répons 3' //. The empty squares in the initial line of the serial table indicate pauses, marked in the score by a fermata at the top of a bar-line, indicating an important break rather than simply an extended pause. Grouped notes on the table correspond to 'versets', and single notes, to 'répons'. The relationship between 'verset 1' and 'répons 1' clearly illustrates these characteristics and the complementary nature of the compositional criteria. On the one hand, the two serial forms that make up the 'verset 1' (I–H) correspond to the initial sets of grouped notes in the serial table but are treated in successive homogeneous serial forms. On the other, the three serial forms of 'répons 1' (E–K–L), derived from successive single notes in the serial table, are intertwined as shown in Example 11.2b.

In the first insert of *Zeitmaße* (bars 29–40), the pitches of the initial series appear as the only sustained notes within a complex musical tissue. From a rhythmic point of view the instruments are completely independent. Register is however rigorously controlled, both in terms of pitch and at the sectional level. This technique is clearly similar to that used by Stockhausen in *Kreuzspiel* (1951), and is comparable to the technique used by Boulez in movements V and IX of *Le marteau sans maître*. In the latter case, acoustic space is organised according to vertical series, eliminating the necessity of ordering pitch succession. In other sections of *Zeitmaße*, composed earlier, Stockhausen used an approximate definition of register (low–medium–high). Sketches pertaining to the pitch organisation in the first insert are to be found on the back side of sketches for the groups of low sounds in *Gesang der Jünglinge*.[22]

Three operations precede the writing out of individual parts. These operations are presented as elements labelled A, B and C of a sketch presented in Example 11.3. (A) The notes of the initial series (transposed to E) are distributed in terms of register. Note the grouping of the tenth and eleventh terms. (B) Complete harmonic fields are established, including sporadic indications concerning duration. (C) The original series is followed by sets of twelve to four notes, among which the series operates as a filter. In field 11, the first serial term (C♯) is omitted; in field 10, the next two (D and A); in field 9, the next three (C, A♭ and E), etc. The sketch also bears witness to moments of doubt: the double registration of C in the third position (sketch element A) and the register modification of C♯ and D in the penultimate

Example 11.3   Karlheinz Stockhausen, *Zeitmaße*, sketches for the first insert, bars 29–40

E	3 5 (1) 4 2 (1) 4 5 2 3
F	2 4 5 3 1 5 3 4 1 2
C	3 3 1 3 5 4 2 3 1 4
E♭	4 4 4 5 3 1 5 2 3 4
B	4 4 4 4 2 3 4 1 5 2
G	3 3 3 3 3 3 4 2 3 1
F♯	4 4 4 4 4 4 2 3 5 3
A	4 4 4 4 4 4 4 5 3 2
G♯	3 3 3 3 3 3 3 3 4 5
D	2 2 2 2 2 2 2 2 2 4
C♯	4 4 4 4 4 4 4 4 4 3

Figure 11.4a   Table for the register deployment of pitch in the first insert of *Zeitmaße*, bars 29–40

harmonic field (sketch element B). In sketch element B, all fields are dodecaphonic except for the last, consisting of a single B♭, which will be superimposed on the introduction of the second structural part. In some fields, one or more pitches may even appear in different registers.

From the initial register disposition (see sketch element B, field one), the pitches change register once they have appeared as a sustained note. For example in sketch element B, the E♭ remains in the upper space of the treble clef until field four, where it is written as a semibreve one octave higher. (In his original draft, Stockhausen indicated the structural importance of these sustained pitches by encircling them.) This change corresponds to the register position of E♭ in sketch element A. The octaves of this section are numbered 1 to 5, from low to high, creating the table in Figure 11.4a.[23]

The choice of five octaves is related to the five-term series used as a function of functions for the organisation of duration governing the interval of entrance between successive events at the beginning of *Zeitmaße*.[24] The register displacement of notes can be explained more or less rigorously by referring to a table based on a five-term series. The notes E and F have ten different positions each, which are determined in a symmetrical manner from the table (see Figure 11.4a). The first serial form, which determines the first five positions on the table, is derived by reading normally from left to right. The second serial form, which determines the last five positions on the table, is derived by rotating the form from the fourth term: 532<u>14</u> becomes 14523. For an analysis of this procedure for E, see lines 1–2, and for F, lines 5–4 of the basic row in Figure 11.4b. The number of positions for C and E♭ is reduced because of shared terms between the end of the first form and the beginning of the second form. For E♭ and B, the last two terms are inverted. For G and F♯, register position is modified by replacing either the terms 5 or 1 by 3. For A and G♯, the term indicating the lowest register has been removed. Finally, D and C♯ have only one register modification each. Though

Basic row and transpositions	Excerpts used for the registration
3-5-1-4-2	E (1): 3-5-1-4-2
	F♯: 4-2-3-5-[3]
5-2-3-1-4	E (2): 1-4-5-2-3
	C (2): 2-3-1-4
1-3-4-2-5	E♭ (2): 1-5-2-[3-4]
	G: 3-4-2-[3]-1
	G♯: 3-4-(2)-5
4-1-2-5-3	F (2): 5-3-4-1-2
	B: 3-4-1-[5-2]
2-4-5-3-1	F (1): 2-4-5-3-1
	C (1): 1-3-5-4-2
	E♭ (1): 4-5-3-1
	A: 4-5-3-(1)-2

Figure 11.4b Analysis of register deployment in relation to the serial table

one could establish a relationship with the table, the operation is not particularly pertinent. Thus, even though the fundamental procedures remain based on the principle of a function of functions, we nevertheless observe Stockhausen moving away from the isomorphism of serial transposition.

TOWARDS AN INTERPRETATION

The above examination of Boulez's technical evolution during the early 1950s has shown that the idea of a 'function of functions' could be variously adapted to produce new configurations while maintaining a link with the compositional point of departure. This link was particularly important at that time because the serialist perspective sought a strong relationship between form and material. A similar concern for consistency can also be observed in the work of other composers from the same period, who, when faced with similar compositional problems, produced variant solutions based on the same fundamental principles. Stockhausen, however, rapidly came to prefer procedures involving permutation that continuously renewed the contours of serial forms. This led him to abandon the isomorphic relationship which remained a cornerstone of Boulez's methods.

The second half of the 1950s witnessed a broadening of serialist conceptions. Composers shifted their focus from elementary serialist techniques, which for many had now become second nature, to concepts of formal unity of ever increasing complexity. Boulez developed the concept of a global structure creating a 'cascade of local structures',[25] and thereby risked losing the link with his compositional point of departure. In fact, the 'danger' was more imaginary than real, because unity was now articulated at the level of overall form: it was achieved through the setting of figures in a musical form rather than through the production of those figures. Stockhausen developed the idea of multi-centred musical organisms. The challenge he faced was to conciliate this multiplicity through mediation. For *Le marteau sans maître*, Boulez established methods based on the dialectical relationships between strict and free writing techniques. With Stockhausen, this opposition became two complementary facets of one complex reality, each allowing for a different exploration of the sound-world proposed by a given composition.

On the one hand, key moments in many of Stockhausen's works contain indicia concerning his basic methods. At rehearsal number 8 in *Gruppen*, the organisation of pitch in terms of frequency bands becomes explicit. In section X of *Kontakte*, a complex sound is decomposed into a beating pulse through a procedure spread over several octaves, by which the pulse is mechanically decelerated. This section illustrates, in reverse logic, how the timbre of much of this composition was produced. On the other hand, Stockhausen's works always transgress the systems initially put in place, revealing their ephemeral nature and suggesting that the work is more than the elementary systems which make it up. As these systems become more open, that is to say 'infinite' (contrary to the definition of 'system' given by Boulez[26]), the complementary relationship between the basic system and the exceptions that confirm the rule becomes more and more difficult to pin down.

To this day, such problems remain unaccounted for in most of the literature dealing with serial music, which is described either as an impenetrable alchemy or as a mechanical unfolding. Whereas the practical problems involved in working out the score can be extraordinarily complex, the ideas behind many of the basic techniques employed by both composers are often quite simple. This simplicity is compensated for by constant innovation in the modes of application, which is present throughout the compositional process and which can even partially suspend the criteria initially established by the composer himself. Most of these composers' writings deal either with the paradigmatic dismantling of mechanical procedures or with aesthetic considerations. So as to extract musical sense from these sources, the analyst must continuously move back and forth between these various levels of information.

CHAPTER 12

Elliott Carter's sketches: spiritual exercises and craftsmanship

Denis Vermaelen

A METHODICAL DISCIPLINE

The sketches of Elliott Carter's works, the majority of which are conserved at the Paul Sacher Foundation, constitute an indispensable source of information for the researcher. More often than not, the analysis of music has proven itself incapable of uncovering the clues scattered throughout the score, which reveal the musical thought governing the choice of organisational procedures. Were this information to be known, it would of course lead to a more elaborate interpretation of compositional technique. The indicia that provide access to these underlying structures will escape even the soundest analytical technique if sufficient consideration is not given to the sketches, drafts and fair copies, which are often all that can shed light on what could be called the composer's craftsmanship. In Carter's case, research has been facilitated by the impressive quantity of source material that he bequeathed for the edification of posterity. Surely he would not have taken this step, had he not been convinced of the interest and usefulness of these documents, as are indeed many of his contemporaries who scrupulously conserve their preparatory work in its entirety, regardless of its relative importance or its degree of completion. And yet, Carter maintains an ambivalent attitude towards this material, to which the following passage from the composer's correspondence bears witness:

> You must realize that all those pages of sketches are truly sketches, in the sense that some technical problem having to do with interval or rhythm or figuration is considered and solutions are worked over until certain artistic demands like 'expression', 'character', 'emphasis' are satisfied in a way that seems to me relatively 'fresh' sounding. Solutions that sound 'dead', 'dry' (unless specifically needed at a certain moment) are discarded and sometimes no 'life-like' solution can be found so the whole process is discarded. All that takes paper and time . . .[1]

In this rather surprising statement, Carter seems eager to anticipate future criticism from researchers examining his source material. A needless precaution to say the least, for do we not expect a composer's sketches to reflect the laborious efforts inherent in creative activity: searching, losing oneself, making mistakes, before finally obtaining an adequate result on paper? In fact, it would seem as though Carter wished to dissuade his future exegetes from placing too much stock in the very material he has taken such care to inventory, classify and conserve. Numerous reasons can be proposed to explain this apparently contradictory attitude. First, the modesty of the artisan, who, having finished his work, does not like having its minutiae dissected so as to reveal his trade secrets and thus lay bare the work's *poiesis*. Second, the dissatisfaction of the creator who believes that strict technical analysis does not do justice to a work. Indeed, Carter has on many occasions expressed reservations about the inherent limitations of analytical techniques:

> I do feel that the approach that many music theorists have taken to composition is not a satisfactory one – I've said this a number of times in different essays. Not that I know a better way, but I do feel that analysis which starts by assuming the artistic value of a work, and then analyses it, seldom tells you what it is that makes the work so interesting to hear. All it does is tell you that the chords are this way and that, and that they're inversions of different sorts and so forth, and I keep feeling that I would rather read theoretical articles that explain why it is that the work, when heard, captures our attention, and what is so valuable about it musically, and then show what it is that contributes to this experience. Now, it could be that at the present stage of musical analysis, it's necessary to carry on the sort of detailed work that you allude to in the case of my sketches, but I'm not sure that it would produce a useful result, because very often the sketches are simply brief passages working out some little problem – about the harmony, for instance.[2]

Lastly, the scepticism that has led Carter to distrust the validity and pertinence of approaches based on source studies, when they limit themselves to the painstaking reconstruction of the compositional process without delving into criteria by which to judge the work's intrinsic features, that is to say the characteristics making up its aesthetic value. No doubt all of the aforementioned factors contribute to Carter's mixed feelings concerning his sketches as well as others not mentioned in the letter.

Carter's sketches can in fact be disconcerting for the researcher interested in retracing the compositional process because much of this material is devoted to the morphological analysis of interval structure and the deployment of groups of pitches in various registers. Often there appears to be no direct relation between these tirelessly repeated preparatory exercises and the writing of Carter's music. Can these daily combinatory gymnastics, with which the composer seems compelled to preface his creative activity, legitimately be called sketches? It would certainly be a mistake to see this activity as nothing more than uninteresting, routine exercises. On the contrary, this preparatory work should probably be considered as a kind of asceticism: a methodical discipline, the full value of which lies in regular repetition. Seen in this light, what could initially be dismissed as a futile habit can be understood as an authentically spiritual endeavour, crucial to the very essence of the composer's work. The rigorous constraints of this discipline constitute a preliminary mental process, the goal of which seems to be to relax and focus the mind so as to prepare the composer for creative work (this type of activity evokes certain age-old meditative practices in which Carter has expressed interest).

A SYSTEMATIC INVESTIGATION

Undertaken with remarkable obstinacy by Carter prior to the actual composition of a work, the methodical examination of pitch combinations available in the tempered chromatic scale was initially motivated by his awareness that, by the second half of the twentieth century, composers had become increasingly responsible for the development of all levels of musical discourse, from the most general to the most specific. From the time he began working on his first string quartet, Carter understood that the disappearance of hierarchical tonal functions signified a considerable enrichment of what he has called the musical vocabulary. All conceivable aggregate structures could be used freely, without bending to pre-existing harmonic rules. It follows that each composer now had to determine which morphological elements would serve as a basis for his musical language, to rigorously circumscribe this material and to conceive procedures capable of generating a syntactic organisation based on logical method. It was during this same period that Carter began to collect the empirical investigations scattered among his sketches in order to establish a systematic index of every possible three- to twelve-pitch structure within the tempered chromatic scale. This rigorous inventory eventually became a kind of musical dictionary. The repertoire is intended to be at once exhaustive (all possible pitch combinations in modulo twelve are included) and synoptic (the scope of a finite catalogue necessarily limits the countless number of possible sound-configurations). Over a twenty-year period, Carter devoted a large part of his time and energy to this ambitious, but by no means utopian, undertaking. Not only was he involved in drawing up a list of pitch structures, he also studied the characteristic morphological properties of each one, applying techniques which were by turns analytic (breaking the structures down into their basic elements) and synthetic (creating combinations of variable density by successively including elements), and which bring to mind the methodologies of linguistics. In an interview given in the late 1960s, Carter briefly referred to this ever-present and time-consuming part of his work:

> This has become for me a whole new field of thought, involving such questions as what two-note groups are contained in three-note groups, and so forth. This way of working allows me to make all sorts of harmonic identities by adding and subtracting notes and so produce a whole gamut of harmonic colors all related to each other.[3]

Sketches for works composed between the early 1950s and the late 1960s (approximately from the First String Quartet to the *Concerto for Orchestra*) contain evidence of this parallel activity that accompanies the creative process without merging with it. The permanent interaction between these two levels of activity is such that it is sometimes difficult to determine whether it is the theoretical explorations which enrich the music of a particular work, or the reverse. Carter attempted to clarify this point by situating his work in the context of research undertaken by composers and theorists since the early 1920s. This is explained in a short typescript with handwritten inserts (placed in square brackets) contained in the copy of the Harmony Book, compiled from 1963 to 1967 and conserved at the Sacher Foundation. It contains the results of the composer's theoretical work and consequently provides information which is essential to a more complete understanding of his musical language:

> The system of [harmonic ordering gradually evolving] in the 'harmony book' was developed after studies of the Aloïs Hába *Neue Harmonielehre* [see my copy pp. 95–119] and J. M. Hauer's *Vom Melos zur Pauke* [see my copy p. 12] and one of the 12-tone technique by Schoenberg, Richard Hill, Leibowitz, Babbitt, Martino, Allen Forte and George Perle. Actually the matter had been on my mind ever since I read the Hauer and Hába books in the early 30s and sporadically tried to work on their ideas. However, after using the all-interval chord idea in the 1st Quartet in 1950 and in a different way in the *Double Concerto* and the 2nd Quartet I decided to expand the chord vocabulary and started developing the charts which took shape as this growing 'harmony book'. I renewed my study of Hába and inserted my own numbering system of chords [built by adding one note] or tropes built on the basis of different starting points, but containing similar patterns.[4]

Though from an epistemological point of view, he would later criticise Aloïs Hába's method for being nothing other than a laborious, redundant and ultimately incoherent taxonomy, and Joseph Hauer's method because it failed to examine the morphological properties of its tropes, Carter nonetheless retained the idea of dividing the chromatic whole into unordered pitch-class sets of variable density. This method is detached from acoustic reality because it takes into consideration neither the deployment of pitches in different registers, nor their order of presentation. As a result, when consulting Carter's source material, one must continuously distinguish between the preliminary formalisation of the musical vocabulary, often simply a list of structures abstracted from any spatial or temporal coordinates, and the writing out of the work itself.

   This methodological dissociation was of course not without its consequences for the orientation of Carter's musical output from the early 1950s onwards. The listed pitch structures, created in advance of every work, are usually undefined entities, which cannot be committed to memory either as thematic elements or as recognisable shapes. They are better understood as charts or pitch matrixes, the transposition and inversion of which generate a potentially infinite number of specific realisations through the permutation of their constituent elements and through change in registral distribution. Thus, a rigorous and supple 'linguistic framework'[5] is created, within which structural homogeneity does not work to the detriment of variety. Apparently dissimilar melodic figures and contrasting harmonic identities can be logically inferred from the same generating principle. These matrixes are mediated through the series of diverse melodic and harmonic manifestations and do not make up part of the musical text *per se*. Though they exercise permanent control over the melodic conduct of individual lines and the building up of the aggregates, they remain latent. However, little by little, the functional structures based on these matrixes eliminated the last traces of thematic development in Carter's works, replacing it with organisational procedures based on the principle of non-repetition.

Following the completion of the first version of the Harmony Book, Carter continued this research, tirelessly exploring the combinatory possibilities within tempered chromatic space. As his ability to analyse the morphological properties of pitch-class sets of variable density developed, Carter began applying this expertise to more complex structures, including the twelve-tone row itself, each row being classified in accordance with its internal ordering. Moreover, these sketches demonstrate the growing importance of problems related to spatial distribution as well as to the study of relationships between different structures created by the same chart or matrix. As a result, the Harmony Book has remained unfinished. It is a work in progress, constantly being revised, enriched and perfected, even though Carter did not initially intend to have it published, or to use it as a theoretical framework for compositional technique. Indeed, it is this aspect of the Harmony Book which distinguishes it from the numerous didactic works written by twentieth-century composers. Developed in close connection to the creative process, its function is strictly personal and essentially pragmatic: that is to say it attempts to resolve questions of pitch organisation, raised in Carter's works since the 1950s. The solutions provided by the book, often precisely dated and annotated in sketches, do however allow researchers to piece together the long-term development of Carter's musical thought, as well as informing them of some surprising alternatives that often open up new perspectives on the work in question. While many of these charts have no precise relation to specific passages in Carter's works and thus seem to become distanced from their origins as they were gradually collated in the independent catalogue, we should not lose sight of the fact that this catalogue remains auxiliary to the compositional process. We now turn to the second, complementary aspect of this essay and consider how the listed pitch structures can be interpreted in terms of specific compositional details of a given piece. To accomplish this we shall focus on 'Anaphora', the first song in the cycle entitled *A Mirror on Which to Dwell*, for soprano and instrumental ensemble.

THE FORMATIVE PROCESS

'Anaphora' is undeniably one of the most carefully wrought pieces to be found in Carter's work list. Of the 750 pages of manuscript material conserved for *A Mirror on Which to Dwell*, no fewer than 168 pages specifically refer to work on 'Anaphora', most of which was completed between 12 July and 10 August 1975. This first group of sketches includes numerous drafts of the successive versions of this song. A subsequent group, produced towards the end of December 1975, bears witness to a later, more advanced stage in the compositional process. On 8 June 1975, just under seven months before the work was completed on 31 December 1975, Carter drew up a list of nine settings of poems by Elizabeth Bishop in order to clarify the general organisation of the cycle and to take stock of his work to that date.[6] At that time, both the rhythmic scheme and vocal line of 'Anaphora' had been sketched and its position as the first song of the cycle was clearly established. Whereas the poem had been conceived as the crowning conclusion to the whole *North & South* anthology, the song represents a kind of portico, inaugurating the cycle with a certain solemnity clearly evident in the opening words: 'Each day with so much ceremony begins . . .'

One part of 'Anaphora' that underwent a particularly large number of revisions is the fragment containing the climax of the soprano line, which was of crucial importance for the composition of the entire piece. To increase the suggestive potential of the adjective 'stupendous' and enhance the violence of its occlusive consonants, Carter wrote an exceptionally disjointed melodic line, putting the articulatory skills of the performer to the test. For each syllable, he adopted a percussive-like articulation: note for instance how the B♭ and the B are doubled respectively by the vibraphone and the piano (bars 57–8), conferring an onomatopoeic expressive value on the word. He then returned to the preceding section (the central part of 'Anaphora'), and recomposed the melodic line, circumscribing it in a restricted range: the high notes of the vocal register were eliminated, making the tonic accents seem deadened, the intonation smoother and the phrasing more uniform. The goal of this levelling of compositional parameters was to put more emphasis on the ensuing renewal of melodic activity, inverting the tendency towards entropy announced at the beginning of the second stanza, where the text evokes the decline of light and energy.

Seen from a technical point of view, the composer's priorities are quite clear: while we might have expected Carter to begin by drafting the soprano melody, which, with its discursive continuity, constitutes the main musical thread, orientating the listening experience, it does seem on the face of it rather more surprising that the rhythmic structure should have been completely predetermined. In fact, the schematisation of the polyrhythmic complex corresponds to a structural phase of Carter's work predating the act of writing out the melody. This phase included calculating metronome frequencies of superimposed pulsations, calculating the length of time separating two consecutive points of synchrony, and establishing rhythmic equivalences for the tempo modulations.

It was precisely at this earlier stage, preceding the actual writing out of 'Anaphora' in July and August 1975 that a functional interdependence – which is the true key to the composition – was established between the separately composed rhythmic scheme and the vocal line, transforming a loose relational fabric into an indivisible whole. In the definitive version of 'Anaphora', the musical hyperbole (bars 57–8), designed to enhance both the sonorous effect and semantic content of 'stupendous', consists of a two-part process, creating a gradated instrumental polyphony in the fifteen bars preceding the melodic climax. On the

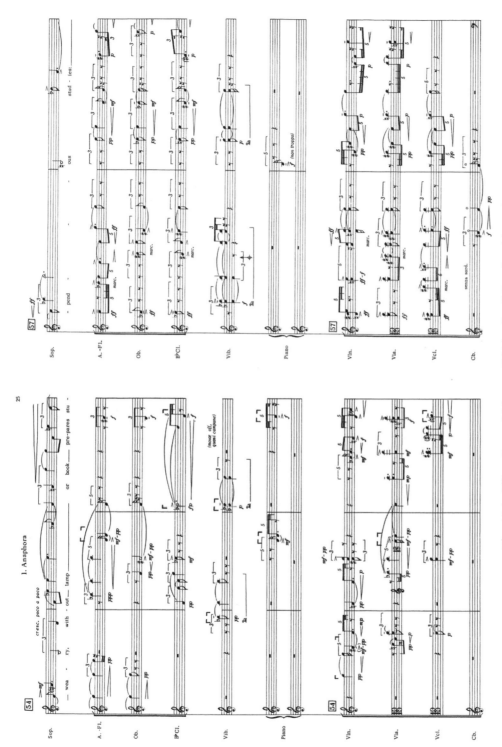

Plate 12.1   Elliott Carter, *A Mirror on Which to Dwell*, 'Anaphora', bars 54–8

one hand, this parallel structure consists of an extension of descending melodic intervals, from the minor second to the diminished fifteenth, which happens to be the interval encompassing the twelve-tone row used as a point of reference in this song (see the staff at the top of Plate 12.2). On the other, an augmenting arithmetic progression is established for the duration values of the polyrhythmic complex. Thus, what at first may appear to be an isolated and somewhat emphatic effect, seeming to have no impact on the overall architecture of the work, draws its legitimacy from the structure of the musical discourse, while still maintaining its ability to surprise the listener. Local contrasts, logically motivated in the syntactic scheme, are articulated in this rigorously structured work. The functional value of these contrasts is thus heightened, allowing for a release of expressive potential, which is both striking and durable. Musical significance is therefore immanent in the form of the melody. The meaning of the work crystallises at that special moment when the vocal line and the instrumental ensemble, both derived from two different structural schemes, are conjoined.

The idea of creating mirror effects between the constituent elements of his musical language is the source of one of the most important compositional challenges Carter faced as he began work on 'Anaphora'. In this song, he sought to put all melodic figures and their aggregates in a scale formed by two sets of six notes distributed symmetrically around a central interval, with every note fixed in a specific register for the duration of the piece. This challenge is of course reflected in the title of the song cycle and was motivated by the structural similarity between the two stanzas of the poem as well as their semantic connections: for instance, the opposition between the clear luminous forms of the morning and their sketchy crepuscular reflections. The function of the dual restrictions (i.e. the placing of pitches in fixed registers and the symmetric deployment of the pitch-class sets) was to severely limit the field of possible interval combinations and thus to reduce the number of possible sound configurations. This quantitative restriction of available aggregates facilitated the organisation of a rigorous harmonic syntax, because the composer's attention was now focused on the relative function of these aggregates and their modes of sequence. In short the composer was able to concentrate on writing the work, gradually transforming the chosen material into musical language. The adoption of these kinds of restrictions has remained a persistent characteristic of Carter's working method, from the *Eight Etudes and a Fantasy* (1950), constructed on a single chord, an interval or even a single note, to the strict canons composed during the 1970s and 1980s, and has stimulated reflexive activity aimed at acquiring a more consistent and flexible compositional technique. This approach brings to mind that adopted by Wassily Kandinsky during his Bauhaus period, when his paintings were composed using only the most elementary shapes such as the circle, the square or the straight line. With Carter there is however no didactic intention. Indeed, it would perhaps be more appropriate to compare 'Anaphora' with the scenes from Act III of *Wozzeck*: a musical invention based on closely circumscribed material, consisting of a polyrhythmic complex, a symmetrical scale of twelve pitches in fixed register and a hexachord.

Of the structures indexed in the Harmony Book, only one received the label 'all-triad', specifying its extraordinary property. The segmentation of this structure into twelve subsets, made up of three elements (triads) each, generates all of the three-note aggregates possible in the tempered chromatic scale. In 'Anaphora', the dual restriction imposed by setting pitches in fixed registers and deploying them symmetrically is compensated by the use of the all-triad structure, which opens up a vast field of possible pitch combinations, because each of the 220 three-note aggregates contained in the twelve-tone structure is present in at least one of the twenty-four six-note aggregates generated by the transposition and inversion of this unique matrix. Restriction and expansion: opposites combine to form a 'linguistic framework', within which the profusion of contrasting harmonic identities does not call into question the coherence of the musical vocabulary. In a sketch dating from 21 December 1975, Carter listed the twenty-four six-note aggregates generated from the 'all-triad' structure, grouping them in pairs. Each pair is made up of an aggregate and its mirror image. This synoptic layout has the advantage of bringing common notes to the fore, suggesting ways of maintaining continuity as the music moves from one aggregate to the next.

The classification of these twelve pairs of aggregates demonstrates the importance attached by the composer to their positioning in relation to the referential row (see the staff at the top of Plate 12.2), which determines their order of succession and their position in the overall course of the melody, that is to say the syntactic function they fulfil in defining the form. Thus, the first three aggregates (1a to 3b), grouped fairly close to each other at the apex of the row, are used mainly in the second section, where we observed the elimination of melodic extremes. This dual contraction is undoubtedly motivated by the textual reference to the feeling of being crushed that overwhelms the entire world as the hours go by. Conversely, the final regeneration is underlined by the use of the last aggregate sets, whose constituent elements are spread over the widest leaps at the end of the referential row. Furthermore, just before the point of synchrony in the first section, the grouping together of several widely spaced aggregates accentuates the musical climax that coincides with an outpouring of questions, creating the feeling of sudden awareness. Clearly, the poetic structure influenced the choice of aggregates, their spatial distribution as well as the positioning of these registrally fixed structures in the course of the piece. Thus, out of a rather rigid framework, we observe the emergence of a dynamic form: an alliance of opposites indicative of the dialectics of Carter's musical thought.

LAST SKETCHES, FIRST PAGE

The genesis of the two-bar instrumental introduction, which begins not only 'Anaphora' but the entire cycle, proved to be laborious. Marked by numerous aborted projects, dead ends, and reworkings, this introduction was one of the last parts of the work to be completed.

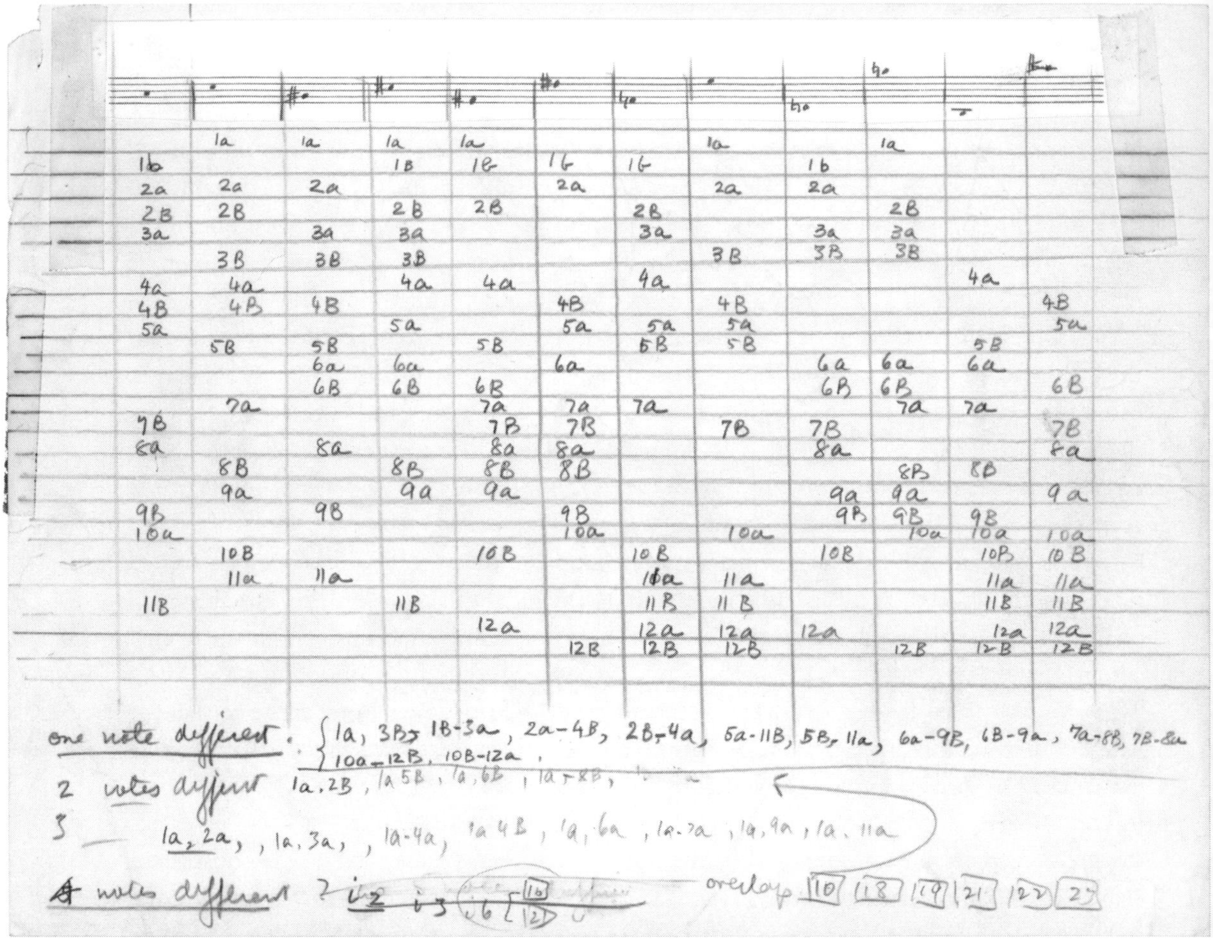

Plate 12.2   Elliott Carter, matrix of the all-triad structure, Elliott Carter Collection,
Paul Sacher Foundation, Basle

Carter seemed unable to resolve the problems encountered in the introduction before he had established a vision of the work as a whole: rather like the writer who composes the preface only after developing an overall plan encompassing both the large- and small-scale aspects of the work and allowing the main themes to emerge. Consequently, even though one already finds a musical continuum based on the idea of a fast-paced polyphony and harmonic material based on the all-triad hexachord in two manuscripts, the former dated 29 July 1975 and the latter dating from 5 August 1975 (see Plates 12.3 and 12.4), the burgeoning polyphony arises from intertwined melodic lines not yet subjected either to the strict control of pitch combinations or to the rigorous contrapuntal style so characteristic of the rest of the song. The impression of intense activity results mainly from a profusion of

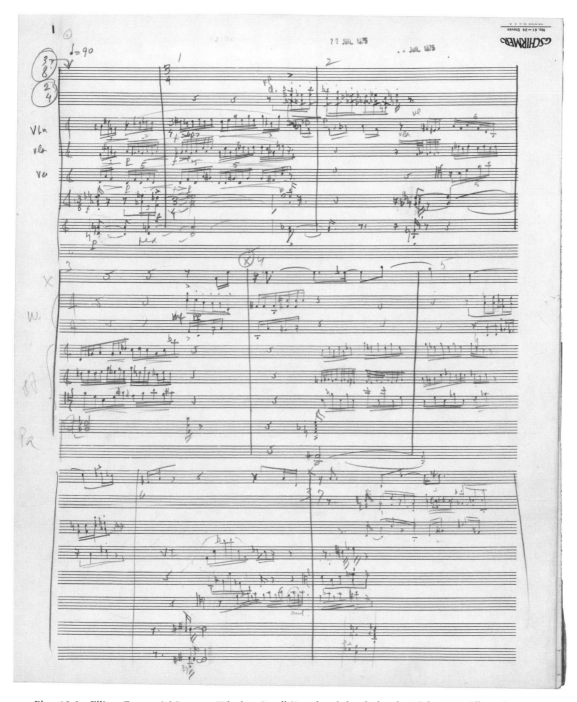

Plate 12.3   Elliott Carter, *A Mirror on Which to Dwell*, 'Anaphora' sketch dated 29 July 1975, Elliott Carter
Collection, Paul Sacher Foundation, Basle

Plate 12.4   Elliott Carter, *A Mirror on Which to Dwell*, 'Anaphora' sketch dating from 5 August 1975, Elliott Carter Collection, Paul Sacher Foundation, Basle

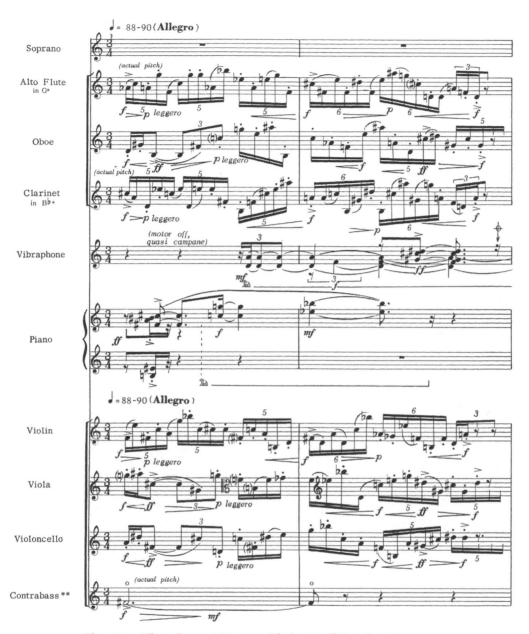

Plate 12.5 Elliott Carter, *A Mirror on Which to Dwell*, 'Anaphora', bars 1–2

Example 12.1   Elliott Carter, *A Mirror on Which to Dwell*, 'Anaphora', bars 1–2,
scheme of pitch relationships

loosely connected ornamental figures (trills, irregular beats). Furthermore, the terracing of two three-part homophonic sound-blocks, characterised by specific aggregates and distinct rhythms, is not as clear as it would become in later versions. Had it remained in this state, the first page of 'Anaphora' would have certainly succeeded in evoking the early morning bustle, with its blurred mingling of birds, bells and factory whistles. Nonetheless, its structure would have remained rather commonplace.

The development of Carter's musical thought during the last six months of his work on *A Mirror on Which to Dwell* becomes clear when we compare these first sketches with the definitive version of the score. Originating from an initial idea, the successive stages of this deductive process gradually evolved in the process of writing out the work. Its development took the shape of increasingly dense structural relationships and, in particular, a heightened concentration of the harmonic material. As is demonstrated in Plate 12.5 and Example 12.1, every single note is part of at least one and often more of the twenty-four aggregates derived from the 'all-triad' hexachord, allowing Carter to establish intersections between the polyphonic blocks, thanks to the minute displacements generated by the polyrhythmic structure.

No less than twenty-seven aggregates follow each other in the space of four seconds. The meticulous development of this page is such that it seems disproportionate when compared to what can be grasped by listening. For Carter, auditory limitations are not to be used as grounds for relaxing the control over compositional technique or as a justification for a summary or superficial ordering that would jeopardise the intrinsic qualities of the work's conception. The existence of small-scale anomalies, found in the sketches, the fair copy and the published score, are not the result of a deliberate attempt to subvert organisational procedures, but rather of mere inadvertence. At the second beat of the second bar, the G♭ in the violin part (second semiquaver of the sextuplet) should be replaced by F♮ in order to form the 11b aggregate. This structural irregularity does not in any way compromise the consistency of this page, which remains one of the most tightly coordinated musical fragments written by the composer.

The virtuoso compositional technique demonstrated here is by no means an end in itself. Were this so, the significance of these two bars would have been restricted to a simple contrapuntal exercise; a structural tour de force, whose rigorous construction and impressive craftsmanship would be sapped by functional contingency and the absence of any legitimacy. The aesthetic value of this page lies in the emergence of musical thought immanent in this composition and can best be evaluated by studying the source material. This musical thought is so perfectly realised in the instrumental introduction that these two bars can be seen as the central core, crystallising the melodic development of the entire song. Everything is contained in this dense and elliptical introduction (the polyrhythmic structure, the harmonic layout, the deployment of pitches in fixed registers). The next sixty bars are nothing but an unfurling of this compact polyphony, terse to the point of anarchy, over a far more extended period of time. Perhaps the composer intended to signify that the unwinding of the day, moving from an ascending phase to a drop and then to regeneration, is already inscribed in the first moment. Carter communicates the rather pleasant idea that no matter how he transforms his musical language, it maintains a permanent connection with something that was present at the very beginning of the work.

CHAPTER 13

E-sketches: Brian Ferneyhough's use of computer-assisted compositional tools

Ross Feller

The American composer and theorist David Schiff has remarked that, 'composers' sketches rarely provide unambiguous evidence of the creative process; they are an incomplete and possibly distorted mirror of a composer's mental activity'.[1] This is especially true of those composers whose sketches partake in preformational or precompositional processes. The expatriate British composer Brian Ferneyhough (*b*. 1943) is one who is well aware that a composer's sketches obliquely refer to the process of creating a piece of music. Because sketches contain traces of an act that is no longer present, and not simply that which is traced, there is an inherent gap between these materials and the analyst's probe. With the recent trend towards computer-assisted composition this gap has widened. Sketches rarely represent all stages of composition. Absence is embedded in the aura that surrounds sketch materials. Computer-assisted sketch materials illuminate this aura. So the 'distorted mirror' can hold many valuable clues for the theorist; it is a mirror upon which to dwell.

Since the late 1980s Ferneyhough has become increasingly involved with computer-assisted composition. The sketches from this period show the computer's impact upon his notational and compositional development.

The year 1994 was a landmark year for Ferneyhough. It was the year in which he began composing the *String Trio*, his first composition to be completely composed with the computer-assistance of PatchWork, a software program from the Paris-based Institut de Recherche et de Coordination Acoustique/Musique (IRCAM). From this year on computer-assistance has become his primary compositional tool. Although his music has changed as a direct result of his involvement with the computer, many of the computer-assisted processes he now uses can be found in his earlier work, albeit in germinal form. Ferneyhough's recent compositional praxis presents us with an appropriate context from which to examine questions about the computer's impact on a composer's sketch process. His computer-assisted work magnifies specific issues and problems related to contemporary practice. The personal, desktop computer has only become widely available since the mid-1980s, yet it is already a standard compositional tool for many composers. The computer has become the primary object on the composer's desktop, impacting not only the composer's compositional practice but also the physical act of composition. Computer-assisted composition leaves different traces from those produced with non-computer-assisted processes. This situation presents new challenges that must be addressed in order for scholars to keep abreast of twenty-first-century compositional developments.

After nearly thirty years of meticulously notating his scores by hand Ferneyhough now uses Coda Music Technology's notation program called Finale. Employing Finale has changed the physical look of Ferneyhough's scores, which, considering the complexity of his music, is not a trivial matter.[2] *Bone Alphabet* (1991) for solo percussion was the first composition in which he utilised computer notation for the final score. Since then Finale has allowed him to take a more distant approach to the act of notation. And it is no doubt a major convenience to no longer calculate complex, fractional beat placements by hand.

Ferneyhough's scores are designed to maximise ambiguity and imprecision, two essential prerequisites for performance interpretation. His scores look extremely precise, but are so highly complex that performers will inevitably fail to realise some aspects that are notated in detail. The level of virtuosity required is just shy of what is currently impossible. This sense of failure is a consequence of his notational practice. It emerges out of a strong conviction he shares with Artificial Life theorists like Marvin Minsky, that it is primarily when systems fail that humans engage consciousness. We tend to be more aware of symbolic processes that do not work well than of those that work flawlessly. According to the composer, 'if things didn't go wrong, if there weren't bugs in the system we probably wouldn't be conscious beings at all . . . the conscious mind is conscious presumably for an evolutionary purpose and that evolutionary purpose is bug fixing'.[3] Ferneyhough's performers are encouraged to develop their own unique interpretative strategies as they attempt to overcome their initial disorientation, largely brought on by notation that is multi-layered, rhythmically complex and gesturally unfamiliar. His computer-generated scores still have these traits, but perhaps the uniform look of Finale's music font, printed on a laser printer, might impart a false, generic sense to the score. The danger here is that the kind of razor-sharp performance that Ferneyhough desires could be compromised. Recently he has developed approaches whereby Finale files are produced automatically from PatchWork files, and vice versa. Thus, the intimate connection between notation and compositional idea, a longstanding attribute of Ferneyhough's style, remains an integral part of his work.

Sketches from his pre-computer work can be found on a plethora of materials including graph and manuscript paper, hotel stationery, personal letters, memos, newspaper clips and photocopies. It seems clear that he sketched on whatever was close at hand. Many of the sketches are well-worn (folded, torn, and/or stained) indicating that they were handled repeatedly. For the most part these sketches consist of single pages, as opposed to sketchbooks. This is largely due to his practice of notating the final score as he is composing,[4] an excruciatingly slow method and one wherein mistakes are spontaneously incorporated, if they occur. The single pages form the environment out of which arise his compositional decisions. Some are arrived at spontaneously. They contain incomplete or partially completed processes, and cryptic notes to himself containing a proliferation of abbreviations, special terms and codes. In many cases the sketched materials are never incorporated into the final score. For example, he might sketch several complete bars to illustrate, or try out, a given procedure rather than to produce a rough draft. In fact he rarely produces rough drafts. These theoretical, or non-teleological, sketches are sometimes used for another piece, written at a later date. Close study of his pre-computer sketches reveals aspects of continuity with his later, computer-assisted work. The techniques employed in the former period exhibit a step-by-step, often binary logic and seem rife for computer processing. His sketch process is especially amenable to computer transfer because of his penchant for using complex parametrical subdivision and material arrays. Both can be easily represented in numeric form.

His sketchbooks are, for the most part, a compilation of single pages, often taped together in an order other than the one implied by the page numbers. Typically, pages are left unnumbered and not dated. In fact Ferneyhough rarely dates any of his sketches. This presents some obvious impediments to establishing a chronology. Furthermore it is not uncommon for him to sketch on the backside of a sketch from a previous work written perhaps many years earlier. Hence, in order to locate all extant sketches for a given piece one would need to look at the sketch materials for his other pieces. Establishing a chronology is a bit easier in the cases where he sketches on dated form letters, hotel stationery (assuming one had access to his itinerary) or newspaper clippings. His self-conscious involvement in a consistent and continuing sense of his own style can help confirm meta-chronological aspects, but may only obfuscate matters on a more local level. Even if one were to simply ask the composer to reconstruct a sketch chronology for one of his compositions, the problem of chronology would still exist because, as he told the Australian musicologist Richard Toop, 'my sketches are sometimes incomprehensible, even to me, the day after'.[5]

In the sketch materials from the late 1980s and early 1990s one finds evidence of Ferneyhough's increased reliance on the computer. The problem of chronology becomes even more acute, however. The compositions from this period have resulted in far fewer sketches than the earlier works. This is because, as he points out, 'the material that's generated by Patch-Work . . . never gets printed out'.[6] This poses some serious challenges to the scholar seeking to reconstruct Ferneyhough's decision-making process. The composer is well aware of this problem, as evidenced in his comment that, 'it will be very difficult for anyone approaching these works in analytical terms to trace the decisions that went into their genesis'.[7] Even if the composer made all of his files available for study, problems of chronology and reconstruction would still exist. Two dates are embedded in computer files: the dates of their creation and most recent modification. If the composer modified and saved his files on more than one occasion (very likely in Ferneyhough's case) there would not be a record of these changes that was easily accessible. In the event that a file began life as another file before being 'saved as' a different name, the creation date would be the date it was renamed, not the date of the original file's creation. Thus, while computers keep accurate track of dates (assuming they were set up correctly to begin with), this is no guarantee that one will be able to reconstruct a complete, or accurate, chronology. When studying conventional paper sketches one might hold the same piece of paper that the composer held. The sketches' physical presence can reveal valuable information to the scholar. With computer sketches this information often never leaves the composer's hard disk drive. Thus, much valuable information is lost because it never leaves the virtual world of the computer. I will use the term 'e-sketch' (electronic sketch) to signify this type of virtual sketch process.

Early E-sketches

The sketch materials from the late 1980s and early 1990s also contain computer print-outs of score fragments and charts, which are produced by laser and inkjet printers. And there are pages that contain ruminations about algorithms to be employed at later stages of his compositional process. Other pages contain the computer-generated results of such processes. Plate 13.1 shows a transcribed rhythmic sketch from *Trittico per Gertrude Stein* (1989) for solo double bass. The small columns of numbers written below each rhythmic layer were generated by a process which Ferneyhough calls a Random Funnel. The Random Funnel process produces a series of numbers with a linear, funnel-shaped random procedure, illustrated in Figure 13.1. The numbers are used to govern filter, permutation and transposition operations among others. These operations produced skeleton structures for the metres, tempos, rhythms and pitches used in *Trittico per Gertrude Stein* and other works from the same period. At its most basic the Random Funnel operates in the following manner: a fixed, unordered number series is randomly permuted until it reaches a contextually pre-determined, final destination. If a number arrives at its destination before the last stage it simply repeats, or remains in place. In his earliest Random Funnel compositions the first or last stage contained a numerical series, incremented by one (see Figure 13.1). Rand Steiger, his colleague at the University of California at San Diego, created the first Random Funnel computer program in 1988 for Ferneyhough. Since then Ferneyhough has expanded the Random Funnel concept to include what he calls 'morphing techniques'. For example a given series might be interpolated into its inversion, or altered in such a way that the first and last stages only partially resemble each other. Other, less obvious, examples occur in instances where he uses one series to filter or permute another. Because the Random Funnel process is cyclic a new number is added to each column every time it cycles back through a pulse or number series. The first numbers added were probably those at the uppermost of each column, i.e. the numbers closest to the rhythmic layer itself. In more recent works, instead of doing this by hand, the computer is used to not only produce data from such procedures, but also to make multiple versions of the same processes. Ferneyhough then selects from these, using this material for reference during the act of composition. The Random Funnel is now only one of many such devices that he has created with the assistance of PatchWork.

Ferneyhough 'palimpsestuously'[8] writes upon his sketches. Some are annotated in such a way as to indicate that he used them as visual reminders of the various processes he employed. For instance in Plate 13.2 ticks are used to keep track of the use and reuse of various filtering procedures. This sketch transcription is from *Terrain* (1992) and involves five rhythmic filters applied, via a Random Funnel, to four lines of material. This kind of procedure can be found

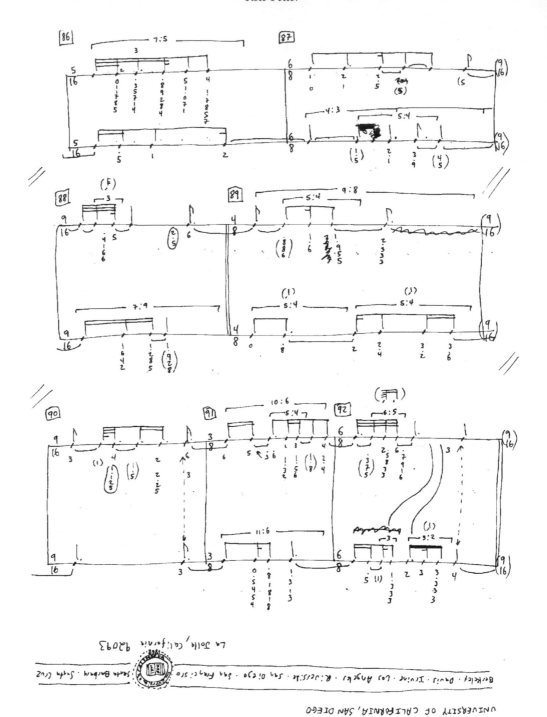

Plate 13.1   Brian Ferneyhough, *Trittico per Gertrude Stein* (1989), rhythmic sketch transcription

3	7	2	1	8	6	4	9	5
8	3	6	2	9	5	4	1	7
5	9	7	4	8	2	3	1	6
2	9	7	5	1	8	3	4	6
2	9	7	4	5	1	3	6	8
4	8	7	1	5	2	3	9	6
4	8	7	6	5	2	3	1	9
1	8	7	6	5	9	3	1	2
1	8	7	6	5	4	3	2	9
9	8	7	6	5	4	3	2	1

Figure 13.1   Random Funnel series

in the sketches from both his pre-computer and his current computer work. In both cases it is an indication of an attempt to forestall the fallibility of memory. Ferneyhough is not the only composer who forgets all the detailed steps of his own compositional process (one thinks of Elliott Carter, for example). From the beginning of the second period his work with the computer has magnified this 'weakness'. As he puts it 'with respect to the *String Trio* . . . I discovered there were insufficient preserved materials to enable the reconstruction of a significant number of procedures'.[9] So when asked to explain these procedures he is forced to 'reinvent' his reasoning. According to Ferneyhough[10] he first employed the Random Funnel while composing *La Chute d'Icare* (1988), doing the necessary calculations by hand. But remarkably similar devices can be found in the sketches for several pieces from the *Carceri d'Invenzione* cycle (1981–6) and in *Lemma-Icon-Epigram* (1981) for solo piano. His first computer-assisted compositional attempts occurred in 1980 while working at the IRCAM facilities in Paris. Although frustrated with the inadequate results produced, evidently due to serious equipment limitations, he managed to generate a series of algorithms, which were subsequently incorporated into PatchWork.

PatchWork

PatchWork is a visually orientated programming environment for graphically creating compositional algorithms. This is done through interconnecting various modules, each with input and output slots. A PatchWork patch is actually a graphic representation of a Lisp program for the Macintosh computer. Lisp is a programming language that is both a formal mathematical language and a programming language. So it is able to process numeric and symbolic data. It is designed to allow symbolic expressions of any degree of complexity to be evaluated by a computer. Making this more palatable to the non-programming musician, PatchWork rewards its end-user with a musically intelligent, 'user-friendly' interface.

PatchWork has enabled Ferneyhough to compose 'more immediately onto the screen'.[11] The distance from e-sketch to final score has been considerably shortened. With both PatchWork and Finale open he is able to toggle back and forth, from one to the other, in rapid

3rd Rereading Filter Sequence

1 = Impulse Group
2 = Tied Sequence
3 = Rest
4 = Single-Value impulse
5 = Single-Value rest

Line 1 Starts: 2 4 3 5 1
Line 2 Starts: 4 1 3 2 5
Line 3 starts: 1 4 3 2 5
Line 4 Starts: 1 2 3 4 5

m. 4, v. 3.
↓
m. 5, v. 1.
↓
m. s. v. 2.

Line 1: (1) Tied Sequence: 2 impulses (2-value + 4-value) ✓
    ✓(2) Single-Value Impulse (1-value) ✓
    (3) Rest: (3-value) ✓
    (4) Single-Value Rest (1-value) ✓
    (5) Impulse Group (2 impulses) ✓
    (6) Single-Value Impulse (1-value) ✓
    (7) Impulse Group (4 impulses) ✓
    (8) Rest (2-value) ✓
    (9) Tied Sequence: 4 impulses (4+3+5+1) ✓✓
    (10) Single-Value rest ✓✓ xa
    (11) Impulse Group (3 impulses) ✓✓
    (12) Single-Value Impulse ✓✓
    (13) Rest (5-value) x2 = 10 ✓✓
    (14) Tied Sequence: 3 impulses (3+5+1) ✓✓
    (15) Single Value rest x2 ✓✓
    (16) Impulse Group (5 impulses) ✓✓
    (17) Tied Sequence: 5 impulses (5+1+4+1+3)
    (18) Rest (1-value) x2
    (19) Single-Value impulse
    (20) Single-Value rest x2

1 = Impulse Group
2 = Tied Sequence
3 = Rest
4 = Single-Value impulse
5 = Single-Value rest

Line 2: (1) Single-value impulse ✓
    (2) Impulse Group: 4 impulses ✓✓✓
    (3) Rest (4-value) ✓✓
    (4) Tied Sequence: 4 impulses (4+1+3+2) ✓✓✓
    (5) Single-value rest ✓✓
    (6) Impulse Group: 1 impulse ✓✓✓
    (7) Single-Value Impulse ✓✓✓
    (8) Rest (1-value) ✓✓
    (9) Tied Sequence: 1 impulse (1) ✓✓
    (10) Single-Value rest ✓✓✓
    (11) Impulse Group: 3 impulses ✓✓✓
    (12) Tied Sequence: 3 impulses (3+2+5) ✓✓✓
    (13) Rest (3-value) ✓✓ x2 ← Parentheses?

Plate 13.2   Brian Ferneyhough, *Terrain* (1992), sketch transcription of '3rd Rereading Filter Sequence'

succession. This is akin to multitasking, a term which adequately describes his compositional process, as well as what musicians go through when performing his work. They are required to perform complex physical gestures that are the result of the piling on of multiple layers of information.

For the most part Ferneyhough uses PatchWork to define various limits and restrictions during the initial stages of composition. He often exploits PatchWork's graphical power by drawing various shaped curves, using PatchWork's 'breakpoint function', and assigning the traversed values to filter operations. For example, rhythmic or pulse selection might be determined by the trajectory of a given shape, as it moves through 24 hierarchically arranged layers of pulse patterns. In this way he is able to create dense, shape-driven pitch or rhythmic series.

Work with any computer program requires a certain degree of formalisation and Patch-Work is no different in this respect. The computer, and programming in general, requires that the composer formalise aspects of the compositional process which formerly might have gone unnoticed or unexamined. At its best, increased formalisation can lead to new musical vistas; at its worst the threat of compositional reification looms large, threatening to turn composers into caricatures of themselves. Many programs force their users to fit what they do into their specific processing formats. However, this is not what happened to Ferneyhough with PatchWork. '[It] didn't force me to change my way of thinking . . . but by formalising those things that I had done in the past I had a very solid basis from which I could extend and vary my practice by creating new patches, and therefore new concepts attached to those patches and new potential for their development in the future'.[12] He has adapted the program to serve his needs and produced a plethora of patches unimaginable without computer assistance.

In his pre-1994 sketches there are only a few patchlike procedures (like the Random Funnel). So the use of the computer has increased the speed of Ferneyhough's procedural invention. It has also helped him to gain, in the composer's words,

> a more profound familiarity with the potential results of complex series of succes-
> sively applied processes than had hitherto been possible . . . PatchWork has opened
> up to me the chance to enhance my intuitive 'feel' for an interactive situation
> through perhaps twenty or thirty runs through a specific conjunction of givens.
> The enhanced feedback from this process has thus brought me closer to a certain
> ideal of creative spontaneity than would presumably otherwise have been possible,
> as well as forcing me to maintain a high degree of rigor and clarity in the initial
> stages of conceptualisation and formalisation.[13]

The importance of spontaneity to Ferneyhough has largely been overlooked. The materials and charts produced with PatchWork form the immediate environment from which his compositions are produced. 'I am able to develop my spontaneity, my sensibility for the possible consequences of any set of algorithmically generated procedures quite significantly.'[14] Although he uses highly pre-determined materials much of the final score is produced via a spontaneous, albeit limited, reaction to them. This is somewhat equivalent to an extremely disciplined improviser performing an elaborate and highly structured improvisation.

In his pre-computer work Ferneyhough's process of creation was intimately bound up with the physical dimension of the compositional act itself. This aspect has been fundamentally altered through his computer employment. In the composer's following statement he addresses the issue of physical disembodiment in the computer-assisted composition process:

> Patchwork by its very nature is a somewhat physically disinvolved medium, it doesn't have a physical dimension, except the computer keyboard, perhaps. What I'm doing is trying to create virtual media. I'm trying to do what I've done in the past but in a much more involved way. But also in a more disembodied way because I don't painfully calculate, and write down, step by step, the different procedures which lead to a final result, such as I did in *Etudes Transcendentales* for instance.[15]

Ferneyhough is working towards the ultimate development of a 'superpatch' which would automatically generate all the dimensions of a piece with one keyboard stroke or push of a button. Whether or not he ever arrives at this point, his push towards it has enabled him to develop new approaches to virtual polyphony. PatchWork has been most important to him for its ability to generate multiple realisations of multi-layered pitch and rhythmic processes. The superpatch would eliminate the ability to spontaneously react to pre-compositional materials during the final stages of his compositional process. The act of selecting from this material would no longer be the composer's. But it is precisely the dialectical engagements between formal and informal creative processes, or between the automatic and the manual that have so characterised Ferneyhough's music, as well as his poetry and paintings. Indeed it is the friction between these approaches that results in the extreme types of musical expression for which he is best known. So, the superpatch would alter some fundamental attributes of his current praxis. It is important to realise that for Ferneyhough, a compositional system does not represent a mechanical means to produce music, but instead is a way to create the context in which compositional decisions are made.

Ferneyhough has compiled about 150 of his most important patches into a booklet entitled, *Patchwork Patches*. The patches are divided into four categories. Ferneyhough calls them: embeddings, iterations, pulse generation, and miscellaneous (a category that includes patches designed to generate values according to factors of density, insertion, inversion, permutation, filters and so on). With so many patches at his disposal it would seem likely that he would, in time, lose track of a given patch's purpose or function. However, he has anticipated this by attaching detailed comments to each patch. Computer programmers routinely use 'comment lines' to explain what their programs are supposed to do. Comment lines are statements within the program text for documentary purposes, which are ignored by the program's compiler. Comment lines are routinely used during the process of debugging a program. And if other programmers come along, at a later date, to extend or improve the original program they will not be completely in the dark as to a program's function. In addition to the comments, Ferneyhough's patchbook contains illustrative examples of each process and screen shots of the patches themselves. But even with all this explicit, documentary material the patchbook might still be incomprehensible to a scholar, because in order to understand what a given comment or example means one needs at least a working knowledge of PatchWork. Plate 13.3 shows a screen shot and sample rhythm from one of his patches called 'Random-Fun perm-to-1 Comb.pw'. This is a fairly basic patch, designed to generate beat values for rhythmic cells with an updated Random Funnel process. The computer randomly selects a number series first. Each number is then gradually reduced to the number one by the end of the process (see Figure 13.2). The number one, in this instance, corresponds with a single beat. So each rhythmic cell would take place over the duration of one beat. To probe deeper, beyond this simple explanation of this particular patch, one would need to examine the specific way in which Ferneyhough constructed it, and what each module is supposed to do. This patch produces results that are not fundamentally different from several other patches. Because he uses patches that contain other patches it would seem almost impossible to trace back from the final score to the patch from which it was generated. In Ferneyhough's music similar material is often produced with different means. Some of his patches are, in his words, 'very ramshackle in elegance terms'.[16] Elegance is a term that programmers use to describe heuristically efficient code, i.e. code that does its work with the minimum amount of program text. This ramshackle quality has always been at the core of his aesthetic, and the formal/informal dialectic. It is one of the primary distinguishing characteristics of his music.

E-sketch Problems

The computer-assisted compositional process challenges our traditional notions about what constitutes a sketch, manuscript and autograph. For example, annotated computer printouts of documents that were typed or coded by hand, could be called 'partial' autographs, because the term autograph only partially applies to this scenario. But is the qualitative difference between using one's hands to click and move a mouse, or pressing a key on a computer keyboard, and making a mark with a pen or pencil so significant as to preclude the former actions from our definition of the term? The composer's 'hand' is present in both instances. If we take autograph to mean an original copy of a completed composition then it would not apply to Ferneyhough's music, because he completes his compositions at the same time as their final scores. His final scores are simply reproduced, not typeset, by his publisher. So his final score is also the fair copy. This has always been the case with his work. The difference is that since the *String Trio* his scores have a 'published' look to them. This situation is true of many of today's composers, most of whom effectively function as their own publishing companies, by taking over typesetting responsibilities that were formerly the

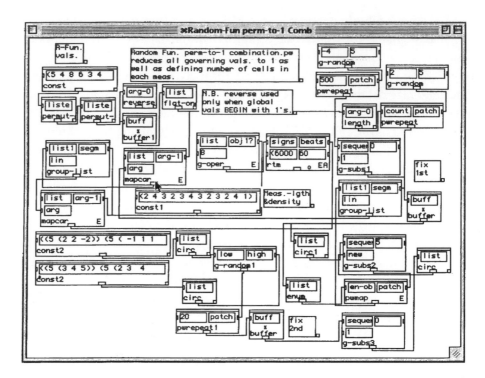

Sample Rhythmic Sequence Generated by this Patch

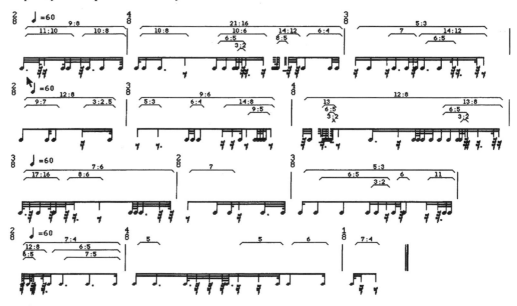

Plate 13.3   Brian Ferneyhough, screen shot and sample rhythm from *Patchwork Patches*, 'Random-Fun perm-to-1 Comb.pw'

((5 4 8 6 3 4 1) (1 3 7 5 3 2 4) (1 1 6 4 2 3 2)
(1 1 3 1 1 2 5) (1 1 1 1 2 1 4) (1 1 1 1 1 1 3) (1 1 1 1 1 1 1)

Figure 13.2   'Perm-to-1' sequence, *Patchwork Patches*

purvey of the publisher. This makes good economic sense for the publisher of non-popular contemporary music. In Ferneyhough's case, his scores are easy to identify but very difficult and time-consuming to typeset accurately.

The computer-assisted compositional process presents scholars with some other difficult problems besides establishing chronology, decoding algorithms, and learning to use specialist software programs. The first and foremost is in regard to obsolescence. While it is true that the computer itself has become a common household object, the programs, platforms and operating systems change so rapidly that it is impossible to keep up with them all. Also, there are so many different programs available that it is not too much of a stretch to conceive of a future wherein studying the work of a composer will be preceded by study of the programs he or she uses.

Another problem is that of transcription. How does one go about transcribing an e-sketch or computer program? In the latter case the source code might be inaccessible. Or, if accessible it would still be a difficult task to decipher this code. It would be like translating from a foreign language that was symbolic and highly formalised. In the extreme case of Ferneyhough's superpatch, where sketch transcription is irrelevant, we can only infer his compositional process from the finished product because the intermediary stages have been eliminated.

Lastly there is the problem of sketch volatility. Preserving a paper sketch is a relatively straightforward procedure; preserving an e-sketch might require frequent changes of disk media and perhaps even an entirely new computer. E-sketches, like any computer files, are subject to crashes. A single crash could conceivably wipe out years of hard work. Or a given file could become so corrupted that no recovery program could fix it, making it permanently inaccessible.

E-sketches challenge the concept of the public document. A composer's hard disk drive has now become the repository of his or her e-sketch materials. Issues of volatility and obsolescence aside, this is fine except for the fact that they are inaccessible to scholars. Ferneyhough, whose manuscript materials are permanently housed at the Paul Sacher Foundation is not obligated to send the e-sketch contents of his hard disk drive. So, the sketches that are preserved are only the ones that happen to be on paper. The PatchWork realisations that he does not use might never materialise in printed form, and may even be deleted from his computer's memory. We are prevented from examining the detritus from decisions to keep some realisations over others. But as cultural anthropologists know so well – garbage holds valuable keys to the past and future. We can learn just as much, if not more, from discarded materials. The use of the computer makes it all too easy to discard unused materials. From the composer's perspective this makes a lot of sense. Why should s/he keep materials that are not used, that simply take up valuable space in memory? After all, the 'right' material might only be a click away.

Brian Ferneyhough's computer-assisted approach is full of unresolved paradoxes and contradictions. He creates and employs algorithms, but he is not an algorithmic composer in a purist sense. He often 'tampers' with the output data produced by his patches. For Ferneyhough the musical idea comes before its realisation. He employs formal as well as informal models, and predetermined as well as spontaneously generated materials. During the last three and a half decades he has conscientiously crafted, as Richard Toop astutely observed, a contemporary musical aesthetic that remains 'faithful to the idea of art as the endless search for the transcendental, and of music as potential revelation'.[17] His work with computer-assisted composition draws attention to the human agent at the threshold between the generation and disintegration of systems, an infinite and unresolved occurrence.

CHAPTER 14

John Cage's Williams Mix *(1951–3):*
the restoration and new realisations of and variations on the first octophonic, surround-sound tape composition

Larry Austin

–for–

Williams [re]Mix[ed]* (1997–2000), for octophonic computer music system, based on John Cage's *Williams Mix* (1951–3), for eight magnetic tapes

The Theme Restored

Six Short Variations

A-city sounds, B-country sounds,
C-electronic sounds, D-manually produced sounds,
E-wind produced sounds, F-small sounds

The Nth Realisation

INTRODUCTION

Creating the first realisation of John Cage's (1912–92) octophonic tape piece, *Williams Mix* (1951–3), involved the precise cutting/splicing of tape-recorded sounds to create eight separate, reel-to-reel, monaural, 15-ips magnetic tape masters for the four-minute, fifteen-second piece. The work's 192-page score is, as Cage referred to it, a kind of 'dressmaker's pattern – it literally shows where the tape shall be cut, and you lay the tape on the score itself' (see Plate 14.1). Cage explained further in a published transcript of a 1985 recorded conversation with author Richard Kostelanetz that 'someone else could follow that recipe, so to speak, with other sources than I had to make another mix'. Later in the conversation Kostelanetz observed, 'But, as you pointed out, even though you made for posterity a score of *Williams Mix* for others to realize, no one's ever done it', to which Cage replied, 'But it's because the manuscript is so big and so little known'.[1]

Intrigued by Cage's open invitation to 'follow that recipe', I embarked on a project in summer 1997 to create just such a new realisation of and variations on the score of *Williams Mix*, the first octophonic, surround-sound tape composition. Presignifying the development of algorithmic composition, granular synthesis and sound diffusion, *Williams Mix* was the third of five pieces completed in the Project for Music for Magnetic Tape (1951–4), established in New York City by Cage and funded by architect Paul Williams.[2] Ongoing collaborators were, first, pianist David Tudor, then electronic music pioneers Louis and Bebe Barron, and finally composer Earle Brown, among others. The score for

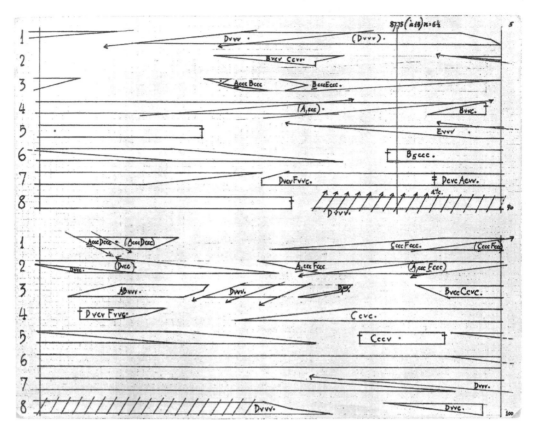

Plate 14.1   John Cage, *Williams Mix*, score, page 5

Williams Mix was completed in October 1952, as well as much of the realisation for the eight magnetic tapes. (Those were finally completed by Cage and Brown on 16 January 1953.)

In early 1998 the John Cage Trust provided me with a colour-xerographic copy of the 192-page score of *Williams Mix*, as well as associated sketches and commentary by Cage on the compositional process involved in the original realisation for eight magnetic tapes.[3] The Trust subsequently provided me with digital audio copies of the eight earliest, extant-generation, reel-to-reel masters of the piece from the Trust's Archive of Cage's works. With the score and tapes I began the restoration and analysis of the precise relation of the recorded sound-events with their *I Ching*-determined parameters in the score. Out of this first, two-year phase came the restoration of the original eight tracks of tape, transferred to the digital, octophonic medium for either digital soundfile output from a computer or playback on an eight-track digital audio tape recorder. This newly restored *Williams Mix*, in fact, becomes the first movement, *The Theme Restored*, of my *Williams [re]Mix[ed]* octophonic tape piece.[4]

Since first starting my project I have continued to collect new sounds for the new, recorded library of nearly 600 sounds, according to Cage's six sound-categories of city, country, electronic, manually produced, wind-produced and small sounds.[5]

Explicated here, the final phase of my project throughout the year 2000, was the design and implementation of an interactive computer music program I have named the *Williams [re]Mix[er]*. Its functionality is modelled on Cage's *I Ching* compositional processes, extrapolated and applied from my years-long analyses of Cage's score, sketches and tapes for *Williams Mix*, as well as his and others' writings and recorded interviews about the piece and Cage's compositional method. In fact, the *Six Short Variations* and *The Nth Realization* realised by the *Williams [re]Mix[er]* – as its subsequent performances are presented – are planned always to be the very latest, computer-generated output of the *Williams [re]Mix[er]*. What took Cage and his collaborators nearly three years of recordings, coin-tosses, notation, and thousands of small pieces of tape measured, cut and spliced together to complete the first realisation of the *Williams Mix* score is accomplished – after collecting the requisite library of recorded soundfiles – in only a few minutes of computation time. Indeed, the settings I have used in designing the *Williams [re]Mix[er]* are Cage's own parameters – as I derived them from my analyses – for the piece's structure and morphology of sound/silence events.

JOHN CAGE AND TAPE MUSIC

John Cage heard tape-music compositions for the first time during a six-month stay in Paris in 1949. There, he came to know the work of composer Pierre Schaeffer, who was experimenting with making musical compositions in the newly emerging magnetic tape recording medium, a genre Schaeffer called *musique concrète*. Cage recalled:

> Schaeffer made every effort he could to get me interested in working along those lines, but I wasn't yet really ready. . . . I was writing my *String Quartet* (1950). . . . I was gradually moving toward the shift from music as structure to music as process and to the use, as a result, of chance operations in composition. I might have been more cooperative with Schaeffer, but I wasn't. It didn't really dawn on me . . . my mind was being used in a different way; so that I wasn't as open as I might have been to the notion of music on magnetic tape then. That was '49.[6]

At the suggestion of the composer Virgil Thomson, Cage looked up the young avant-garde composer Pierre Boulez, who was also in Paris. That meeting grew into a friendship through the next several years, manifested in their exchange of letters between November 1949 and August 1954 about their respective works and compositional approaches. This correspondence fortunately included detailed descriptions about Cage's new tape-music composition *Williams Mix*, as it was planned, realised and presented in its première performance.[7]

UNIVERSITY OF ILLINOIS
SCHOOL OF MUSIC

———

FESTIVAL OF CONTEMPORARY ARTS

———

JOHN CAGE

LECTURE: Music for Magnetic Tape

———

Recital Hall, Sunday, March twenty-second
Nineteen hundred fifty-three
Four o'clock

PROGRAM

Etude pathétique.................................*Pierre Schaeffer*
Batterie fugace...................................*Pierre Henry*
Symphonie pour un Homme seul...*Pierre Schaeffer and Pierre Henry*
    Part IV: Héroïca
             Apostrophe
             Strette

Fantasy in Space..................................*Otto Luening*
Low Speed.......................................*Otto Luening*
Sonic Contours...................................*Vladimir Ussachevsky*
For an Electronic Nervous-system, No. 1.....*Louis and Bebe Barron*
    (First performance)

INTERMISSION

Antiphonie.......................................*Pierre Henry*
Timbres-Durées (excerpt).........................*Olivier Messiaen*
For Magnetic Tape (Part I).......................*Christian Wolff*
    (First performance)
Etude for a Single Sound.........................*Pierre Boulez*
Etude II...*Pierre Boulez*
Williams Mix.....................................*John Cage*
    (First performance)
Octet..*Earle Brown*
    (First performance)

Plate 14.2   John Cage, programme of the première of *Williams Mix*

THE PROJECT FOR MUSIC FOR MAGNETIC TAPE

Returning from Paris to New York in November 1949, Cage composed throughout 1950 several chamber works for soloists, completing his *String Quartet in Four Parts* and the *Concerto for Prepared Piano and Chamber Orchestra*. These were followed in 1951 by his seminal piano work *Music of Changes* using the *I Ching* and chance operations and his next live electronic piece, *Imaginary Landscape No. 4*, for 12 radios and 24 performers. Then came *Imaginary Landscape No. 5* followed by *Williams Mix*, Cage's first two tape pieces, both composed as part of the Project for Music for Magnetic Tape, an experimental music initiative conceived and organised by Cage and David Tudor in New York in 1951 and funded by a grant from architect and arts patron Paul Williams.[8]

David Tudor recalled that the initial idea and motivation for the Project came from Cage. They worked closely together during the Project's first phase in 1951 to create and categorise what Cage called an all-inclusive collection of tape-recorded sounds. They met and then engaged electronic music pioneers Louis and Bebe Barron to work as sound-engineers for the Project, beginning in the summer of 1951, contracted and paid by architect Paul Williams for a year's work.[9] The collecting and recording of sounds for *Williams Mix* continued until summer 1952. Tudor recalled that the Barrons helped to record and prepare all the material, making contributions based on their studio resources, technical knowledge and recording methods. The established method of working for Cage and Tudor at first primarily involved the categorisation of the recorded sounds and the initial cutting and splicing of tape for *Williams Mix* in Cage's downtown New York loft at 326 Monroe Street overlooking the East River. In summer 1952, composer Earle Brown joined the Project. The score for *Williams Mix* was completed in October 1952, the cutting and splicing of the eight tapes completed, according to Cage's inscription on the last page of the score, on 23 January 1953 (see Plate 14.3). In the next two and what turned out to be the final active months of the Project, Cage and Brown worked together to complete Brown's tape piece *Octet* using left-over cuttings from the library of tape sounds collected for *Williams Mix*.

The Project effectively culminated with the 22 March 1953 lecture/concert curated and produced by Cage as part of the Festival for Contemporary Arts at the University of Illinois, Urbana. Three of the Project's five tape works created thus far were presented, as well as tape pieces Cage had collected from other American and French composers (see Plate 14.2).

Cage had planned *Williams Mix* to be a multi-part work lasting twenty minutes, not just the four-minute, fifteen-second duration of 'Part I', as he referred to it on the last page of the score (see Plate 14.3). 'The piece as planned is 20 minutes, but 4 minutes alone (the first "movement") will be 192 pages!' Funding for the Project had been exhausted and, in his letter to Boulez in the summer of 1952, he wrote, 'I have the sad news that the building in which I live [on Monroe Street] will be torn down in a year; but you will be here before that happens'.[10] The imminent destruction of the Project's main workplace – and the fact that he tried but could not find sponsorship in universities and other institutions for his vision of

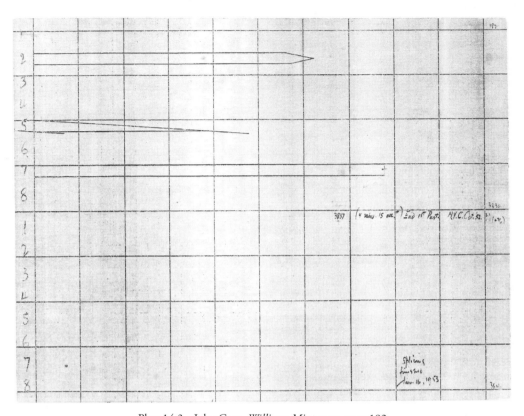

Plate 14.3 John Cage, *Williams Mix*, score, page 192

a centre for experimental music – discouraged Cage and must have convinced him that the Project and the completion of *Williams Mix* and other creative research in tape music could not be realised at that time as he had envisioned. Though the Project, *per se*, did not continue after 1954, Cage did use the library of recorded sounds left over from those collected for *Williams Mix* over a decade later for more than half of the 88 tape loops for his *Rozart Mix* (1965) tape-loop installation at the Rozart Museum, Brandeis University.[11]

On a typewritten draft of an information page describing the *Williams Mix*, when it was to be published by Henmar Press (Peters Edition) in New York in 1960, Cage acknowledged all the original collaborators who had assisted with its creation as part of the Project for Music for Magnetic Tape:

> The composing means derived from the method of obtaining an oracle from the *I-Ching*, devised by John Cage, carried out by John Cage and David Tudor with assistance from Jay Watt and Lucille Dlugoschevsky. Sound engineering and recording of all sounds was by Louis and Bebe Barron. Splicing was done by John Cage, Earle Brown and David Tudor with assistance from Ben Johnston, Nicola Cernovitch, Remi Charlip, M. C. Richards, Merce Cunningham and Carroll Brown.[12]

CAGE AND THE *I CHING* (THE BOOK OF CHANGES)

In *Williams Mix* John Cage invoked *I Ching* chance operations for compositional decisions: (1) the duration of successive time-segments, which are the 'structural division of the whole into parts' of the piece; (2) the density and relation of sounds-to-silences, which is the form and 'morphology of continuity' of the piece; (3) the choice of which sounds in which of six categories of sounds; (4) the determination of the duration of sounds and silences; (5) the single or double combination of these sounds; (6) the attack/sustain/decay ramps of each sound; (7) the timbral variation (v) of the frequency, overtone structure, and amplitude or the timbral constancy (c) of each sound; (8) the striation (pulsation) or not of each sound; and (9) the panning among tracks and/or the overlapping of sounds on the same track.[13]

Cage's method of mapping numbers to parameters of the piece derived from consulting the *I Ching* three-coins oracle, where heads = '1' and tails = '0': three coins are tossed six times to create, from bottom to top, two trigrams combining to form a hexagram or *gua*. Where the compositional choice to be made was simply yes or no, Cage tossed one coin, heads or tails, to obtain the answer; in other situations he drew a number from a deck of cards like the Tarot deck to replenish the numbers in the 8 by 8 charts with numbers 1 to 64. For *Williams Mix*, Cage explained:

> The composing means employed chance operations derived from the *I Ching* (Chinese Book of Changes). . . . Briefly, three coins tossed six times give one or two numbers from 1 to 64. Separate charts were made having 64 elements, one to determine the rhythmic structure (11 times 6 divided 5, 6, 16, 3, 11, 5), another to determine factors which shortened or lengthened the structural parts, 16 for sounds and silences, 16 for durations, 16 for attack and decay of sounds. Another chart determined how many of the 16 were active within a given structural division. There being only 8 tracks, 8 active at one time brought about maximum density, 16 maximum fragmentation. At the beginning of each of the 11 structural units [which I have named 'hexads', because they each have six measured time-segments], it was determined which of the 16 charts (the even or the odd numbered) were mobile and which immobile. If a chart was mobile, an element in it, once used, disappeared, giving rise to a new one; if immobile and used, remained to be used again. The replenishing of the mobile charts was from a deck of appropriate cards (giving a sound, a duration or a pattern of attack or decay, each obtained by permutation of possibilities but not previously employed in the charts). These cards had been shuffled in a way continual to the Tarot. The vertical bar in the first system [see Plate 14.1] indicates the beginning of the third structural part. The following information is given above it: its position in inches from the beginning (5.85 seconds); the number of charts to be used; and the factor (n) which multiplied by 16 (the third number of the rhythmic structure) established the length in inches of the third section.[14]

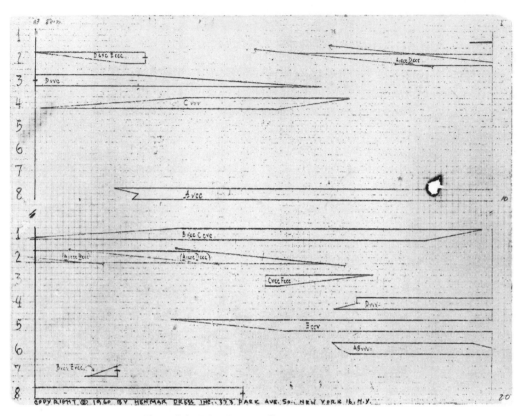

Plate 14.4   John Cage, *Williams Mix*, score, page 1

When consulting the *I Ching*, the four possible coin-toss results are:

2 heads and 1 tail	=	solid line	=	——	(111)
2 tails and 1 head	=	broken line	=	– –	(101)
3 tails	=	solid line	=	——	(111)
3 heads	=	broken line	=	– –	(101)

Tossing three coins six times, the results of each set of tosses are recorded from the bottom up to obtain a hexagram or *gua* and, hence, a number between 1 and 64, as designated in the *I Ching* as the 'upper canon' (1–30) and the 'lower canon' (31–64).

THE *WILLIAMS MIX* MANUSCRIPTS

The extant original manuscripts for John Cage's *Williams Mix* are housed in the John Cage manuscript collection of the American Music Section of the Lincoln Centre Library branch of the New York City Public Library. Colour and black-and-white xerographic copies of the original manuscripts – in a 77.27 per cent reduction in size from the originals – are housed in 'Box 9' in five file folders in the Archive of the John Cage Trust, New York City. For my project, I was provided with copies of the Cage Archive manuscripts, described below:

File folder 1: An $8\frac{1}{2}''$-by-11'' typewritten title page prepared by Cage for the publication of the score including detailed descriptions about the meaning of the special score notation, the categories and nomenclature of the sounds as notated, the 'shape' of the sounds on each of the eight tracks and what the shapes indicate about how the tape is spliced, and at the bottom of the page the copyright inscription. Cage's explanatory text follows below, including a reference – Cvvv – to page 1 of the score itself. (See Plate 14.4.)

WILLIAMS MIX for magnetic tape
John Cage

This is a score for the making of music for magnetic tape. Each page has 2 'systems' comprising 8 lines each. These 8 lines are 8 tracks of tape and they are pictured full-size, so that the score constitutes a pattern for the cutting of tape and its splicing. It has been found by experiment that various ways of cutting the tape affect the attack and decay of the sounds recorded on the tape. Therefore these are all indicated exactly when they involve simple or double cuts across the tape. When the desired cutting to be done exceeds this simplicity one sees in the score a cross (in green pencil). It is then the business of the splicer to freely cut the tape, even to 'pulverize' it, in a complicated way. When arrows appear in the score on diagonal lines, this refers to a way of splicing on the diagonal at the angle and in the direction notated which produces an alteration in all the characteristics of the recorded sound.

Within each enclosed shape, one may read a designation of the sound to be spliced. These (all audible phenomena) are categorized as A, B, C, D, E or F and according to whether the frequency, overtone structure and amplitude are predictable or not, c or v. Thus Cvvv (4th track, 1st system) is a sound of the category C (electronically produced or 'synthetic' sounds) in which all the three characteristics mentioned above are v or variable, i.e. unpredictable. Cccc will be a sound of the same category, the 3 characteristics being c or constant, i.e. predictable.

When a sound is described as double, e.g. DcvcEccc, electronic mixing has produced the combination. When a sound has an underlined designation, e.g. A1cccDccc, the A1 part has been made into a loop, thus bringing about a rhythmic pattern characteristic and then electronically mixed with the D constituent.

Red dots indicate that the actual splicing was completed.

This score is written for tape travelling at 15 inches per second. Therefore, each page is the score for 1 and one-third seconds. Thus the 192 pages constitute the score of a piece only a fraction over $4\frac{1}{4}$ minutes.

A: city sounds; B: country sounds; C: electronic sounds;
D: manually produced sounds, including the literature of music;
E: wind-produced sounds, including songs;
F: small sounds requiring amplification to be heard with the others.

The library of sounds used to produce the Williams Mix numbers around 500 to 600
sounds.

File folder 2: An $8\frac{1}{2}''$-by-11″ typewritten page, apparently a much earlier, marked-up draft in Cage's hand of the title and explanation page by Cage with the hand-printed title simply 'Wms. Mix'. This is followed by three typed paragraphs detailing in slightly different language than *File folder 1* the score notation, the splicing techniques and marking, the categories of sounds, and – not in the final draft – a paragraph naming the *I Ching* as the 'composing means' and all the persons who collaborated with and assisted Cage in the various areas in the course of creating the piece. There is no copyright inscription at the bottom of the page.

File folder 3: Twelve (of thirteen) $8\frac{1}{2}''$-by-11″ sheets of graph paper with eight horizontal and vertical grid marks per inch. Each sheet is landscape orientated with handwritten numbers from 1 to 8 appearing in four groups or systems on the far left side of the $8\frac{1}{2}''$ side of each page, each number separated by one grid and each group of numbers by two grids. These numbers refer to the eight individual tape tracks in the score. Each page is numbered in the upper right corner, starting with '2' and ending with '13'. Page '1' is missing. Clearly, each horizontal grid mark equals one second of lapsed time through each of the four systems from left to right and top to bottom. Several vertical lines per page demark structural time-segments in the piece. At the bottom of each vertical line appears the number of lapsed seconds from the beginning of the structural plan. At the top and to the right of each vertical line appear letter and number designations derived by Cage for the *I Ching* charts, which control time-segment lengths and density of the sounds in each time-segment track. These same vertical lines and designators appear in the score itself, demarcating the time-segments and the structural plan of the piece.

File folder 4: Four large 11″ by 17″ cardboard poster sheets, one side announcing a concert by pianist David Tudor, the other blank side used by Cage as a sketch sheet for number calculations and letter designations of single and double source sounds.

File folder 5: (see Plate 14.1) 192 8 1/2"-by-11" sheets of graph paper with eight horizontal and vertical grid marks per inch, pages 1 to 32, and with four horizontal and vertical grid marks per inch, pages 33 to 192 (see *File folder 1* above for Cage's explanation of the score notation). Eight of the 192 pages are in inked notation, the remainder in black pencil notation with some use of green and red pencil notations as well.[15]

THE *WILLIAMS MIX* TAPES

As far as I have ascertained, the eight, first-generation, 15-ips, monaural, reel-to-reel tapes of the eight separate tracks of *Williams Mix* – literally thousands of very short recorded tape segments, separated alternately from one another with and spliced to very small tape leader segments – no longer exist, having been stored in some unknown location, misplaced or simply discarded after being copied to eight production master tapes. Copies of the earliest generation tape recordings believed to exist of the eight separate tracks for Cage's *Williams Mix* are housed in the Archive of the John Cage Trust and in the Edition Peters catalogue collection of Cage's published works available for performance from C. F. Peters Corporation in New York City. There very well could be other extant copies of such tapes that have survived. For instance, Cage, in his letter to Pierre Boulez dated May 1953, wrote that, 'the "Williams Mix" is on its way to you [in Paris]. I have sent 9 tracks [i.e. nine separate monaural tapes]: one is all 8 mixed and the others are the single tracks . . .'[16] Also, since the piece was not published by Edition Peters until 1960, Cage must have had other copies made of the tapes to send to other presenters of the work after its first performance in 1953.

The extant tapes in the Cage Trust Archive, which were placed there directly from Cage's personal collection after his death, exist in two formats. The first format consists of eight separate, 30-ips, monaural, reel-to-reel, production master tapes, each tape assigned to one of the eight separate tracks of three octophonic pieces on each reel, in order: *Intersection* by Morton Feldman, *Octet* by Earle Brown and *Williams Mix* by John Cage. There are no known copies of the eight 15-ips, monaural, reel-to-reel tapes of the format used in the first performance of *Williams Mix* at the University of Illinois, where eight monaural Magnecorders were used for playback (*Were these the tapes, perhaps that Cage sent to Boulez?!*). The second format consists of four separate, 15-ips, stereo, reel-to-reel, master tapes, each tape assigned to two of the eight separate tracks (i.e. 1–2; 3–4; 5–6; 7–8) and including only Cage's *Williams Mix*. After the Illinois première in subsequent performances, such stereo format copies must have become the format of choice, since eight monaural tape machines would not be nearly as practical to find as 15-ips stereo machines, only four of which would be needed.

For my project the John Cage Trust provided me with digital recorded copies of both the monaural and stereo formats, transferred from contemporary, professional quality, reel-to-reel tape machines (for example, the Tascam SV-3700) to the compact disc audio format. I then made a digital transfer of both the monaural and stereo format versions input to my computer workstation (a Silicon Graphics O2 computer with an eight-channel digital/ analogue sound input/output PCI), each monaural track stored as a separate digital soundfile.

The eight separate tracks begin with – as Cage put it in his letter to Boulez of May 1953 – 'synchronization marks (audio frequency oscillator sine waves) 1 kilocycle; 1 second silence; 400 cycles per second; 1 second silence; 1 kilocycle; 1 second silence; 2.5 kilocycles; 4 seconds silence and then the music'.[17] These signals were used to cue the individual tapes in the tape machines (either eight monaural or four stereo machines), so that they could be cued to start simultaneously by one operator per two machines, that person pressing the two play buttons on cue from a person acting as the coordinator. The tape machines were most likely not electronically synchronised (though such technology was feasible) in the early performances; thus, the synchrony of their combined playback was relatively imprecise, depending on the accuracy of the playback speed of each machine matching the others. Cage knew this, of course. He knew that, even though his score was realised with a high degree of accuracy on each of the tape tracks, there would always be a degree of variance from the score in actual performance with multiple tape machines. I suspect that Cage rather enjoyed this relatively variable 'chance operation' (*sic*) of tape machines in every performance. To my knowledge a synchronised version of *Williams Mix* for an eight-track tape machine was never made nor experienced by Cage in his lifetime, though the technology had become readily available by the 1960s. Now, with my present restoration of the *Williams Mix* tapes and the subsequent transfer to and careful reconciliation of the timing of the eight tracks to eight-track soundfiles and then to eight-track ADAT recordings, the piece is heard as the tracks were meant to be precisely synchronised in the score.[18]

THE DIGITAL RESTORATION/SYNCHRONISATION OF THE *WILLIAMS MIX* TAPES

From the beginning of my commission to create a new realisation of and variations on *Williams Mix*, I have endeavoured to gain a thorough knowledge and appreciation of its original score and tapes through intensive analyses of the relatedness of the written references, the score notations and the aural effect of the piece. First, in February 1998, I received a copy from the Cage Trust of the score and associated sketches, beginning their review and analysis. Meanwhile, I had also asked for digital copies of the tapes from the Trust. This step took longer to accomplish correctly, since the extant tapes available to me at that time existed only in their analogue, reel-to-reel formats and had to be carefully and faithfully transferred to digital media. Thanks to the patiently expert efforts of Laura Kuhn, Director, and Mikel Rouse, technical consultant, of the Trust, I did receive the correctly transferred digital copies the next year, in March 1999. I had, by that time, learned much from the score and sketches about the nature of Cage's intent for the realisation of the score into sound. I had also, in my composer travels, continued since the summer of 1997 to record city and country sounds (New York, London, Birmingham (UK), Bellagio, Bourges, Saarbrucken, Strasbourg, Luxembourg, York, Paris, Tokyo *et al.*) to add to my growing library of sounds for my planned new realisation of the score.

Now, with the digital copies of the *Williams Mix* stereo pairs of the eight tracks transferred to my computer as soundfiles, I first separated each track to an individual monaural soundfile. With the computer system sound-editor I could compare each successive sound in each track to Cage's notated designation in the score, including each sound's duration/placement, its category, the type of variation, if any, of the sound, and its combination, if any, with a second sound. From the score, I had already compiled statistics on Cage's six categories of sounds, their characteristics and combination. I had found, for instance, that there were 350 different sounds and a total of 2,128 separate iterations of these sounds in all eight tracks, the iterations ranging from as few as one iteration to as many as 46, averaging six iterations. Now, with the ability to isolate and hear an individual sound, I could test whether successive iterations of a sound were the same or not. What I did find was that successive iterations were indeed the same aural category but were not an actual continuation of one another, even though they would have been cut from the same piece of tape. Apparently, these segments of tape were cut from the tape for different tracks at different times by Cage and Brown, as the score required and was progressively rendered, inch by inch, track by track.

There was also the aural and visual means to determine the actual sounding duration of each recorded track and to compare that duration with its duration and placement in the temporal continuum specified by the score. I found in the 15-ips stereo format of pairs of tracks that the durations and placement of the recorded tracks were comparatively close to the durations of the tracks in the score. What I discovered in the 30-ips monaural tracks was a greater disparity between the duration of the recorded sound and the score. I also found, surprisingly, that the 30-ips monaural tracks had more system noise, hum and tape hiss than 15-ips stereo pairs of tracks. In fact, the recorded track-2 soundfile in the stereo format was virtually the same length as it was notated in the score. The other seven recorded tracks in the stereo format varied in their actual recorded duration and the duration designated in the score, but not by too much. For track-1, for instance, the specified duration in the score of the entire track, from the onset of the first sound to the precise end of that track's last sound made that track's sounding duration exactly 252.94834 seconds. With the sound-editor, I found that the corresponding duration of the soundfile of track-1 was 254.878 seconds, making the recorded track-1 1.92966 seconds or .07628 per cent longer than the score. In the sound-editor a soundfile's duration can be uniformly shortened or lengthened and its pitch correspondingly raised or lowered. For track-1, then, I set the 'pitch' or 'transposition factor' of its soundfile to be multiplied by 1.07628, making track-1 shorter by .07628 per cent and uniformly 7.628 cents of a semitone higher. Then, according to the score, .6333 seconds of silence was added to the beginning of the soundfile and correspondingly 1.6116 seconds was added to the end of the soundfile to have the correct total track of 255.1932 seconds. In this way all eight soundfile tracks could be and were adjusted to conform to the score durations and be in proper synchrony and pitch with one another.

Now that the pitch and duration of all eight soundfile tracks had been reconciled with the score and with one another, the first step in the restoration/synchronisation of *Williams Mix* had been completed. The next step was to reduce as much as possible the system hum, tape hiss and any bleed-through of sound from one layer of tape to the next on the reels. Experimentation with professional digital noise-reduction techniques on the soundfiles revealed that, while the noise during each silence could be reduced significantly, the sounding events themselves lost relatively too much high-frequency content, so that the brightness of the original sounds was unacceptably diminished. I decided first not to use digital noise reduction, deciding instead to undertake the formidable task of digitally clearing each noisy 'silence' between each sound-event in every track with the sound-editor. There were well over 2,000 such noisy silences! The benefit, though, was twofold: not only was I successful in clearing the silences and keeping the sound-events as rich as possible, but in the process I heard each individual sound in the entire piece, comparing that sound to the score, its category, duration and transformations, if designated. Thus, the restoration/synchronisation of *Williams Mix – The Theme Restored –* had begun, a process that took over four months in late 1999 to complete before I could experience the piece as Cage intended in the score for it to be heard and now with enhanced sound-quality.

THE *WILLIAMS* [RE]MIX[ER]

It was during this intensive period of restoration and analysis of the relation between the score and Cage's realisation that my concepts about the nature of my own new realisation of *Williams Mix* focused more clearly. They had evolved towards what I perceived Cage would have done himself in creating new realisations of *Williams Mix*. Cage had referred to the score in the 1985 interview with Kostelanetz as a kind of 'dressmaker's pattern – it literally shows where the tape shall be cut, and you lay the tape on the score itself'. In the same interview he further explained that 'someone else could follow that recipe, so to speak, with other sources than I had to make another mix'.[19] Cage's mixed use of a dressmaker's pattern and a cook's recipe metaphor gives a clue. An earlier clue about how he might, himself, have made a new realisation was given by Cage in an unpublished portion of a 1966 interview with Kostelanetz about the nature of the process of creating the first *Williams Mix* realisation. Explaining the process of deriving numbers from the *I Ching* by tossing three coins six times, he suddenly exclaimed, 'Now, this is all remarkably like a computer!'[20] Indeed!

Cage, by 1966, already understood that a computer program could be written which would invoke the *I Ching* and could, for example, yield ever-new *Williams Mix* scores. Such new realisations could be based on the same protocols of music composed by process and chance operations that Cage had created in his pre-compositional sketches for *Williams Mix*, a program that creates ever-new 'dress patterns' and 'recipes' modelled on the *compositional process* – itself derived from the *I Ching* – of creating that first 'pattern' or 'recipe'. In fact, in 1968 he and Lejaren Hiller engaged programmer Ed Kobrin of the University of Illinois to write such an *I Ching* program as one of the key subroutines in the main program, 'HPSCHD', to use in their collaborative computer music composition, *HPSCHD*.[21] It happens that I interviewed Cage and Hiller in June 1968 in Urbana, Illinois, about their collaboration and about the use of the computer to both make compositional decisions according to the computer subroutine, 'ICHING', and to generate the harpsichord-like sounds for the 51 monaural tapes – each twenty minutes long, interestingly the same length as *Williams Mix* had been planned to be – called for in the piece.

> CAGE: . . . [I have been] teaching the computer to toss coins as I had been doing manually, following the mechanism of the *I Ching* – to produce that subroutine took six weeks. To produce this whole piece [*HPSCHD*], which is not yet operating, has taken ten months, which is one month longer than I spent on *Music of Changes*, or on *Williams Mix*. . . . AUSTIN: I'm interested in your comment [before] that your work here might introduce a possibility for music for everyone. . . . CAGE: I'm just saying that more and more people will be using computers and that more and more routines will exist, and that the possibility of making programs which utilize a routine made here, for instance, with one made there, with one made in some other place and adding others to it, will produce a music which has not yet been heard; and this can be enjoyed, surely by some, maybe by many. . . . I think that, if I were to go on with this business of computer programming, one of the first things I would do would be to extend the uses of the subroutine ICHING so that it would become practical to use it for all kinds of choices . . .[22]

Cage did, indeed, go on to use that 'ICHING' program and subsequently other *I Ching* programs written for him as a compositional tool for many other pieces. In my own project I had already begun to enter concepts in my composing journal for just such a universal *I Ching* program as the basic compositional choice source for a *Williams [re]Mix[er]*:

> Feb. 9, 1999 – Make an algorithmic *WM(ixer), which can create, proliferate realizations with a soundfile database and I Ching engine.*[23]

As my analysis of the score continued – determining the incidence of different individual sounds in Cage's six categories and their combination as double-sounds – I began to see trends in my findings, asking questions of myself about the score in my journal, such as:

March 16, 1999 – What is the shortest sound? What is the longest sound? What is the shortest silence? What is the longest silence? Why do certain sounds occur frequently over several score pages and other sounds only once? Why do a number of sounds occur much more than others? Why, ostensibly by chance, does the same sound pan between tracks? Which track has the most sounds, which the least? Significance? Did John ask the *I Ching* to devise alternative results during the course of making the score?[24]

By April 1999, I had completed my compilation and analysis of sounds in Cage's score. In the course of that compilation, I had noted anomalies in the score that would be factors in my design of the 'WM(ixer)'. By October 1999, I had begun the restoration of the eight tape-tracks and had already heard and presented in lectures in Europe and the USA the properly synchronised – though not yet noise-free – ADAT version of *Williams Mix*. In my composition journal I noted on 10 October 1999:

Rome, American Academy, sitting in the AA garden on a sunny afternoon, awaiting a marathon of concerts to begin.

Williams [re]Mix[er]

(1) 8-in/8-out in any combination: a real-time re-mixer.

(2) A 'sound-splicer' algorithm, which with the *I Ching* determines the duration of the whole piece, which of 6 categories, then selects: (a) the soundfile from a soundfile database; (b) the segment duration/locus which is to be spliced; (c) the number (0, 1, or 2) of rise and decay ramps, also including length and angle of ascent and descent; (d) whether there is one sound selected or two mixed of same duration; (e) whether the timbre will be constant (c) (unchanged) or variable (v) (transformed); (f) whether the frequency will be constant (c) (unchanged) or variable (v) (transformed); (g) whether the amplitude will be constant (c) (unchanged) or variable (v) (transformed); (h) whether the sound will be striated (pulsed) and, if so, at what rate; (g) whether the sound will continue in another track(s) and at what rate of 'panning' change, i.e. during, immediately after, or shortly after.

(3) 'Immediate' output.

(4) The soundfile database will contain 6 categories (types) of sounds per Cage . . .

(5) The 'electronic' sounds will be produced in real-time (w/csound or cmix calls) – maybe.[25]

Thus, the design stage of the *Williams [re]Mix[er]* had begun. I would in the coming months go through Cage's score and sketches over and over, in each parameter analysing the characteristics and statistical distribution of each parameter of the piece. First, I established programming protocols with which the programmer I had engaged, Michael Thompson, could implement an effective *I Ching* algorithm as close to the way Cage used it as I could determine. Then, I could design the protocols for its use in making all the compositional decisions.

THE *WILLIAMS [RE]MIX[ER]* COMPUTER PROGRAM EXECUTION PROTOCOLS

Through the tossing of coins, Cage asked the oracle of the *I Ching* to answer the questions he had about the morphology – *form* – of *Williams Mix*, what events were to occur and when and how they were to relate. *Form* – the sound, the silence and the space of the piece – subsumed all: form was the wholeness of the piece, the shaping of musical time and space through change. From the number and duration of the *Williams Mix* 'structural units' – *time-segments* – to the duration of each of the recurrent pattern of six time-segments in each group – *hexads* – to the density of sound/silence events in each hexad to the selection of sounds, their category, combination and transformation through the course of the piece, chance operations and how they would be invoked – asking the oracle – determined the piece's form and effect. I found through intensive analysis of the morphology of the *Williams Mix* score that Cage formulated the right questions: the answers are the genius of the piece.

Through analysis – mainly listening, comparing, counting and measuring – I uncovered trends in the piece's morphology that established distributive weightings of its parameters statistically, shaping the form of the piece. These perceived, counted, measured trends became models for the protocols I designed that, when extrapolated and implemented in the *Williams [re]Mix[er]* computer program, could replicate the original piece with new choices, freshly made: ever-new realisations and variations. What follow are summaries of the protocols I designed for the computer program algorithms, which composer-programmer Michael Thompson implemented effectively for the *Williams [re]Mix[er]*.[26]

SCORE TO SOUND OUTPUT

The *Williams [re]Mix[er]* computer program functions in two overall phases: (1) the first phase, as described below in protocol steps 1–47, where the *I Ching* sub-programs calculate and write their data to a software sound-synthesis *csound* score textfile; and the second and final phase, where the *csound* orchestra 'plays' or 'perfs' the csound score to an eight-channel digital soundfile, ready to be performed to eight speakers surrounding the listener in a 360° circle.

PROGRAM EXECUTION

1. At execution time the program orders and labels all soundfiles in the soundfile library folders, A, B, C, D, E and F, then generates 16, 8 × 8, 1–64, non-repeating *gua* charts (arrays).
2. The program now asks the user for the number of time-segments to be generated from the *gua* charts, in multiples of six – called *hexads*. The time-segment (TS) default parameters *WM* come from Cage's 66 successive 'structural units', time-segments marked by Cage

at intervals by a vertical line through the score system. *Hexads* are successive patterned groups of six time-segments. The default is Cage's number of eleven multiples of six hexads or 66 time-segments.

3. The program now generates the parameters of each successive time-segment, including the density of sound-events in each successive time-segment following the determination of the number and parameters of the time-segment *hexads*.

4. The program now determines the category (A, B, C, D, E or F) combination (single or double sound), variation type (constant (c) or varied (v) in its frequency (f), overtone structure (os) and amplitude (a)), and length of sound-sources in each successive time-segment, tracks 1–8, with each sound followed and preceded by a silence of N duration, including zero silence.

5. After the category, combination, variation and length of sound-events in each successive time-segment, tracks 1–8, have been determined, the program now determines the type and duration of the attack and decay ramps of each sound-event, track by track.

6. The program now determines which sound-events in which of the tracks will be panned to which other tracks through its duration.

7. After the program has determined the durations, category, ASD of each sound-event in all the tracks, the program now determines whether a sound-event in a time-segment in a track will be striated (pulsated) completely or partially and at what rate.

8. The program now compiles the parameter data and writes the final *csound* score, ready to be 'perfed' by the WRM csound 'orchestra', with its numerous 'instruments' for playing the selected soundfile extractions, processed (v) or not (c) by various filter instruments (comb, bandpass, hi/lo pass, alpass, etc.). At output the eight-channel soundfile is generated, ready to be played and heard.

PERFORMANCE

The single, direct reference by Cage to the performance configuration of the necessary eight speakers for *Williams Mix* is his description in his letter to Boulez of the première at the 1953 University of Illinois concert, that the speakers were 'situated around the audience'. Brown's description was that the speakers surrounded the audience, 'equidistantly'.[27] So, the speakers are to surround the audience equidistantly, but in what track arrangement? There is, it turns out, a bias as far as the number of sounds in each track: there are progressively fewer sounds and more and longer silences from track-1 to track-8. I do not know how this progressive symmetry came to be in a chance compositional process, except by Cage's particular questions he put to the *I Ching* in that regard. Be that as it may, I have chosen the most direct configuration for performances of *Williams [re]Mix[ed]*, the eight-speaker configuration surrounding the listener(s) in a 360° circle, as follows: track-1: 0°; track-2: 45°; track-3: 90°; track-4: 135°; track-5: 180°; track-6: 225°; track-7: 270°; and track-8:

315°. The most practical orientation for the audience in a typical concert-hall arrangement, then, would be for the track-1 speaker to be centre front, for the track-2 speaker to be right front, then clockwise equidistantly around the hall, ending with the track-8 speaker at left front of the audience. Or the arrangement could be counter-clockwise. But I can imagine other non-symmetrical, but equidistant arrangements, depending entirely on the space and the context of the performance event. Cage spoke, in fact, of experimenting with placing speakers above the audience as well, leaving us with some enticing options in future performances.

> I also think that another architecture than the concert hall will be needed for a hearing that is excellent. The loudspeakers around the audience should also be above the audience. Perhaps no architecture at all: out of doors with the loudspeakers on the tops of buildings. A magnetrillon! . . .[28]

MONAURAL AND STEREO IMAGING

The sounds originally recorded for Cage's *Williams Mix* were monaural. Each sound was heard from a single speaker on a single track. The sounds I recorded for the *Williams [re]Mix[er]* library are stereo and are heard in adjacent speaker pairs, projecting a rich stereo image all around the circle of eight speakers, depending on the track for the sound-event.

THE 'LIBRARY OF SOUNDS' FOR *WILLIAMS MIX*

'The library of sounds used to produce *Williams Mix* numbers around 500 to 600 sounds', wrote Cage on the information sheet of the score. The apparent reason that Cage did not know the precise number of sounds in his 'library' is not that he did not care to be exact or even that he could have *been* exact. It was more that he needed only to know that he had an adequate supply of relatively short lengths of tape-recorded sounds prepared and obtained from the Barrons in each of the six sound-categories to realise the score, week by week as it progressed. He originally meant to make a piece that was in four parts and twenty minutes long, and so he needed an extensive supply to satisfy the compositional requirements ahead. For the completed 'first part' of *Williams Mix*, I counted the number of different single source sounds and double source sounds (two single source sounds, mixed together) that appear in the score, so that I could understand their type, incidence and distribution in planning my own new realisation. The total different sounds called for in the score for *Williams Mix* is 353; the total single source sounds is 150; the total double source sounds is 203; and the total iterations of all sounds are 2,128, by categories, as follows:

A: 88 city sounds (25 single sources, 63 double sources) with 525 iterations
B: 66 country sounds (20 single sources, 46 double sources) with 380 iterations

C: 66 electronic sounds (26 single sources, 40 double sources) with 380 iterations
D: 56 manual sounds (25 single sources, 31 double sources) with 371 iterations
E: 44 wind sounds (24 single sources, 20 double sources) with 270 iterations
F: 30 small sounds (30 single sources, 3 double sources) with 202 iterations.

Neither Cage nor Tudor did the actual tape recording of sources for the library. That, the mixing of sources, and any looping and processing was done by the Barrons, who had been engaged for the project from summer 1951 to summer 1952. As Cage had written in his letter to Boulez in the summer of 1952: 'I allow the engineers making the sounds total freedom. I simply give a list of the sounds needed. . . . I do not specify how a sound shall be interpreted [in this regard] but leave it to the engineers.'[29] Apparently, though, Cage did provide the Barrons with sound-effects records he had acquired (probably from his experiences in previous years with radio broadcasting) plus other records he must have brought to them (for example, radio dramas, jazz records, etc.), so that they could transfer these sounds to tape. On one of Cage's sketch pages appears a handwritten description of just such a 'Single source record' with various sounds in each of the six categories, reading:

Single source record
traffic Avvv (superpositions and au[t]o h[or]ns; but no other variation.)
speech Evvv (radio ditto)
jazz Dvvv (   )
E[lectronic] S[ounds] full variation Cvvv (freq. superb o.s. amp)
Rain Bcvv orig[inal] (amp & o.s. changed)
Cellophane manual agitation F vcv orig[inal] fr. & amp changed

THE SOUNDS OF *WILLIAMS MIX*

In his dialogue with Joan Retallack, John Cage reflected on *Williams Mix* just months before his death on 12 August 1992, that,

> I'm still attracted, even at this point in technology, I'm attracted to the idea of cutting things up and putting them together. I think that the principle of collage is very important in all aspects of the century, hmm? . . . in our hearts. One of the troubles with some technology is that it makes it almost impossible to use collage. It makes it so easy to produce an effect with a blurring-over . . . smoothes out all the difficulties. So that you get your finished work before you've even begun.[30]

Williams Mix is certainly not smooth sounding: the sounds are heard in a prickly, spatial collage surrounding us, the briefest sound just .016666 second long, the longest sound only 1.309 seconds long. In the restoration process of clearing the noise in all the brief silences (the briefest was 0 second, the longest on a single track was 6.266 seconds) between the 2,128 sounds on the eight tracks of *Williams Mix*, I isolated and listened to each sound, however brief. The briefest sound is, in fact, no more than a click, labelled 'Avvv', a city sound with the *flos/a* varied. It was a tiny sliver cut from the longer 'Avvv' source tape. The longest sound, labelled 'Fvcc' in the score, comes from the 'small sound' category and is equally difficult to recognise: a complex, low-pitched sound, whose frequency slides down about a minor third with a rumbling, saw-like oscillation – like many noises we hear but find difficult to identify, if at all. I suspect it is a small, noisy sound whose frequency has been lowered an octave. But that is as far as I can quantify its nature.

During my months of restoring the piece I listened progressively to each of the sounds in *Williams Mix*. I kept a log of the kinds of single and double sounds that were particularly recognisable and striking and/or which seemed representative of the types of sounds in the six categories. 'Small sounds', in category F, were the most difficult to identify, while 'electronic sounds', C, were the most readily identified. The sounds in categories A, B, D and E were relatively recognisable much of the time. Of course, the human voice – a wind-produced sound in category E – was usually quite recognisable, when it was heard at the original pitch: Eccv, 'Thirty-five . . .' or Evvv, 'In this thing . . .'. Those vocal sounds whose frequencies were transposed an octave higher were too fast to recognise at once. So, out of curiosity, I transposed several down an octave to discover just what the person was actually saying. One voice was particularly familiar to my ears, Ecvv: Humphrey Bogart demanding, 'Tell me where the money came from!' Another, Evvv, cried out, 'These seven-year-old olives are rotten!'

The sounds of the city, category A, were mostly traffic noise, its constant roar punctuated by auto horns. Sounds in category B, country sounds, were variously crows cawing, birds singing, crickets and frogs making their sounds, and a creaky wagon rolling down a dirt road. Electronically generated sounds, C, were high and low sine and pulse waves – sustained in clusters or single tones, modulated, or sweeping up or down. Interestingly, many of the manually produced sounds of category D were recordings of jazz piano solos of the 'stride' era.

Thus, Cage's library of sounds for *Williams Mix* was a diverse collection, related – by chance – only in the special non-relatedness that the tossing of coins brings from invoking the *I Ching*. Further, the library exists now only in the sounds – brief portions of the original sound-sources – heard in the now-restored *Williams Mix* . . . not so for the new library of sound-sources I have recorded for the second and subsequent interpretations of the score of *Williams Mix*, which Cage invited to be realised and which the *Williams [re]Mix[er]* and its evolving soundfile library provides.

THE *WILLIAMS [RE]MIX[ER]* COMPUTER SOUNDFILE LIBRARY

'I think that the principle of collage is very important in all aspects of the century, hmm? . . . in our hearts', Cage mused.[31] The heart of the *Williams [re]Mix[er]* is the computer soundfile library of sounds I have found and continue to find for its ever-new, *I Ching*-determined spatial collages of sounds. Cage, too, intended his own library of sounds to be a dynamic, not static, collection.[32]

As I write this, in January 2001, there are 548 total stereo soundfiles in the *Williams [re]Mix[er]* library, specifically by category: A, 127; B, 92; C, 81; D, 60; E, 146; F, 42. As time goes on, I can choose or not to remove or add soundfiles to each category. Or, as is the case of this present composition, *Williams [re]Mix[ed]*, in its six middle movements, I have chosen to place just one category of sounds in all six categories to create the *Six Short Variations* for *A-city sounds, B-country sounds, C-electronic sounds, D-manually produced sounds, E-wind produced sounds*, and *F-small sounds*.

In the present *Williams [re]Mix[er]* library, the duration of each different soundfile ranges from as short as 20 seconds to as long as 90 and averages about 60 seconds. These nominal durations have been found to allow a variety of different sound-events. In each run of the program, of course, the *I Ching* chooses a different number and combination of soundfiles and durations of sound-events to be selected from the soundfile library. When a particular soundfile with a particular duration is chosen from a particular category, the program extracts that duration from the current beginning of the soundfile. If the soundfile has been previously selected and a sound-event duration extracted, the new sound-event duration is extracted from the end of the previous selection's sound-event duration, so marked or 'flagged'. If subsequent selections of that soundfile reach the end of the soundfile, the program 'wraps around' or 'loops back' to the beginning of the soundfile selection. This process is modelled on the tape-segment cutting/extraction system that Cage and Brown described. That is, such extractions would always be measured and cut from the head of the particular tape segment pulled out of the appropriately labelled envelope, which apparently contained a sizable number of such tape segments.[33] Of course, there was no way to 'loop back', once a tape-segment length was exhausted or the duration of the sound-event called for was longer than the remaining tape segment.[34]

The sounds found, categorised and collected for either Cage's 'library of sounds' or its modelled incarnation as the *Williams [re]Mix[er]* 'computer soundfile library' were subject both to chance and taste in gathering their collection. Cage's six broad categories were conceived and selected by him, even though he, the composer, gave great freedom to the Barrons to choose the actual sound-sources of the recordings themselves. I embraced Cage's categories but was nevertheless selective in what sounds or sound-situations I recorded and included in each category. In both, the final arbiter of choice for the material chosen was the *I Ching*.

I have described the nature of the sounds in *Williams Mix*. My own library of sounds include, in A, city sounds recorded by me on my visits to cities in the USA, Europe and Japan, including, for instance, the Trevi Fountain in Rome; a motorcyclists' open market rally in Bourges, France; the sounds, up and down, of an antique elevator in an apartment house in Paris; the city clamour of the Ikebukuro and Kunitachi sections of Tokyo;

horse-drawn carriages in New York's Central Park, the sounds of a Jim Dine exhibit at Guggenheim Museum, the New York subway downtown; the security guards' warning whistles at a Parisian public park at closing time; Piccadilly Circus at noontime in London; trains arriving/leaving the Shinjuku station in Tokyo; fireworks on a Sunday evening in Bourges; the London Underground; and the Rome Corso – all sounds with many different sonic 'shots' of each location.

In my B category, country sounds, I collected water fowl at daybreak on the central campus lake at York University, UK, and birds singing in a quiet forest near Bourges. I found that country sounds not 'polluted' with traffic noises – air or auto/truck – were very difficult to find and so, like Cage and the Barrons did before, I explored my classic BBC Sound Effects Library of 40 compact discs and found swarms of bees, a rainforest in Ecuador, roosters crowing at dawn, horses, cattle, a lemur, pigs in a shed, a remote country village, a wren, and so on – all very rich, pristine recordings.

I interpreted the C category of electronic music more personally in my collection. I have composed more than 70 electronic and computer-music compositions since 1964 and decided to select choice moments from several of my earlier solo computer-music pieces to include in my library. Also very personal, I managed to get a copy of the videotape that was made for a recent echocardiogram stress test of my heart, yielding the electronic 'beeps' of the machine following the beats of my heart. But most personal of all, I included a large number of electronic, sonic artefacts from the recording David Tudor made with me of my composition for him, *Accidents* (1967), for electronically prepared piano.[35] Also, I included the electronic sounds made by my telephone when I placed my call to Bebe Barron in January 1999, to record my interview with her.

My D category of manually produced sounds is a mix of found and composed sounds. They include Sunday change-ringing of the magnificent bells of the twelfth-century St Etienne Cathedral in Bourges; a street conga player in London's Piccadilly Circus; stroked and struck granite sculpture sounds from my tape piece, *Rompido!* (1993); brief excerpts from each of the ten percussion orchestra cycles of my *Life Pulse Prelude* (1984), based on sketches Ives left to be realised and completed for his *Universe Symphony* (1911–51); a Manhattan street band of drummers and clappers; bells at Mass in the Vatican; a bowed saw performer in the subway at Times Square in New York; clapping by thousands of people for the Pope at his Sunday audience in Piazza San Pietro in the Vatican; two claves struck together from my *Variations . . . beyond Pierrot* (1993–5); and excerpts from my string-bell sounds from my recently composed *Ottuplo!, four inter-episodes for real and virtual string quartet* (2000).

The wind-produced sounds of my category E include 26 one-minute excerpts from my telephone interview with Bebe Barron about her recollections of her and Louis's *Williams Mix* work with Cage, as well as 33 one-minute excerpts from Richard Kostelanetz's 1966 interview with Cage about how *Williams Mix* was composed. Other E sounds include children happily playing in a Bourges school play-yard; alto saxophone improvisations by

Stephen Duke from my *BluesAx* (1995–6), for saxophones and computer music; a Parisian woman greeting me, 'Monsieur', and my response, 'Madame'; gusty, howling, moaning, high winds and a tornado from my BBC collection; a busy outdoor bar of internationals speaking many languages at once in Luxembourg; the crowd, chanting 'Papa, Papa . . .' at the Pope's Sunday audience in the Vatican; organ and choir music from celebrations of the Mass at Notre Dame in Strasbourg, France, Saint Patrick's in New York, and St Peter's in the Vatican; a train blowing its horn; and my only borrowing from Cage's original library of sounds, transposed down an octave, 'These seven-year-old olives are rotten!'

The F category of 'small sounds that have to be amplified to be heard' is my smallest collection but the most varied. It includes the sound of Cage's pencil as he writes, very quietly talking to himself in undertones as he demonstrates to Kostelanetz the tossing of the three coins six times to obtain *guas* from the *I Ching*; the quiet creaking of one of the Jonty Harrison family's kitchen chairs; the ticking of a clock; a faucet dripping; the faint sound of the circulating Freon refrigerant dying away after the refrigerator had finished its cooling cycle and shut off in the kitchen of the Composers' House of the IMEB in Bourges; a match lit; the distant, mysterious, sporadic thumping sound I heard through the heating/cooling system in my room at the Skyline Hotel in New York; a teapot filled; teeth polished; and – the sound closest to my heart [*sic*] – the actual sound of my blood pumping through my heart . . . shuush-shuush, shuush-shuush, shuush-shuush, shuush-shuush. . . .

For this composer's heart . . . every run of the *Williams [re]Mix[er]* brings me a new, stimulatingly joyful, spatial collage of these sounds from my personal library . . . the kind of joy Cage experienced when he heard the first complete performance of *Williams Mix*, writing ecstatically to Boulez that, 'The experience of the 8 loudspeakers is extraordinary. There is no room for anything but immediate listening. The air was so alive one was simply part of it.'[36]

THE NON-CONCLUSION: THE NTH REALISATION

> It is thus possible to make a musical composition the continuity of which is free of individual taste and memory (psychology) and also of the literature and 'traditions' of the art. The sounds enter the time-space centred within themselves, unimpeded by service to any abstraction, their 360 degrees of circumference free for an infinite play of interpenetrations. Value judgments are not in the nature of this work either as regards composition, performance or listening. The idea of relation being absent, anything may happen. A 'mistake' is beside the point, for once anything happens, it authentically is.[37]

When asked by my long-time friend and colleague Joel Chadabe in October 2000, during an intermission talk with me and Earle Brown that he was moderating, 'Why are you doing this, Larry?', I was nonplussed. I had just presented a preview of my *Williams [re]Mix[ed]* and had described my project and Cage's open invitation to 'follow the recipe'. As a composer and noted historian of electronic music, I thought to myself that Joel certainly should appreciate the legendary primacy of *Williams Mix* as the first octophonic tape piece in the history of electronic music and the first important work in the genre by the great American composer of experimental music, John Cage. But, as I was making my response to the question, repeating what John Cage had said that 'someone else could follow that recipe, so to speak, with other sources than I had to make another mix', I began to understand why Joel had posed what seemed to me to be a rhetorical question. Joel had sensed what was perhaps in the back of the audience's mind, that is, 'What a great idea . . . but what an enormous amount of work for a composer to work three years to restore a four-minute piece of another composer, then to analyze its 192-page score, to collect nearly 600 new sounds, and then to design a computer program to make a new version of it'. Then, I reflected for a moment on my earlier and much larger project to realise and complete Charles Ives's *Universe Symphony*, a project begun in 1974 and finally completed in 1993. Of that similar project I offered the following *apologia* that,

> I believe that Ives always intended to complete the *Universe Symphony* but invoked a caveat in his Memos that '. . . in case I don't get to finishing this, somebody might like to try to work out the idea . . . ,' later appealing to Cowell to work with him to finish the work. . . . It is done. . . . I have realised the musical material of the sketches and finished the *US* in what I have felt is a genuine musical and even spiritual collaboration with Ives's music of the *US*, Ives's words about the music, and with the conductors, performers, scholars, and sponsors of my two-decade long personal commission to finish the *Universe Symphony*. Envision. Listen.[38]

I then expressed to Joel that my current *Williams Mix* restoration, realisations and variations continue in that same spirit of discovery and fulfilment I had for my previous *Universe Symphony* research and realisation of Ives's sketches for his last, largest, most compelling, but unfinished work. Now, with *Williams [re]Mix[ed]* and its *Williams [re]Mix[er]* program providing ever-newer realisations, I continue as Cage's student and collaborator, much as Tudor, the Barrons and Browne were in creating the 'first part' of *Williams Mix*.

On the last page of the score for *Williams Mix*, Cage inscribed, '*(4 min. 15 sec. +) End 1st Part. N.Y.C. Oct. '52 Splicing finished Jan. 16, 1953*' (see Plate 14.3, page 192, score.) Dare I imagine that John's spirit is slyly laughing now, asking the oracle, 'Is this the 2nd Part, the 3rd or the 4th?' Once more, envision. Listen and enjoy, again and again.

Appendix: Select list of composer institutes

The following presents a representative list of institutions devoted to the promotion and study of the work of twentieth-century composers. The term 'composer institute' was coined at the First International Symposium of Composer Institutes organised by the Orff-Zentrum and held in Munich from 29 June to 2 July 2000. These institutions 'share the common task of maintaining cultural awareness of the work of their particular composer, both today and in the future, as well as communicating the intellectual and artistic dimensions of his [or her] creative work to their own era and to posterity.'[1] Many of the listed institutions conserve important manuscript collections (musical manuscripts, as well as letters, diaries, annotated books and other documents related to the composer's career) and have made or are making these collections available for academic research. Those institutions that do not house manuscript collections know where such collections are to be found, as well as whether and to what extent these collections are available for study. Whereas the overwhelming majority are built around the work of one particular composer, a few have established multiple collections. Among these the four most important are the Paul Sacher Foundation (Basle), the Stiftung Archiv der Akademie der Künste (Berlin), the Fondazione Giorgio Cini – Institute of Music (Venice) and the Getty Research Library (Los Angeles). The list does not include national or regional libraries (the British Library, the Bibliothèque nationale de France, the Bayerische Staatsbibliothek, etc.), which have traditionally been and continue to be the repositories for the estates of deceased composers of national stature.

The information presented below is of course inherently unstable. Though much will remain valid for the foreseeable future, some of the addresses and numbers will have changed by the time this book is published. In spite of these problems we felt the list should be published because, as a historic document, it bears witness to the explosive growth of this type of institution during the last quarter of the twentieth century.

ALBAN BERG STIFTUNG
Established in 1967
Trauttmansdorffgasse 27
A-1130 Vienna
Austria
Tel.: Int + 43 1 877 7164
Fax: Int + 43 1 877 7164 22

adamiak@albanbergstiftung.at
www.albanbergstiftung.at

ARCHIVES OF THE ERIK SATIE
FOUNDATION
Established in 1981
IMEC

Abbaye d'Ardenne
F-14280 St Germain la blanche herbe
France
Tel.: Int + 33 2 31 29 37 37
Fax: Int + 33 2 31 29 37 36
e-mail@imec-archives.com
(A web site is currently in production.)

ARCHIVIO CONTEMPORANEO
'ALESSANDRO BONSANTI'
(Houses the Fondazione Luigi
Dallapiccola)
Established in 1975
Palazzo Corsini Suarez
Via Maggio 42
I-50125 Florence
Italy
Tel.: Int + 39 55–290131/32
Fax: Int + 39 55–213188
archivio@vieusseux.fi.it
www.vieusseux.fi.it/archivio.html

ARCHIVIO LUIGI NONO
Established in 1993
Guidecca 795
Fondamenta S. Biagio
I-30133 Venice
Italy
Tel.: Int + 39 041 520 9713
Lnono@unive.it
www.luiginono.it

ARCHIVO MANUEL DE FALLA
Inaugurated in 1978
Paseo de los Mártires
E-18009 Alhambra Granada
Spain
Tel.: Int + 34 58 22 83 18/22 84 63
Fax: Int + 34 58 21 59 55

archivofalla@retemail.es
www.servicom.es/archivo-falla

ARNOLD SCHÖNBERG CENTER
The Arnold Schönberg Institute of the
University of Southern California was
established in 1973. In 1997 the holdings
were transferred to the Arnold Schönberg
Center.
Palais Fanto
Schwarzenburgplatz 6
A-1030 Vienna
Austria
Tel.: Int + 43 1 712 1888
Fax: Int + 43 1 712 188888
office@schoenberg.at
www.schoenberg.at

BARTÓK ARCHIVES OF THE
INSTITUTE OF MUSICOLOGY
OF THE HUNGARIAN ACADEMY
OF SCIENCES
Opened in 1961
Táncsics Mihály utca 7
Budapest I
H-1250 Pf. 28
Hungary
Tel./Fax: Int + 36 1 375 2139
Fax: Int + 36 1 375 9282
Info@zti.hu
www.zti.hu/bartok.htm

BOHUSLAV MARTINŮ INSTITUTE
IN PRAGUE
Established in 1995
Náměstí Kinských 3
CZ-15000 Prague 5
Czech Republic
Tel.: Int + 420 2 57 31 31 04

Tel./Fax: Int + 420 2 57 32 00 76
martinu@martinu.cz
www.martinu.cz/bmi.htm

BRITTEN–PEARS LIBRARY
Established in 1963
The Red House
Aldeburgh
Suffolk IP15 5PZ
United Kingdom
Tel.: Int + 44 1728 452615
Fax: Int + 44 1728 453076
bpl@britten-pears.co.uk
www.britten-pears.co.uk

CARL NIELSEN MUSEUM
Opened in 1988
Claus Bergs Gade 11, Odense
DK-5000 Odense C
Denmark
Tel.: Int + 45 65 51 46 01
Fax: Int + 45 65 90 86 00
www.odmus.dk

CENTRE DE DOCUMENTATION
CLAUDE DEBUSSY
Established in 1974
2 Rue Louvois
F-75002 Paris
France
Tel.: Int + 33 1 42 96 35 50
contact@debussy.fr

CENTRE DE DOCUMENTATION
MUSICALE, BIBLIOTHÈQUE GUSTAV
MAHLER
Established in 1986
11bis, rue de Vézelay
F-75008 Paris

France
Tel.: Int + 33 1 53 89 09 10
Fax: Int + 33 1 43 59 70 22
popoff@mediathequemahler.org
www.mediathequemahler.org

CENTRO STUDI MUSICALI
FERRUCCIO BUSONI
Established in 1976
Piazza della Vittoria 16
I-50053 Empoli (Florence)
Italy
Tel.: Int + 39 0571 711122
Fax: Int + 39 0571 78236
csmfb@centrobusoni.org
www.centrobusoni.org

DARIUS MILHAUD COLLECTION OF
MILLS COLLEGE
Established in 1984
Mills College
5000 MacArthur Blvd.
Oakland CA 94613
United States
Tel.: Int + 510 430 2047
Fax: Int + 510 430 2278
www.mills.edu/library/LIB_SVCS/
LIB_COLL/pcoll_desc/milhaud.html

ERNST KRENEK INSTITUT
Founded in 1997
Hanuschgasse 3
A-1010 Vienna
Austria
Tel.: Int + 43 1 513 94 47
Fax: Int + 43 1 512 08 11
krenek@krenek.com
www.krenek.com

FONDAZIONE GIORGIO CINI –
INSTITUTE OF MUSIC
(Houses numerous manuscript collections,
notably those of Alfredo Casella, Gian
Francesco Malipiero and Nino Rota)
Established in 1985
Island of San Giorgio Maggiore
I-30124 Venice
Italy
Tel.: Int + 39 041 271 0211
musica@cini.it
www.cini.it

FONDAZIONE ISABELLA SCELSI
(Houses the manuscripts of Giacinto
Scelsi)
Established in 1987
Via di San Teodoro, 8
I-00186 Rome
Italy
Tel.: Int + 39 06 6992 0344
Fax: Int + 39 06 6992 0404
fondazione@scelsi.it
www.scelsi.it

FRANZ SCHREKER FOUNDATION
Established in 1986
c/o Christopher Hailey
22 Western Way
Princeton NJ 08540
United States
Tel.: Int + 609 683 4893
kienzle@schreker.org or Cthailey@cs.com
www.schreker.org

GETTY RESEARCH LIBRARY
(Houses, among other collections, David
Tudor Papers, John Cage Musical

Notebooks, Leonard Stein Collection of
Musical Scores)
Opened in 1997
1200 Getty Center Drive, Suite 1100
Los Angeles CA 90049-1688
United States
Tel.: Int + 310 440 7335
griweb@getty.edu
www.getty.edu/research/institute

INTERNATIONALE HANNS EISLER
GESELLSCHAFT
Founded in 1994
Eisenbahnstr. 21
D-10997 Berlin
Germany
Tel.: Int + 49 30 612 884 61
Fax: Int + 49 30 612 804 63
IHEG@aol.com
www.hanns-eisler.com

INTERNATIONALE ISANG YUN
GESELLSCHAFT e.V.
Established in 1996
Nassauische Str. 6
D-10717 Berlin-Wilmersdorf
Germany
Tel.: Int + 49 30 873 47 44
Fax: Int + 49 30 873 72 07
office@yun-gesellschaft.de
www.yun-gesellschaft.de

ISTITUTO DI STUDI MUSICALE
GOFFREDO PETRASSI
Established in 1993
Università Pontina
Viale Le Corbusier 379
I-04100 Latina (Rome)

Italy
Tel.: Int + 39 0773 605550
Fax: Int + 39 0773 628498
istituto.petrassi@panservice.it
www.istitutopetrassi.it

JOHN CAGE TRUST
Established in 1993
666 Greenwich Street, Suite 416
New York NY 10014
United States
Tel.: Int + 212 807 0646
Fax: Int + 212 807 0443
lkuhn@johncage.org

KARL SZYMANOWSKI
MUSEUM
Opened in 1967
Willi 'Atma' [The Atma Villa]
ul. Kasprusie 1
PL-34500 Zakopane
Poland
Tel.: Int + 48 18 201 34 93
Fax: Int + 48 18 201 45 54
glowa@tatrynet.pl
www.muzeum.krakow.pl/prawe/
oddzialyf.htm

KODÁLY ARCHIVES AND MEMORIAL
MUSEUM
Opened in 1990
Andrássy út 89
H-1062 Budapest VI
Hungary
Tel.: Int + 36 1 342–8448/352-7106
Fax: Int + 36 1 322-9647
kodalyzm@axelero.hu
www.kodaly-inst.hu

KURT WEILL FOUNDATION FOR
MUSIC, INC
Established in 1962
Weill-Lenya Research Center
7 East 20th Street
New York, NY 10003
United States
Tel.: Int + 212 505 5240
Fax: Int + 212 353 9663
kwfinfo@kwf.org
www.kwf.org

KURT WEILL GESELLSCHAFT
Established in 1993
Meisterhaus Feininger
Ebertallee 63
D-06846 Dessau
Germany
Tel.: Int + 49 340 619595
Fax: Int + 49 340 611907
weill-zentrum@t-online.de
www.kurt-weill-fest.de

LEOŠ JANÁČEK FOUNDATION
Established in 1991
Marešova 14
CZ-60200 Brno
Czech Republic
Tel.: Int + 420 5 41 24 68 24
Tel. and Fax: Int + 420 5 41 24 68 25
E-mail: janacek-nadace@janacek-nadace.cz
www.janacek-nadace.cz/envers/e-sidlo.htm

MAX-REGER-INSTITUT/ELSA-
REGER-STIFTUNG
Established in 1947
Alte Karlsburg Durlach
Pfinztalstr.7

D-76227 Karlsruhe
Germany
Tel.: Int + 49 721 854501
Fax: Int + 49 721 854502
mri@uni-karlsruhe.de
www.uni-karlsruhe.de/kultur/
Max-Reger-Institut

ORFF-ZENTRUM MÜNCHEN
Opened in 1990
Kaulbachstrasse 16
D-80539 Munich
Germany
Tel.: Int + 49 89 288105-0
Fax: Int + 49 89 280356
kontakt@orff-zentrum.bayern.de
www.orff-zentrum.de

PAUL-HINDEMITH-INSTITUT
Established in 1974
Eschersheimer Landstr. 29-39
D-60322 Frankfurt/Main
Germany
Tel.: Int + 49 69 5970362
Fax: Int + 49 69 5963104
institut@hindemith.org
www.hindemith.org

PAUL SACHER FOUNDATION
(Housing over 90 manuscript collections
primarily of twentieth-century
composers)
Established in 1973
Auf Burg
Münsterplatz 4
CH-4052 Basel
Switzerland
Tel.: Int + 41 61 269 6644

Fax: Int + 41 61 261 9183
www.paul-sacher-stiftung.ch

RICHARD STRAUSS INSTITUT
Established in 1999
Schnitzschulstraße 19
D-82467 Garmisch-Partenkirchen
Germany
Tel.: Int + 49 8821-910 950
Fax: Int + 49 8821-910 960
rsi@garmisch-partenkirchen.de
www.richard-strauss-institut.de

SIBELIUS MUSEUM
Founded in 1926, the institution became
the Sibelius Museum in 1949
Biskopsgaten 17
FIN-20500 Åbo (Turku)
Finland
Tel.: Int + 358 2 2154494/2154388
Fax: Int + 358 2 5218528
sibeliusmuseum@abo.fi
www.sibeliusmuseum.abo.fi

SOCIÉTÉ INTERNATIONALE FRANZ SCHREKER
Established in 1964
24, rue des Petites Ecuries
F-75010 Paris
France
Tel.: Int + 33 1 48 24 21 97
Fax: Int + 33 1 48 24 18 62
jorge.zulueta@wanadoo.fr
www.zulueta-romano.com/bio/jacobo.htm

STIFTUNG ARCHIV DER AKADEMIE DER KÜNSTE, BERLIN
(Houses numerous manuscript collections
concerning twentieth-century music: Boris

Blacher, Paul Dessau, Harald Kaufmann,
Heinz-Klaus Metzger, Hans-Heinz
Stuckenschmidt, etc.)
(The music archive was established
in 1993)
Robert-Koch-Platz 10
D-10115 Berlin-Mitte
Germany
Tel.: Int + 49 30 30884 261
Fax: Int + 49 30 30884 102
musikarchiv@adk.de
www.adk.de

STOCKHAUSEN STIFTUNG FÜR
MUSIK
Established in 1994
Kettenberg 15

D-51515 Kürten
Germany
Fax: Int + 49 2268-1813
stockhausen.foundation@stockhausen.org
www.stockhausen.org/foundation.html

WILLIAM WALTON
TRUST/FONDAZIONE WILLIAM
WALTON
Established in 1984
3 Park Street
Windsor, Berkshire SL4 1LU
United Kingdom
Tel.: Int + 44 1753 714364
Fax: Int + 44 1753 866845
enquiries@waltontrust.org.uk
www.waltontrust.org.uk

Notes

INTRODUCTION

1 Louis Hay, 'History of Genesis?' *Yale French Studies*, 89 (1996), 199–200. For a remarkable study of the working manuscripts and procedures of Renaissance composers, see Jessie Ann Owens, *Composers at Work: The Craft of Musical Composition 1450–1600*, Oxford University Press, 1997.

2 See Lydia Goehr, *The Imaginary Museum of Musical Works: An Essay in the Philosophy of Music*, Oxford University Press, 1992.

3 See for example Timo Virtanen, 'Pohjola's Daughter – "L'aventure d'un héros"', in *Sibelius Studies*, ed. Timothy L. Jackson and Veijo Murtomäki, Cambridge University Press, 2001, pp. 139–74; and Rachel Beckles Willson, *György Kurtág: The Sayings of Peter Bornemisza Op. 7 (1963–68)*, Aldershot: Ashgate, 2003.

4 Walter Benjamin, 'The Task of the Translator: An Introduction to the Translation of Baudelaire's *Tableaux parisiens*', in *Illuminations*, ed. Hannah Arendt, trans. Harry Zohn, New York: Schocken Books, 1969, p. 79.

5 *Ibid.*, p. 73.

6 Matthew Gurewitsch, 'Finding the Truth in the Composer's Hand', *The New York Times* (14 May 2000).

7 See for instance Richard Taruskin's oft-repeated remarks in 'Reply to Brown and Dempster', *Journal of Music Theory*, 33/1 (1989), 156. These remarks have not stopped Taruskin from referring to manuscript material whenever he sees fit in his study of Stravinsky's music, notably in *Stravinsky and the Russian Traditions: A Biography of the Works Through 'Marva'*, Oxford University Press, 1996.

8 Douglas Johnson, 'Beethoven Scholars and Beethoven Sketches', *Nineteenth Century Music*, 2 (1978–9), 3–17. Gianmario Borio has noted that Johnson's fallacious argument is based on a belief in the thaumaturgical power of musical analysis to read the structure of a given work as though it were transparent in the published score. Gianmario Borio, 'Sull'interazione fra lo studio degli schizzi e l'analisi dell'opera', in *La nuova ricerca sull'opera di Luigi Nono*, ed. Gianmario Borio, Giovanni Morelli and Veniero Rizzardi, Venice: Leo S. Olschki, 1999, p. 3.

I SKETCHES AND SKETCHING

1 Gottfried Boehm, 'Prekäre Balance', *Cézanne Vollendet Unvollendet*, ed. F. Baumann, E. Benesch, W. Feilchenfeldt and K. A. Schröder, Zurich: Kunsthaus, 2000, pp. 29–31.

2 Walter Benjamin, *The Origin of the German Tragic Drama*, London: Verso, 1998, p. 55.

3 *Ibid.*, p. 166.

4 Paul Mies, *Die Bedeutung der Skizzen Beethovens zur Erkenntnis seines Stils*, Leipzig: Breitkopf & Härtel, 1925.

5 Ulrich Mosch, 'Zum Formdenken Hans Werner Henzes. Beobachtungen am Particell der 6. Symphonie', *Quellenstudien II Zwölf Komponisten des 20. Jahrhunderts*, ed. Felix Meyer, Winterthur: Amadeus, 1993, pp. 169–73.

6 Hans Heinz Stuckenschmidt, *Schönberg: Leben, Umwelt, Werk*, Zurich: Atlantis, 1974, p. 491.

7 Rainer Cadenbach, *Max Reger und seine Zeit*, Laaber Verlag, 1991, p. 183.

8 For an exhaustive examination of this aspect of Ives's work, see J. Peter Burkholder, *All Made of Tunes: Charles Ives and the Uses of Musical Borrowing*, New Haven: Yale University Press, 1995.

9 Eric Hobsbawm, *Age of Extremes: The Short Twentieth-Century 1914–1991*, London: Abacus, 1995, p. 519.

10 Brian Newbould, 'Introduction', Franz Schubert, *Symphony No. 10 in D major D. 936A*, London: Faber Music, 1995, p. v. For more on Newbould's endeavour see Brian Newbould, *Schubert: The Music and the Man*, Berkeley: University of California Press, 1999, pp. 385–8.

11 Peter Gülke, 'Neue Beiträge zur Kenntnis des Sinfonikers Schubert', in *Franz Schubert, Musik-Konzepte, Sonderband* [Special issue], ed. Heinz-Klaus Metzger and Rainer Riehn, Munich: edition text+kritik, 1979, pp. 193–203. Curiously, Newbould makes no mention of Gülke's earlier work with the same sketch material.

12 David Osmond-Smith, 'La mesure de la distance: *Rendering* de Berio', *Inharmoniques*, 7 (1991), 150.

2 PRELIMINARIES BEFORE VISITING AN ARCHIVE

Translated by J. Bradford Robinson

1 See, for example, David Osmond-Smith, *Berio*, Oxford University Press, 1991, p. 36, or Gavin Thomas, 'Musica e musica . . .', *Musical Times*, 137/1 (1996), 15.

2 *Luciano Berio: Musikmanuskripte*, Inventare der Paul Sacher Stiftung, 2, ed. René Karlen, Winterthur: Amadeus, 1988; available from Schott Musik International, Mainz.

3 *Luciano Berio: Musikmanuskripte*, Inventare der Paul Sacher Stiftung, 2, rev. and enlarged 2nd edn, ed. Ulrich Mosch, Mainz: Schott Musik International, forthcoming.

4 As examples of a great many catalogues we might mention *Musikhandschriften aus der Sammlung Paul Sacher: Festschrift zu Paul Sachers siebzigstem Geburtstag*, ed. Ernst Lichtenhahn and Tilman Seebass, Basle: Editiones Roche, 1976; *Musikhandschriften der Bodmeriana: Katalog*, ed. Tilman Seebass, Cologny-Geneva: Fondation Martin Bodmer, 1986; Aleš Březina, 'Die Martinů-Manuskripte in der Paul Sacher Stiftung', *Schweizer Jahrbuch für Musikwissenschaft/Annales Suisses de Musicologie*, 13–14 (1993–4), 157–274; and more recently Günther Weiss *et al.*, *Gustav Mahler: Briefe und Musikautographen aus den Moldenhauer-Archiven in der Bayerischen Staatsbibliothek*, Patrimonia, vol. 157, Munich: Kulturstiftung der Länder, 2003.

5 At the time of writing there is no catalogue of the musical manuscripts in the Luciano Berio Collection at the Paul Sacher Foundation, Basle. The following description was specially prepared for the present article on the model of standard catalogues for purposes of illustration.

6 That further pages existed after p. 6, though not wholly inconceivable, is rather unlikely as the draft stops in the middle of the page.

7 Several pages in the sketches and drafts contain cross-references to page numbers that relate to none of the existing manuscripts, not even the fair copy in full score. We may therefore safely posit the existence of at least one further large-scale manuscript, perhaps the initial fair copy. No other traces of this manuscript have yet been discovered.

8 Hugo Loetscher, 'Vorläufiges zu einer Hinterlassenschaft: Ein Archivar in eigener Sache', *Neue Zürcher Zeitung*, 219/225 (29 September 1997), 29.

9 The question of how to safeguard sources when a collection is entrusted to an archive during the composer's lifetime is discussed by Ulrich Mosch, 'Musikverlage, "Komponisten-Institute" und das zeitgenössische Schaffen', *Der Musikverlag und seine Komponisten im 21. Jahrhundert: Zum 100-jährigen Jubiläum der Universal Edition*, Studien zur Wertungsvorschung 41, ed. Otto Kolleritsch, Vienna and Graz: Universal Edition, 2002, pp. 30–43, esp. pp. 35 ff.

10 Berio's copyrights will not expire until the year 2073!

11 See p. 25 above. For the moment we must leave open the question of what Berio meant by the term 'episode'.

12 The première of the complete version was given by the composer himself at the Aspen Music Festival, Colorado, on 13 August 1985.

13 Luciano Berio, 'Requies (1984)'; quoted here in the composer's own English translation from the CD booklet to *Luciano Berio: World Premiere Recordings: Requies – Voci – Corale*, London Sinfonietta, cond. Berio, RCA Victor, Red Seal RD87898. © BMG Music, p. 3.

14 This only becomes possible, at least in a first approximation, when the materials are definitively catalogued and filmed. But even here we soon encounter obstacles if the composer used several sketches simultaneously.

15 There are certain cases in the Hans Werner Henze Collection at the Sacher Foundation where the sketches and drafts were paginated by the composer *ex post facto* and obviously not in the order in which they originated.

16 Exhibition held in the Basle Kunstmuseum from 25 April to 20 June 1986; Hans Jörg Jans (ed.), *Komponisten des 20. Jahrhunderts in der Paul Sacher Stiftung*, Basle: Kunstmuseum, 1986, pp. 335–40 (currently distributed by Schott International).

17 Exhibition held in the Pierpont Morgan Library, New York, from 13 May to 30 August 1998; Felix Meyer (ed.), *Settling New Scores: Music Manuscripts from the Paul Sacher Foundation*, Mainz: Schott International, 1998, p. 160.

18 Felix Meyer (ed.), *Quellenstudien II: Zwölf Komponisten des 20. Jahrhunderts*, Winterthur: Amadeus, 1993, pp. 77, 82, 87 and 90 (currently distributed by Schott International).

19 *Luciano Berio: Two Interviews with Rossana Dalmonte and Bálint András Varga*, ed. and trans. David Osmond-Smith, New York and London: Boyars, 1985, Plates 4, 9 and 12 after p. 94.

3 ARCHIVAL ETIQUETTE

Translated by Friedemann Sallis

1 Coined by Christiane Thomas, the term 'preventive conservation' refers to the prophylactic nature of 'passive conservation', a term widely used in specialised literature. Christiane Thomas, 'Was erwarten Archivarinnen und Archivare von Restauratoren', *Dritte Tagung der Österreichischen Archivrestauratorinnen und Restauratoren, 18–19 November 1996*, Vienna: Österreichisches Staatsarchiv, 1996, p. 58.

2 Helmut Bansa, 'Papierchemie', *Dauerhaftigkeit von Papier. Vorträge des 4. Internationalen Graphischen Restauratorentages*, Zeitschrift für Bibliothekswesen und Bibliographie Sonderheft 31, ed. Helmut Bansa *et al.*, Frankfurt am Main: Vittorio Klostermann Verlag, 1980, pp. 5–8.

3 Fibril signifies small fibre and is normally understood as its subdivision.

4 Thomas Krause, 'Warum altert Papier? Begriffsdefinition, Untersuchsmethoden', *Dauerhaftigkeit von Papier*, pp. 28–9.

5 Guido Dessauer, 'Das Papier im Archiv', *Das Papier*, 43/11 (1989), 607.

6 Anna Haberditzl, 'Kleine Mühen – große Wirkung: Maßnahmen der passiven Konservierung bei der Lagerung, Verpackung und Nutzung von Archiv- und Bibliotheksgut', *Bestandserhaltung in Archiven und Bibliotheken*, ed. Hartmut Weber, Stuttgart: Verlag W. Kohlhammer, 1992, pp. 71–83.

7 The quality of cardboard and paper for the long-term conservation of source material has been standardised internationally. The technical basis for the manufacture of paper products with a high degree of durability is set out in *American National Standard. Permanence of Paper for Publications and Documents in Libraries and Archives*, Bethesda: NISO Press, 1993.

8 This supposes that the institution has established a complete inventory of its holdings and that the inventories are readily available. This is in fact not always the case when dealing with twentieth-century sketch material.

9 Philip C. Brooks, *Research in Archives: The Use of Unpublished Primary Sources*, University of Chicago Press, 1969, p. 36.

4 COMING TO TERMS WITH THE COMPOSER'S WORKING MANUSCRIPTS

1 David Perkins, *Is Literary History Possible?* Baltimore: The Johns Hopkins University Press, 1993, pp. 72–3.

2 See, for instance, Peter Benary's attempt to distinguish four sketch types: (1) thematic-motivic sketches; (2) combinatorial sketches, in which various compositional parameters are dealt with simultaneously; (3) independent sketches with or without a demonstrable link to a known work or work project; (4) continuity sketches. Peter Benary, 'Skizze – Entwurf – Fragment', *Die Musik in Geschichte und Gegenwart: allgemeine Enzyklopädie der Musik, Sachteil*, vol. 8, ed. L. Finscher, Kassel: Bärenreiter–Metzler, 1994, p. 1508.

3 Nicholas Marston, 'Sketch', *The New Grove Dictionary of Music and Musicians*, vol. 23, ed. Stanley Sadie and John Tyrrell, London: Macmillan, 2001, p. 472.

4 An exception would be the case of a composer working with an assistant or as part of a team. During the last ten years of his life, Luigi Nono spent a great deal of time working with technicians and musicians at the Heinrich-Strobel-Stiftung in Freiburg. In this case, many of his sketches may well have been used to communicate ideas within a small group of collaborators. This however does not invalidate the point that sketches are private documents not intended to be read by the public at large.

5 Joseph Kerman, *Musicology in the 1980s: Methods, Goals, Opportunities*, New York: Da Capo Press, 1982, p. 58.

6 The section of Plate 4.1 written in pencil can be distinguished (note the differences in texture and the lighter shade of grey). Furthermore, if the reader looks carefully, the parts of the documents written in blue and orange ink can also be differentiated. A careful examination of this aspect of the sketch would allow the scholar to establish the order in which Kurtág wrote his ideas on this page.

7 The vast majority of over 200 sketches and drafts conserved at the Paul Sacher Foundation pertaining to Kurtág's *Kafka-Fragmente* are carefully dated. These data have allowed the present author to establish a detailed chronology of the surviving sketch material.

8 The English term 'short score', not to be confused with 'piano score', is an exception in that in most languages, the original Italian term has simply been transferred (i.e. *Particell* in German).

9 For more on this aspect of Ligeti's compositional technique, see Friedemann Sallis, 'Reading György Ligeti's *Lux aeterna*: An Exercise in Musicological Border-Crossing', *Muualla, täällä. Kirjoituksia*

elämästä, kuttuurista, musiikista. Juhlakirja Erkki Salmenhaara (Festschrift for Erkki Salmenhaara), ed. Helena Tyrväinen, Seija Lappalainen, Tomi Mäkelä and Irma Vierimaa, Jyväskylä: Atena Kustannus Oy Jyväskylä, 2001, pp. 137–52.

10 One such system is the so-called 'elastic talea', derived from his study of the music of Guillaume de Machaut and which he claims to have used in the Requiem and *Lux aeterna*. Pierre Michel, *György Ligeti. Compositeur d'aujourd'hui*, Paris: Minerve, 1985, pp. 160–1. Plate 4.5 may well provide information leading to an elucidation of this aspect of Ligeti's compositional technique.

11 Roman Ingarden, *The Work of Music and the Problem of its Identity*, ed. J. G. Harrell, London: Macmillan, 1986, pp. 149–53.

12 For a recent survey of the field, see Georg Feder, *Musikphilologie. Eine Einführung in die musikalische Textkritik, Hermeneutik und Editionstechnik*, Darmstadt: Wissenschaftliche Buchgesellschaft, 1987.

13 See for example, Robert Schumann, 'Über einige muthmaßlich corrumpierte Stellen in Bach-schen, Mozartschen und Beethovenschen Werken', *Gesammelte Schriften über Musik und Musiker*, vol. 2, ed. Gustav Jansen, Leipzig: Breitkopf & Härtel, 1891, pp. 344–8.

14 Schleiermacher was referring to the visual arts, however he explicitly states that this function was valid for sketch material in all forms of art. Friedrich Schleiermacher, *Vorlesungen über die Ästhetik*, Berlin: Walter de Gruyter, 1974, pp. 262–3.

15 Carl Dahlhaus, *Foundations of Music History*, Cambridge University Press, 1985, p. 4.

16 Otto Jahn, letter written to Gustav Hartenstein on 12 December 1852, cited in Thomas Whelan, *Towards a History and Theory of Sketch Studies*, Ann Arbor: UMI Dissertation Services, 1990, p. 115.

17 Gustav Nottebohm, cited in *ibid.*, pp. 125–6.

18 László Somfai, *Béla Bartók: Compositions, Concepts and Autograph Sources*, Berkeley: University of California Press, 1996, p. 24.

19 *Ibid.*, p. 61.

20 Martha Hyde, 'Musical Form and the Development of Schoenberg's Twelve-Tone Method', *Journal of Music Theory*, 29/1 (1985), 85–98.

21 Martha Hyde, 'Format and Function of Schoenberg's Twelve-Tone Sketches', *Journal of the American Musicological Society*, 36/3 (1983), 454–5.

22 Gianmario Borio, 'Sull'interazione fra la studio degli schizzi e l'analisi dell'opera', *La nuova ricerca sull'opera di Luigi Nono*, ed. G. Borio, G. Morelli and V. Rizzardi, Venice: Leo S. Olschki, 1999, pp. 5–6.

23 Umberto Eco, *The Open Work*, Cambridge, Mass.: Harvard University Press, 1989, p. 100.

24 *Ibid.*, p. 163.

25 Jean-Louis Lebrave, 'La critique génétique: une discipline nouvelle ou un avatar moderne de la philologie?' *Genesis: manuscrits, recherche, invention*, 1 (1992), 67.

26 Laurent Jenny, 'Genetic Criticism and its Myths', *Yale French Studies*, 89 (1996), 14.

27 Friedemann Sallis, Ulrich Mosch and Christina Dreier, *György Kurtág. Musikmanuskripte*, Inventare der Paul Sacher Stiftung, Mainz: Schott Musik International, forthcoming. The inventory does not contain information concerning either the composer's correspondence or hundreds of pages of drawings made by the composer and also conserved at the Foundation.

28 Friedemann Sallis, 'The Genealogy of György Kurtág's *Hommage à R. Sch*, op. 15d', *Studia Musicologica*, 43/3–4 (2002), 311–22.

29 Carl Dahlhaus, 'Plea for a Romantic Category: The Concept of the Work of Art in the Newest Music', *Schoenberg and the New Music*, Cambridge University Press, 1987, p. 218.

5 THE CLASSIFICATION OF MUSICAL SKETCHES EXEMPLIFIED IN THE CATALOGUE OF THE ARCHIVIO LUIGI NONO

Translated by Friedemann Sallis

1 The ALN was founded three years after the composer's death by his widow, Nuria Schoenberg Nono, in 1993.
2 The ALN counts its manuscript holdings in terms of sheets of paper, referring to both the recto and verso sides of a leaf of paper. Though widespread, this procedure is not universal. The Paul Sacher Foundation counts pages containing some form of written information.
3 The generally accepted guide for the cataloguing of music manuscripts in Italy is: *Guida a una descrizione catalografica uniforme dei manoscritti musicali*, ed. Massimo Gentili Tedeschi, Rome: Instituto centrale per il catalogo unico delle biblioteche italiane e per le informazione bibliografiche, 1984.
4 This title is in the Rhaeto-Romance dialect spoken in Friuli-Venezia Giulia, a region north-east of Venice. In Italian the title would read 'I turchi del Friuli'.
5 The first performance of *La fabbrica illuminata* took place in Venice on 15 September 1964.

7 TRANSCRIBING SKETCHES

Translated by Michael Graubart, revised by Friedemann Sallis and Marion Macfarlane

Author's note: For this chapter I provided a German text and an exact translation by Michael Graubart. The English version printed here, which is based on Graubart's work, was made by Friedemann Sallis and Marion Macfarlane. Special circumstances made it impossible for me to scrutinise the relationship of this English text to the German original. The few passages that came to my notice made it clear that the English version differs from the German text in more than mere nuances. I have nonetheless, bearing in mind the subject matter dealt with in the text, agreed to publication in its present form. Readers wishing to consult the German original may find it in Regina Busch, "Über die Transkription einer Skizzenseite von Anton Webern', *TEXTkritische Beiträge* 9 (2004) pp. 25–45.

1 Edgar Allan Poe, 'Marginalia – No V' [*Graham's Magazine*, March 1846], *Marginalia*, Charlottesville, University Press of Virginia, 1981, p. 98.
2 This would be true even if the material nature and the special features of script and writing material (colours, smells, consistency of paper, ink, pens, etc.) were to be copied in every detail and with all errors faithfully reproduced.
3 This observation does not refer to the transcription of pictograms into alphabetic script or to various types of transliteration. In this chapter we will examine the same repertoire of signs presented in different media (i.e. in manuscript, in print or via photographic processes).
4 Roland Reuß, 'Schicksal der Handschrift, Schicksal der Druckschrift. Notizen zur "Textgenese"', *Textkritische Beiträge* (Textgenese 1), 5 (1999), 16. For a definition of the term 'poetic text' see *ibid.*, 15. This and all subsequent quotations have been translated by Michael Graubart.
5 The speed with which a text is written will have different effects depending on the means used to produce the document. Rapidity and haste in typewritten texts often results in errors, whereas in handwritten texts the result is usually a sketchy and illegible script. In manuscript material misspellings occur far less frequently than garbled or slurred word-endings, the omission of parts of letters and incomplete punctuation.
6 Roland Reuß, 'Textkritische Editionen und Dateiformate. Notizen', *Jahrbuch für Computerphilologie*, ed. Volker Deubel, Karl Eibl and Fotis Jannidis, Paderborn: Mentis, 1999, pp. 101–6. The text is also available at http://www.textkritik.de/technik/formate.htm.

7 It should be noted that the work of a professional copyist can scarcely be distinguished from the printed version of the same text, and if differences do occur they usually concern letters rather than musical notation.

8 Pre-printed staff paper provides a 'justified' spatial framework in advance, which is then not always completely filled with written music. Moreover, what may seem justified in manuscript will not necessarily be justified in print.

9 Reuß, 'Textkritische Editionen und Dateiformate. Notizen', p. 102.

10 Among the published facsimiles there are a few exceptions, for example the pencil manuscript of *Aufblick* (without opus number) designated as *Partitur, Entwurf* (full score, draft) in Hans Moldenhauer, 'Excelsior! Die Genese des Webern-Archivs', *Komponisten des 20. Jahrhunderts in der Paul Sacher Stiftung*, ed. Hans Jörg Jans, Felix Meyer and Ingrid Westen, Basle: Paul Sacher Stiftung, 1986, pp. 130–47. The draft of the arrangement for two pianos of Schoenberg's Op. 16, presented in the same publication (p. 142) can hardly be classified as a sketch.

11 We can assume that Webern took great care in preparing the pagination and the graphic image (*Notenbild*) of his fair copies in accordance with various criteria, and occasionally brought this to the attention of close friends and associates, notably Hildegard Jone and Erwin Stein (for example, in the case of the printed score of the String Quartet, Op. 28). It is important that the empty staves indicating the silence of instruments be maintained throughout the score. This is particularly striking in the first movement of the Concerto, Op. 24, and has nothing to do with making the score appear longer or fuller. In the scores of Berg and Schoenberg, great care must also be taken with the details of the printed score (cf. the different editions, with and without the empty staves, of Berg's *Fünf Orchester-Lieder* [Five Orchestral Songs], Op. 4, the Chamber Concerto, or of Berg's and Schoenberg's violin concertos). Musicians know full well that the graphic image of the score can have an impact on technical and intellectual aspects of both the rehearsal and the performance of what has been notated.

12 Felix Meyer suspects that they may have been torn from notepads (conversation with the author).

13 Kathryn Bailey, 'Webern's Row Tables', *Webern Studies*, ed. Kathryn Bailey, Cambridge University Press, 1996, pp. 172 ff.

14 Felix Meyer, 'Anton Webern: Kinderstück M. 266, 1924', *Canto d'Amore: Classicism in Modern Art and Music 1914–1935*, ed. Gottffied Boehm, Ulrich Mosch and Katharina Schmidt, Basle: Kunstmuseum, 1996, pp. 356–7; Hans and Rosaleen Moldenhauer, *Anton von Webern. Chronik seines Lebens und Werks*, Zurich and Freiburg im Breisgau: Atlantis, 1980, pp. 280 ff.; Anne C. Shreffler, '"*Mein Weg geht jetzt vorüber*": The Vocal Origins of Webern's Twelve-tone Composition', *Journal of the American Musicological Society*, 47/2 (1994), 309–12.

15 The document is currently conserved at the Pierpont Morgan Library, New York, Robert Owen Lehman Collection, No. 115912 (32 pages).

16 The following account adopts the pagination of the Paul Sacher Foundation. The fifteen leaves in folder 49 include three sheets of sketches for Op. 16, numbered pages [1] to [6]. Even numbers have been placed at the bottom right, odd numbers to the left. We do not know which side of these sheets Webern considered recto and which verso.

17 The second attempt is almost identical with the final version. In the following pages, we also find the definitive version left unmarked in favour of a different later attempt. Drafts of bars 8–11 are found on all six pages. The formulations on page [6] are closest to the ones on page [3] (cf. also the cross-reference signs).

18 Webern interrupted work on Op. 16 No. 5 at the end of August 1924 because of other commitments (the first performance of his *Fünf geistige Lieder* [Five Sacred Songs], Op. 15, and rehearsals of Schoenberg's *Die glückliche Hand*, Op. 18, and Alexander Zemlinsky's String Quartet No. 3,

Op. 19). The fifth canon was completed two days after the first performance of the Zemlinsky quartet and it is quite possible that Webern had not yet begun to compose the first canon. According to his own statements, he was also working on the first song of the *Drei Volkstexte* (Three Folk Texts), Op. 17, and the *Kinderstücke* in the autumn of 1924.

19 The document is currently conserved at the Pierpont Morgan Library, New York, Robert Owen Lehman Collection, Nos. 11586 and 11587; the latter comes from the estate of Marya Freund.

20 'Now I want to work on something different.' Webern, in a letter to Berg written on 23 August 1923, and in a letter to Schoenberg written on 24 August 1923, cited in Moldenhauer, *Chronik*, p. 247.

21 The 'reverse' side of this page only contains sketches for Op. 16 No. 1, and also bears its own title.

22 The sketching procedure described by Ernst Krenek for the sketchbooks (verso sides are used to supplement or correct work done on the facing recto sides) may also apply to loose sheets. Thus later drafts may appear at an earlier point in a sketchbook or sheaf of sketches. Ernst Krenek, 'Commentary', in Hans Moldenhauer, *Anton von Webern: Sketches (1926–1945)*, New York: Carl Fischer, 1968, p. 2.

23 Felix Meyer adheres to this interpretation, inferring that the *Kinderstück* was drafted before Op. 16 No. 1 was completed on 12 November 1924. Meyer, 'Anton Webern: *Kinderstück*', p. 356.

24 In fact, there are ten bars all together. The third bar of the second system (staves 10–11) is circled, which, according to Anne Shreffler, signifies a deletion. Shreffler, '*Mein Weg*', 310; see also Meyer, 'Anton Webern: *Kinderstück*', p. 356. However, not all notes and passages that are to be deleted in Webern's sketches are encircled, and not everything that is encircled counts as a deletion.

25 Webern quoted in a letter to Emil Hertzka, *die Reihe*, 2. *Information über serielle Musik. Anton Webern*, 2nd edn, ed. Herbert Eimert, Vienna: Universal Edition, 1955, pp. 20 ff.

26 Moldenhauer, *Chronik*, p. 282. A facsimile of the fair copy (M. 267) is published in Meyer, 'Anton Webern: *Kinderstück*', p. 356. The piece was published under the title *Kinderstück* opus postumum, New York: Carl Fischer, 1967.

27 I believe that the piano piece entitled *Klavierstück* (Piano Piece), Op. posth. and bearing the heading *Im Tempo eines Menuetts* (In the tempo of a minuet) (M.277) (© Universal Edition 1966, U.E. No. 13490) from the first sketchbook, composed during the second half of July 1925, may also have been intended for the collection of children's pieces. In his letter to Hertzka, Webern only mentioned an interruption in the work. It is true that this piece is more difficult than the two known *Kinderstücke*. Nevertheless, both its piano texture and row technique resemble that of the *Kinderstücke*. The rows also show common features.

28 From here onwards, staves will be counted from the beginning of the *Kinderstück* sketches (see Plate 7.3).

29 Private communication from Felix Meyer; see also Plate 7.2.

30 See note 23 above.

31 Meyer, 'Anton Webern: *Kinderstück*', p. 356; Moldenhauer, *Chronik*, p. 282. On this point, Shreffler presents further arguments, resulting from her reconstruction of Webern's journey towards twelve-tone composition. Shreffler, '*Mein Weg*', 309–12.

32 See for instance the repeated resumptions of the initial rhythmic configuration, particularly in the second part of the draft; their similarity to the beginning of the first draft; the fermata on f#″ at the end of the last variant (staff 14); and the fermata on the same pitch near the beginning of the first draft (staff 3).

33 Arnold Schoenberg, *Aus einem Gutachten für die Akademie* (4.XII.1929; Mus [195]), Arnold Schönberg Center, Vienna, T 35.30 (facsimile and English translation in Leonard Stein, 'Schoenberg: Five Statements', *Perspectives of New Music*, 14 (Fall/Winter 1975), 172 ff.

8 A TALE OF TWO SKETCHBOOKS: RECONSTRUCTING AND DECIPHERING ALBAN BERG'S SKETCHBOOKS FOR *WOZZECK*

1 Alban Berg, *Letters to his Wife*, trans. Bernard Grun, New York: St Martin's Press, 1971, p. 229.

2 The ultimate source for reconstructing Beethoven's sketchbooks is of course D. Johnson, A. Tyson and R. Winter, *The Beethoven Sketchbooks: History, Reconstruction, Inventory*, Berkeley: University of California Press, 1985. J. Grier, *The Critical Editing of Music History: Method, and Practice*, Cambridge University Press, 1996 is invaluable for its explanation of terminology like pagination, foliation, etc.

3 Ernst Hilmar, *Wozzeck von Alban Berg*, Vienna: Universal Edition, 1975.

4 Peter Peterson, *Alban Berg: Wozzeck*, Munich: edition text + Kritik, 1985, pp. 77–80, and David Fanning, 'Berg's Sketches for *Wozzeck*: A Commentary and Inventory', *Journal of the Royal Musical Association*, 112 (1986–7), 285–8. Melchior von Borries and Donald McLean discuss F 21 Berg 13/II primarily in its relation to sketches for the *Marsch*, Opus 6/II, which appear in the first half of this sketchbook. See Melchior von Borries, *Alban Bergs Drei Orchesterstücke Op. 6 als ein Meisterwerk atonaler Symphonik*, Weimar: Verlag und Datenbank für Geisteswissenschaften, 1996, and Donald McLean, 'A Documentary and Analytical Study of Alban Berg's Three Pieces for Orchestra', Dissertation, University of Toronto, 1997.

5 Rosemary Hilmar, *Katalog der Musikhandschriften, Schriften und Studien Alban Berg im Fond Alban Berg*, Vienna: Univesal Edition, 1980.

6 My chronology of the sketchbook is based on a detailed examination of the source documents, and differs significantly from Peterson and Fanning. See Patricia Hall, 'The Inception of *Wozzeck*: 1914–18', forthcoming.

7 For a study of the reconstruction of a home-made sketchbook formed from cut leaves of large-format paper, see Patricia Hall, 'Two Sketches for Alban Berg's *Lulu*', *Music History from Primary Sources: A Guide to the Moldenhauer Archives*, ed. Jon Newsom and Alfred Mann, Washington: Library of Congress, 2000, pp. 115–20.

8 See also Ulrich Krämer's impressive study, *Alban Berg als Schüler Arnold Schoenberg*, Vienna: Universal Edition, 1996, in which he analyses Berg's paper types based on the orientation of the shield to the staff.

9 For some of Berg's sketchbooks, for instance ÖNB Musiksammlung F 21 Berg 65, neither shield nor 10-linig is present. However, the margins for the 'A' leaves are significantly different than those for the 'B' leaves.

10 The text for this letter appears in Juliane Brand and Christopher Hailey, *The Berg–Schoenberg Correspondence: Selected Letters*, New York: Norton, 1987, pp. 312–13.

11 Harald Küppers, *DuMont's Farbenatlas*, Cologne: DuMont Buchverlag, 1999.

12 See, for instance, Johnson, Tyson and Winter, *Beethoven Sketchbooks*, p. 136.

13 For instance, Harald Süss, *Deutsche Schreibschrift*, Augsburg: Augustus Verlag, 1995. See particularly his discussion of Kurrent and Sütterlin handwriting beginning on p. 51.

14 In this regard, I would like to again thank Professor Herwig Knaus, for generously checking my transcriptions and suggesting alternative readings. Martha Hyde made many valuable editing suggestions for the entire chapter.

9 'WRITTEN BETWEEN THE DESK AND THE PIANO': DATING BÉLA BARTÓK'S SKETCHES

1 Dezső Kosztolányi, Hungarian writer and poet, interviewed Bartók, see *Pesti Hírlap*, 31 May 1925.

2 See Plates 1, 4–5, 12, etc., in Anton von Webern, *Sketches (1926–1945)*, commentary by E. Krenek with a foreword by H. Moldenhauer, New York: Carl Fischer, 1968.

3 László Somfai, *Béla Bartók: Composition, Concepts, and Autograph Sources*, Berkeley: University of California Press, 1996, pp. 34, 69–78.

4 Bartók sent such pages for example to his wife Ditta with sketches for the first movement of the Sonata for Piano and Nos. 1–2 of *Outdoors* in summer 1926, cf. Somfai, *Béla Bartók,* p. 48, and facsimiles in Somfai, *Tizennyolc Bartók-tanulmány* (Eighteen Bartók Studies), Budapest: Zeneműkiadó, 1981, pp. 73–4.

5 Somfai, *Béla Bartók,* pp. 35–7.

6 These 125×170 mm notebooks were printed by J. Eberle in Vienna (trademark No. 70) and sold in Budapest. For a survey of the music papers used in Bartók's manuscripts see Somfai, *Béla Bartók*, p. 97.

7 The Budapest Bartók Archive keeps fifteen such field-books, the American estate (Peter Bartók's collection) two more.

8 Among the manuscript pages of the Harvard Lectures (1943) there is a sketchy plan of the topics. The last lecture, one that Bartók, due to his sudden illness, could not write, was planned to discuss the 'General spirit (connected with folk music)': see Somfai, *Béla Bartók*, p. 15.

9 For a diplomatic transcription see Somfai, 'Bartók vázlatok II.' (Bartók sketches II), *Zenetudományi Dolgozatok*, Budapest: MTA Zenetudományi Intézet, 1985, pp. 30–5.

10 According to a letter to Michel-Dimitri Calvocoressi, 24 September 1921, Bartok was unsure whether playing with Jelly in England would be professionally advantageous for him; shortly after this he met her in Budapest. Adrienne Gombocz and László Somfai, 'Bartók Briefe an Calvocoressi (1914–1930)', *Studia Musicologica*, 24 (1982), pp. 204, 208. The Arányis left the Hungarian capital on 6 October, see Joseph Todd Gordon Macleod, *The Sisters d'Arányi*, London: Allen & Unwin, 1969, p. 137.

11 Béla Bartók Jr., *Bartók Béla családi levelei* (Béla Bartók's family letters), ed. A. Gombocz-Konkoly, Budapest: Zeneműkiadó, 1981, p. 325.

12 Cf. the Sotheby auction catalogue, 15/16 May 1967, 112 (the original Hungarian text is unavailable; the translation is not authenticated).

13 The printed rehearsal numbers are not above a whole bar but above the bar-line, therefore we mark, for example, the second bar after no. 2 not as 2^{+1} but 2^{+2}.

14 Due to the $\frac{6}{8}$ time and the melodic contour, in spite of the different pitch level and different chords, there is a certain resemblance between this idea and the two *calmandosi* bars before no. 13 in the second movement.

15 BB 28 Sonata for Piano and Violin 1903 (*BB* is the abbreviation of the work numbers in Somfai, *Béla Bartók Thematic Catalogue*, in preparation).

16 Somfai, *Béla Bartók*, pp. 60–1.

17 See the facsimile of the two pages and the explanation of the sketching process in Somfai, *Béla Bartók*, pp. 71–4.

18 A scientific examination of ink-types and colours based on the use of a multi-graded colour scale as suggested by John Arthur for Mozart studies, see Arthur, 'Some Chronological Problems in Mozart: The Contribution of Ink-Studies', *Wolfgang Amadè Mozart: Essays on his Life and his Music*, ed. Stanley Sadie, Oxford: Clarendon Press, 1996, pp. 35–52, seems to be out of proportion in the case of Bartók. Different colours of inks can easily be distinguished and described; the meaning of fine nuances of shades of the same fountain-pen ink can be explained only subjectively.

19 See Béla Bartók Jr., *Apám életének krónikája* (The chronicle of my father's life), Budapest: Zeneműkiadó, 1981.

20 See Bartók's correspondence with his publishers (Universal Edition Vienna; Boosey & Hawkes London and New York); the indexed version of this huge and mostly unpublished material is on computer in the Budapest Bartók Archive.

21 See Somfai, *Béla Bartók*, pp. 56–61.

22 See the 11 July 1919 unpublished letter in which Bartók informed Universal Edition that he finished the one-act pantomime 'in sketches'.

23 See Bartók's 30 March 1920 unpublished letter to Universal Edition.

24 See Bartók's 18 April 1920 unpublished letter to Universal Edition.

25 See Direktor Hertzka's 27 August 1920 letter to Bartók (the proofs of *Three Studies* were sent two weeks before) and Bartók's 1 September 1920 unpublished letter to Universal Edition (he sent the proofs back on that day).

26 See Bartók's 26 March 1921 unpublished letter to Universal Edition.

27 See Bartók's 20 August 1921 unpublished letter to Universal Edition.

28 See, in detail, László Somfai, 'Progressive Music via Peasant Music? Revisiting the Sources of Bartók's Style and Compositional Process', *The Past in the Present*, Proceedings of the IMS Inter-congressional Symposium and the 10th Meeting of the Cantus Planus, Budapest & Viségrad, 2000, ed. László Dobszay, Budapest: Liszt Ferenc Academy of Music, 2003, pp. 499–513.

29 The outlines of the sonata form of the first movement: exposition (up to No. 10), development (Nos. 10–20), recapitulation (from No. 20). In the exposition, the primary theme area is a complex section including a return of a variant of the opening theme (one of Bartók's favourite strategies, see, for example, Piano Concerto No. 1): violin theme; waltz-rhythm transition theme (from 2^{-6}); *vivo* variant of the opening violin theme (from 4); syncopated-rhythm transition theme (from 5^{+2}). The secondary theme area includes the arpeggiando *Sostenuto* (from 6) and the *Vivo appassionato* piano theme (from 7). The closing theme area (from 8), dominated by the piano, has an *agitato* theme (with *sul ponticello* accompaniment) and a *sostenuto* (with *quasi-trillo* figure in the violin).

30 Following Alistair Wightman's essay, 'Szymanowski, Bartók and the Violin', *Musical Times*, 122 (1981), 159–63, Malcolm Gillies reopened the case in 'Stylistic Integrity and Influence in Bartók's Works: The Case of Szymanowski', *International Journal of Musicology*, 1 (1992), 139–60. Based on a minute examination of circumstantial evidence and picked-up textural details of the music, Gillies seriously questions the stylistic integrity of the First Sonata, and discusses the dropping of the opus number and the belated publication as a possible consequence of Bartók's 'embarrassment and guilt towards Szymanowski', suppositions which the present writer cannot share.

10 DEFINING COMPOSITIONAL PROCESS: IDEA AND INSTRUMENTATION IN IGOR STRAVINSKY'S *RAGTIME* (1918) AND *PRIBAOUTKI* (1915)

Translated by Friedemann Sallis

1 Igor Stravinsky, cited in Hermann Danuser, *Gustav Mahler und seine Zeit*, Laaber Verlag, 1991, p. 54.

2 Igor Stravinsky, *Poétique musicale sous forme de six leçons*, Cambridge, Mass.: Harvard University Press, 1979; English trans., Igor Stravinsky, *Poetics of Music in the Form of Six Lessons*, trans. Arthur Knodel and Ingolf Dahl, Cambridge, Mass.: Harvard University Press, 1979.

3 Hans Jörg Jans, 'Strawinskys Musik und ihr Schrift-Bild', *Strawinsky. Sein Nachlass. Sein Bild*, Basle: Kunstmuseum, 1984, pp. 23–32.

4 Best known among these is Igor Stravinsky and Robert Craft, *The Rite of Spring: Sketches 1911–1913*, London: Boosey & Hawkes, 1969. After the composer's death in 1971, a number of

facsimile editions were published: for example, Igor Stravinsky, *L'oiseau de feu: fac-similé du manuscrit Saint-Pétersbourg 1909/1910*, ed. Louis Cyr, Geneva: Minkoff, 1985.

5 See, for instance, Barry Cooper, *Beethoven and the Creative Process*, Oxford: Clarendon Press, 1990.

6 This isolated remark was noted by Sibelius in Swedish. Jean Sibelius, 'Diary 1909–1943', Jean Sibelius Collection, Helsinki, The National Archives of Finland.

7 Lindberg's remarks on this subject are recorded in Tomi Mäkelä, 'Viewpoints on Orchestration – Talks about Texture', *Finnish Musical Quarterly*, 3 (1992), 45.

8 Joseph Kerman, *Concerto Conversations*, Cambridge, Mass.: Harvard University Press, 1999, pp. 89–90.

9 Volker Scherliess, *Igor Strawinsky und seine Zeit*, Laaber Verlag, 1983, p. 139. Comparing Stravinsky's music and Eisenstein's films can produce plausible results as long as we ignore the contrary political opinions which underlie their works.

10 Edward T. Cone, 'Stravinsky: The Progress of a Method', *Perspectives of New Music*, 1/1 (1962), 18–26.

11 Gretchen Horlacher, 'Sketches and Superimposition in Stravinsky's *Symphony of Psalms*', *Mitteilungen der Paul Sacher Stiftung*, 12 (1999), 22–6.

12 Roman Ingarden, *Das literarische Kunstwerk: eine Untersuchung aus dem Grenzgebiet der Ontologie, Logik und Literaturwissenschaft*, Halle: Niemeyer, 1931.

13 Carl Gustav Jung, among others, speaks of 'extroversive' and 'introversive' art. Jolande Jacobi, *The Psychology of C. G. Jung*, New Haven: Yale University Press, 1962, pp. 23–4. See also the idea of 'extroversive semiosis' in Kofi Agawu, *Playing with Signs: A Semiotic Interpretation of Classical Music*, Princeton University Press, 1991.

14 Performers also sketch their 'artistic production' (interpretations and improvisations) and often alter melodic details. The creative process begun by the composer is thus prolonged in a dynamic dialogue and the composition achieves its final form through a 'second hand'. Thanks to an increased interest in the art of interpretation in general and a tendency to consider the sound of a composition in performance as the true form in which music exists, performers' notes and working documents are currently perceived as being historically relevant sources of information.

15 For more on this subject see Tomi Mäkelä, *Virtuosität und Werkcharakter. Eine analytische und theoretische Untersuchung zur Virtuosität in den Klavierkonzerten der Hochromantik*, Berliner musikwissenschaftliche Arbeiten 37, ed. Carl Dahlhaus and Rudolf Stephan, Munich: Katzbichler, 1989.

16 Rainer Cadenbach, *Max Reger und seine Zeit*, Laaber Verlag, 1991, p. 203; and Tomi Mäkelä, '"Verunglückt auf der Reise". Das "Erste Concert" (Fragment) von Max Reger mit Blick auf sein Klavierkonzert opus 114', *Musikalische Moderne und Tradition*, ed. Alexander Becker, Gabriele Gefäller and Susanne Popp, Wiesbaden: Breitkopf & Härtel, 2000, pp. 37–54.

17 Theodor Adorno underlined this point when he wrote during his years of exile that 'the only works which really count are those which are no longer works at all'. Theodor Adorno, *Philosophy of Modern Music*, trans. Anne G. Mitchell and Wesley V. Blomster, New York: Seabury Press, 1973, p. 30.

18 The Swedish recording company BIS recently decided to prepare a complete commercial edition of Jean Sibelius's unfinished pieces, fragments and even early versions of major works such as the Fifth Symphony and the Violin Concerto, which the composer had explicitly withdrawn but forgotten to destroy. Interesting as these documents may be for the analyst, they will do little to help the Sibelius-enthusiast when arguing with the mean-spirited critic.

19 Arnold Whittall, 'Music Analysis as Human Science? Le Sacre du Printemps in Theory and Practice', *Music Analysis*, 1/1 (1982), 33–5.

20 Max Weber, *Die rationalen und soziologischen Grundlagen der Musik*, Tübingen: J. C. B. Mohr, 1972; English trans., Max Weber, *The Rational and Social Foundations of Music*, Carbondale: Southern Illinois University Press, 1958.

21 This situation explains in part the marked increase, during the second half of the twentieth century, of facsimile publications of the autograph fair copy.

22 Tomi Mäkelä, 'Comprehending Chromaticism: Structural Semantics in Anton Webern's *Wiese im Park* Op. 13 No. 1', *Hudební Veda a Výchova* 8, Acta Universitas Palackianæ Olomucenisis Facultas Pædagogica, Musica VI, Olomouc: Univerzita Palackého v Olomouci, 2000, pp. 95 ff.

23 Nicolai Rimsky-Korsakov, *Grundlagen der Orchestration mit Notenbeispielen aus eigenen Werken*, trans. Alexandr Elukhen, Berlin: Russischer Musikverlag, 1922.

24 Igor Glebow (alias Boris Asaf'yev), *Kniga a Stravinskom* (Leningrad: Triton, 1929); in English, Boris Asaf'yev, *A Book About Stravinsky*, Russian Music Studies 5 trans. Richard F. French, Ann Arbor: University of Michigan Press, 1982, p. 80.

25 *Ibid.*

26 For a more detailed examination of this point see Tomi Mäkelä, 'Die Konfigurierung des Klanges. Die Angaben zur Instrumentation von *Ragtime* für elf Instrumente und *Pribaoutki* in Igor Strawinskys Skizzen', *Mitteilungen der Paul Sacher Stiftung*, 13 (2000), 26–32.

27 Taking account of the number of staves in Stravinsky's sketches is not a simple task. Early in his career, the composer invented the Stravigor, a small, five-track set of wheels, which, when dipped in ink, could be rolled over empty paper, creating staves. The instrument allowed him a more flexible use of paper, which during World War I became quite expensive. Later, this flexibility would become a hallmark of the composer's published scores; see *Movements* for piano and orchestra, 1958–9.

28 Using the latest developments in criminology, these documents can now be reconstructed.

11 FLOATING HIERARCHIES: ORGANISATION AND COMPOSITION IN WORKS BY PIERRE BOULEZ AND KARLHEINZ STOCKHAUSEN DURING THE 1950S

Translated by Friedemann Sallis and John Boulay

1 For a general description of the development of serial music from the early 1950s to the mid-1960s, see Pascal Decroupet, 'Konzepte serieller Musik', *Im Zenit der Moderne. Die Internationalen Ferienkurse für Neue Musik Darmstadt 1946–1966*, ed. Gianmario Borio and Hermann Danuser, Freiburg im Breisgau: Rombach, 1997, pp. 285–425. The present chapter is based on archival research undertaken principally at the Paul Sacher Foundation in Basle, which I would like to thank for its generous assistance.

2 Boulez began asserting the necessity of distinguishing between strict and free writing techniques in serial music as early as 1954. Pierre Boulez, '. . . Near and Far', *Stocktakings from an Apprenticeship*, trans. Stephen Walsh, Oxford: Clarendon Press, 1991, pp. 150–1. For the original text, see Pierre Boulez, '. . . auprès et au loin', *Relevés d'apprenti*, Paris: Seuil, 1966, pp. 194–5.

3 In mathematics, a function is defined as a relation or an expression involving one or more variables.

4 Boulez, *The Boulez–Cage Correspondence*, ed. Jean-Jacques Nattiez, trans. and ed. Robert Samuels, Cambridge University Press, 1993, p. 102.

5 Among the many documents on *Structures I*, see in particular György Ligeti, 'Pierre Boulez. Entscheidung und Automatik in der Structure Ia', *die Reihe*, 4 (Vienna: Universal Edition, 1958), 38–63; Marc Wilkinson, 'Pierre Boulez *Structure Ia*. Bemerkungen zur Zwölfton-Technik', *Gravesaner Blätter*, 4/10 (1958), 12–29; Robert Piencikowski, 'Nature morte avec guitare', *Pierre*

Boulez. Eine Festschrift zum 60. Geburtstag am 26. März 1985, ed. Josef Häusler, Vienna: Universal Edition, 1985, pp. 66–81.

6 Boulez, '. . . Near and Far', *Stocktakings*, p. 153; Boulez, '. . . auprès et au loin', *Relevés d'apprenti*, p. 198.

7 Pierre Boulez, *Boulez on Music Today*, trans. Susan Bradshaw and Richard Rodney Bennett, Cambridge, Mass.: Harvard University Press, 1971, p. 40. For the original text, see Pierre Boulez, *Penser la musique aujourd'hui*, Geneva: Gonthier, 1964, p. 41.

8 Georg Friedrich Haas, 'Disziplin oder Indisziplin? Anmerkungen zu der von Ulrich Mosch veröffentlichten Reihentabelle von Pierre Boulez', *Musiktheorie*, 5/3 (1990), 271–3. This article was published in response to Ulrich Mosch, 'Disziplin und Indisziplin. Zum seriellen Komponieren im 2. Satz des *Marteau sans maître* von Pierre Boulez', *Musiktheorie*, 5/1 (1990), 39–66.

9 The last line of the table in Example 11.3 contains the number 2 twice. The one in square brackets is correct in relation to the system. The one in parentheses results from a displacement towards the left instead of towards the right, an error contained in Boulez's sketch as reproduced by Mosch.

10 The serial forms used at the beginning of the sixth movement are the lines 2-6-4R-10-8R-11-3R respectively. The particular intersections are between 6 and 4R, with a shared Bb and D, and between 11 and 3R (beginning of the first vocal intervention) with a shared Bb.

11 Pascal Decroupet, 'Renverser la vapeur . . . Zu Musikdenken und Kompositionen von Boulez aus den fünfziger Jahren', *Musik-Konzepte*, 89/90 (1995), 112–31.

12 Elena Ungeheuer, 'Statistical Gestalts – Perceptible Features in Serial Music', *Music, Gestalt, and Computing*, ed. Marc Leman, Berlin: Springer, 1997, pp. 103–13.

13 Karlheinz Stockhausen, 'Gruppenkomposition: Klavierstück I (Anleitung zum Hören)', *Texte 1*, Cologne: DuMont, 1963, p. 63.

14 On the subject of frequency multiplication, see Boulez, 'Possibly . . .', *Stocktakings*, pp. 128–9; Boulez, 'Eventuellement . . .', *Relevés d'apprenti*, p. 168; Boulez, *Boulez on Music Today*, pp. 79–80; Boulez, *Penser la musique*, pp. 88–9; Josef Häusler, 'Klangfelder und Formflächen. Kompositorische Grundprinzipien im II. Band der *Structures* von Pierre Boulez', text accompanying the record Wergo 60011 (1965); Lev Koblyakov, 'Pierre Boulez: *Le marteau sans maître* – Analysis of the Pitch Structure', *Zeitschrift für Musiktheorie*, 8/1 (1977), 24–39; Lev Koblyakov, *Pierre Boulez: A World of Harmony*, Contemporary Music Studies 2, Chur: Harwood Academic Publishers, 1990.

15 Boulez, 'Stravinsky Remains', *Stocktakings*, p. 61; Boulez, 'Stravinsky demeure', *Relevés d'apprenti*, p. 83.

16 Boulez, 'Possibly . . .', *Stocktakings*, pp. 128–9; Boulez, 'Eventuellement . . .', *Relevés d'apprenti*, p. 168 (see Example XII); see also Koblyakov, 'Pierre Boulez: *Le marteau sans maître*', pp. 24–5, and Koblyakov, *Pierre Boulez: A World of Harmony*, pp. 4–6.

17 As noted above, within these limits the composer retains control over numerous aspects of the compositional process: the vertical disposition of the harmonic specificities of a given cell, the order of pitch succession within a given cell, the subdivision of global values of duration and the addition of grace notes.

18 In total, three errors in pitch appear in the Philharmonia pocket edition, at bars 8, 36 and 37 respectively. The pencil manuscript conserved at the Paul Sacher Foundation contains only the deviation at bar 8. The facsimile edition prepared by Universal Edition for the Donaueschinger Musiktage 1954, where the work should have been premièred, corresponds to the previously finished first ink manuscript and contains an error at bar 37 (the semiquaver sounding E instead of Eb as it should). This same error is included in the first printed edition (UE 12450, 1956). The Philharmonia edition then adds a further error at bar 36 (the grace note in the flute part sounding E instead of Eb).

19 *Antiphonie* is one of the three movements of the Third Piano Sonata that remain unpublished to this day. The present analysis is based on documents conserved in the Boulez Collection at the Paul Sacher Foundation. Two distinct versions of *Zeitmaße* exist. The first was made up of three structural parts (A–B–C); in the second version, Stockhausen cut up this initial structure by adding four sections, here called inserts (in accordance with the composer's own terminology). The published version of the score is thus divided as follows: A (bars 1–28); insert 1 (29–40); B1 (41–72); insert 2 (73–103); B2 (104–152); insert 3 (153–206); B3 (207–229); insert 4a (230–265); B4 (266–271); C1 (272–274); insert 4b (275–289); C2 (290–352).

20 Boulez, *Boulez on Music Today*, pp. 81–2; Boulez, *Penser la musique*, pp. 91–2.

21 Boulez, *Boulez on Music Today*, p. 135; Boulez, *Penser la musique*, p. 157.

22 At the beginning of the 1980s, Stockhausen published the sketches and manuscripts of his works from *Kreuzspiel* to *Momente* in a limited photocopy edition. Partial and complete copies of this edition are accessible in libraries and other institutions. The present research has been made on the basis of the complete copy, housed at Paul Sacher Foundation. For a detailed analysis of *Gesang der Jünglinge* based on the sketches, see Pascal Decroupet and Elena Ungeheuer, 'Through the Sensory Looking-Glass: The Aesthetic and Serial Foundations of *Gesang der Jünglinge*', *Perspectives of New Music*, 36/1 (1998), 97–142.

23 The spelling of pitches follows the sketches. For graphic reasons, Stockhausen chose to use only sharps in the printed score.

24 For a detailed analysis of *Zeitmaße*, based on the sketch material, see Pascal Decroupet, 'Une genèse, une œuvre, une pensée musicale – en mouvement. *Zeitmaße* de Karlheinz Stockhausen', *Revue belge de musicologie*, 52 (1998), 347–61.

25 Boulez, *Boulez on Music Today*, pp. 104–6; Boulez, *Penser la musique*, pp. 120–3.

26 Boulez, *Boulez on Music Today*, p. 35; Boulez, *Penser la musique*, p. 35.

12 ELLIOTT CARTER'S SKETCHES: SPIRITUAL EXERCISES AND CRAFTSMANSHIP

Translated by Friedemann Sallis and John Boulay

1 Unpublished letter addressed to Jonathan Bernard, dated 7 January 1982 and conserved in the Elliott Carter Collection of the Paul Sacher Foundation.

2 Jonathan Bernard, 'An Interview with Elliott Carter', *Perspectives of New Music*, 28/2 (1990), 205.

3 Allen Edwards, *Flawed Words and Stubborn Sounds: A Conversation with Elliott Carter*, New York: Norton, 1971, p. 108.

4 Elliott Carter, Harmony Book, conserved in the Elliott Carter Collection at the Paul Sacher Foundation. The document has recently been published: Elliot Carter, *Harmony Book*, ed. Nicholas Hopkins and John F. Link, New York: Carl Fischer, 2002.

5 Elliott Carter cited in Edwards, *Flawed Words*, p. 86.

6 In the definitive version of *A Mirror on Which to Dwell*, Carter reduced the number of songs to six and changed the order.

13 E-SKETCHES: BRIAN FERNEYHOUGH'S USE OF COMPUTER-ASSISTED COMPOSITIONAL TOOLS

1 David Schiff, 'A Paper Mountain: Eliott Carter's Sketches', *Settling New Scores: Music Manuscripts from the Paul Sacher Foundation*, ed. Felix Meyer, Mainz: Schott Musik International, 1998, p. 115.

2 See Ross Feller, *Multicursal Labyrinths in the Work of Brian Ferneyhough*, Ann Arbor: UMI Dissertation Services, 1994; and Feller, 'Strategic Defamiliarization: The Process of Difficulty in Brian Ferneyhough's Music', *The Open Space*, 2 (Spring 2000), 197–202.

3 Ross Feller, 'Elevated Bug Fixing: Brian Ferneyhough in Conversation with Ross Feller', forthcoming.

4 See Paul Griffiths, 'Interview with Paul Griffiths', *Brian Ferneyhough: Collected Writings*, ed. James Boros and Richard Toop, Amsterdam: Harwood Academic Publishers, 1995, p. 242.

5 Richard Toop, 'Interview with Richard Toop', *Brian Ferneyhough: Collected Writings*, p. 255.

6 Feller, 'Elevated Bug Fixing'.

7 *Ibid.*

8 Palimpsest, derived from the Greek word *palimpsëstos* meaning to rub, or rubbed again, generally signifies a kind of writing whereby an 'original' text has been partially erased or written over by another text. The first text usually leaves only a faint trace. Ferneyhough seems to have used this process in *Lemma-Icon-Epigram* and in various unpublished poems, one of which is book-length in size and entitled, *Palimpsests*.

9 Email to the author, 19 April 2001.

10 Letter to the author, 22 June 1996.

11 Email to the author, 19 April 2001.

12 *Ibid.*

13 Brian Ferneyhough, 'Temporal Patterning and Process Mapping', Paris, paper read at IRCAM, 1996.

14 Feller, 'Elevated Bug Fixing'.

15 *Ibid.*

16 Email to the author, 1 May 2001.

17 Richard Toop, 'On Complexity', *Perspectives of New Music*, 31/1 (Winter 1993), 54.

14   JOHN CAGE'S *WILLIAMS MIX* (1951–3): THE RESTORATION AND
     NEW REALISATIONS OF AND VARIATIONS ON THE FIRST
     OCTOPHONIC, SURROUND-SOUND TAPE COMPOSITION

* Commissioned by the International Institute for Electroacoustic Music, Bourges, France, with sponsorship and support from the John Cage Trust and C. F. Peters Corporation.

1 Richard Kostelanetz, *John Cage (Ex)plain(ed)*, New York: Schirmer Books, 1996, pp. 72–5.

2 The other tape pieces were, in order of completion, *Imaginary Landscape No. 5* (Jan. 1952) by John Cage; *For Magnetic Tape* (1952) by Christian Wolff; *Octet* (1953) by Earle Brown; and *Intersection* (1953, withdrawn) by Morton Feldman.

3 The original manuscripts, which I have studied, are housed in the American Music Section of the Lincoln Center Library branch of the New York City Public Library.

4 Larry Austin, *Williams [re]Mix[ed]*, New York: C. F. Peters Corp., 2001.

5 Cage stated in various interviews and writings that he had collected and drawn from a library of 500 to 600 sounds; the actual number of different recorded sounds used in the Cage score for *Williams Mix* is 350, their iterations totalling 2,128.

6 Richard Kostelanetz, *Conversing with Cage*, New York: Limelight Editions, 1988, pp. 161–2.

7 Jean-Jacques Nattiez (ed.), *The Boulez–Cage Correspondence*, Cambridge University Press, 1993, p. 130.

8 The first piece Cage completed in the Project – also the first tape piece he had ever composed – was *Imaginary Landscape No. 5* (1951–Jan. 1952, four minutes' duration), 'a score for making a [monaural] recording on tape, using as material any 43 phonograph records'. Cage further

described the score and tape realisation of *Imaginary Landscape No. 5*: 'Each graph unit equals three inches of tape (15 ips). Differences of amplitude (1–8) are given. The rhythmic structure is 5 times 5. The composing means involved chance operations derived from the I Ching. The recording on magnetic tape used in the first performances was made by the composer and David Tudor with the technical assistance of Louis and Bebe Barron.' ('Notes on Compositions II' (1950–63), from *John Cage: Writer*, selected and introduced by Richard Kostelanetz, New York: Limelight Editions, 1993, p. 52.)

9 Joel Chadabe, *Electric Sound*, Upper Saddle River, NJ: Prentice-Hall, 1997, pp. 54–5.

10 Nattiez (ed.), *Boulez–Cage Correspondence*, p. 130.

11 Richard Kostelanetz (ed.), *John Cage: An Anthology*, New York: Da Capo, 1970, pp. 18–19.

12 John Cage, *Williams Mix*, New York: Henmar Press, 1960.

13 'I Ching' means 'truth of change', its creation originating from the Chinese Zhou I dynasty (1122–221 BC). Developed by the ancient sages Fu Xi and King Wen and later refined and commented on by the Duke of Zhou and Confucius, the *I Ching* was brought to a high level through over 3,000 years. The commentaries that are associated with each of the 64 *gua* are consulted for the divination of what one should or should not do, their purpose to resolve doubt and confusion. The main theme of the *I Ching* is that everything is in a process of continuous change, rising and falling in a progressive evolutionary advancement. Alfred Huang, *The Complete I Ching*, Rochester, Vermont: Inner Traditions, 1998.

14 George Avakian, producer, *The 25-year Retrospective Concert of the Music of John Cage*, Mainz, Wergo compact disc, WER 6247-2, 1994, 53–4.

15 Inked page 5 was used as an illustration in the programme notes for *Williams Mix* for Cage's 25-year retrospective concert on 15 May 1958.

16 Nattiez (ed.) *Boulez–Cage Correspondence*, 130.

17 *Ibid.*, p. 142.

18 My restored, synchronised ADAT version of *Williams Mix* is now available for performance rental as part of the Edition Peters catalogue from the C. F. Peters Corporation, New York.

19 Kostelanetz, *John Cage (Ex)plain(ed)*, pp. 72–5.

20 Untranscribed portion of the 1966 Kostelanetz recorded interview of Cage, which I transcribed in its entirety.

21 Ed Kobrin, 'I Ching', Davis, California, *Source*, Composer/Performer Edition 7/4-2 (1970), 1–7.

22 Larry Austin, John Cage, Lejaren Hiller, 'HPSCHD', Davis, California, *Source*, 4/2-2 (1968), 12–13.

23 Austin's personal composition journal, 2 March 1998 to 4 June 1999.

24 *Ibid.*

25 Austin's personal composition journal, 4 June 1999 to 3 September 2000.

26 A compact disc recording of *Williams [re] Mix[ed]* has been produced and released by the Electronic Music Foundation, EMF CD 039.

27 Chadabe, *Electric sound*, p. 57.

28 Nattiez (ed.), *Boulez–Cage Correspondence*, p. 142.

29 *Ibid.*, 131.

30 Joan Retallack (ed.), *MUSICAGE: Cage Muses on Words, Art, Music*, Hanover and London: Wesleyan University Press, 1996, pp. 93–4.

31 *Ibid.*

32 *Williams Mix* was only Cage's first 'mix' of a 'library of sounds'. Others followed with other collections – mixes – using other sources, other means of collection: *Fontana Mix* (1958), *Rozart Mix* (1965), *Newport Mix* (1967), *Instances of Silence* (1982), and so on.

33 It is interesting to note here that I detected no 'backwards' sounds in *Williams Mix*. This means both that Cage and Brown always cut from the proper end of the tape, that is the head, and that the Barrons never prepared any 'backwards' sounds for the library, nor were any notated in the score.

34 I imagine that such remaining short cuttings of tape segments left in the envelopes, once 'part 1' of *Williams Mix* was completed, became the material that Brown and Cage used subsequently in Brown's *Octet*.

35 Larry Austin, 'Accidents' (including *Source* Record, No. 1), Davis, California, *Source*, 4/2-2 (1968), 20–2.

36 Nattiez (ed.), *Boulez–Cage Correspondence*, p. 143.

37 John Cage, 'Four Musicians at Work', *Trans Formation: Arts, Communication, Environment: A World Review*, 1/3 (1952), p. 172.

38 Larry Austin, 'The Realization and First Complete Performances of Ives's Universe Symphony', *Ives Studies*, ed. Philip Lambert, Cambridge University Press, 1997, pp. 215–16.

APPENDIX: SELECT LIST OF COMPOSER INSTITUTES

1 Hans Jörg Jans, 'Preface', *The Future in the Present: Composer Institutes in the 21st Century*, ed. Graham Lack, Munich: Orff-Zentrum, 2000, unpaginated.

Select bibliography

Adorno, Theodor W., *Philosophy of Modern Music*, trans. Anne G. Mitchell and Wesley V. Blomster, New York: Seabury Press, 1973

Agawu, Kofi, *Playing with Signs*: *A Semiotic Interpretation of Classical Music*, Princeton University Press, 1991

American National Standard. Permanence of Paper for Publications and Documents in Libraries and Archives, Bethesda: NISO Press, 1993

Arthur, John, 'Some Chronological Problems in Mozart: The Contribution of Ink-Studies', *Wolfgang Amadè Mozart: Essays on his Life and his Music*, ed. Stanley Sadie, Oxford: Clarendon Press, 1996

Asaf'yev, Boris (Igor Glebow), *Kniga a Stravinskom*, Leningrad: Tritor, 1929; in English, Boris Asaf'yev, *A Book About Stravinsky*, Russian Music Studies 5, trans. Richard F. French, Ann Arbor: University of Michigan Press, 1982

Austin, Larry, 'Accidents' (including Source Record, No. 1, 1968), *Source, 4/2-2* (1968), 20–3
    'The Realization and First Complete Performances of Ives's *Universe Symphony*', *Ives Studies*, ed. Philip Lambert, Cambridge University Press, 1997, pp. 179–232
    Williams [re]Mix[ed], New York: C. F. Peters Corporation, 2001

Austin, Larry, John Cage and Lejaren Hiller, 'HPSCHD', *Source*, 4/2-2 (1968), 10–19

Avakian, George (producer), *The 25-year Retrospective Concert of the Music of John Cage*, Mainz: Wergo compact disc, WER 6247-2, 1994

Bailey, Kathryn (ed.), *Webern Studies*, Cambridge University Press, 1996

Bansa, Helmut, *et al.* (eds.), *Dauerhaftigkeit von Papier. Vorträge des 4. Internationalen Graphischen Restauratorentages*, Zeitschrift für Bibliothekswesen und Bibliographie Sonderheft 31, Frankfurt am Main: Vittorio Klostermann Verlag, 1980

Bartók, Jr., Béla, *Apám életének krónikája* [The chronicle of my father's life], Budapest: Zeneműkiadó, 1981

Bartók Jr., Béla, and A. Gombocz-Konkoly (eds.), *Bartók Béla családi levelei* [Béla Bartók's family letters], Budapest: Zeneműkiadó, 1981

Beckles Willson, Rachel, *György Kurtág: The Sayings of Peter Bornemisza Op. 7 (1963–68)*, Aldershot: Ashgate, 2003

Benary, Peter, 'Skizze – Entwurf – Fragment', *Die Musik in Geschichte und Gegenwart: allgemeine Enzyklopädie der Musik, Sachteil*, vol. 8, ed. L. Finscher, Kassel: Bärenreiter Metzler, 1994– , pp. 1506–19

Benjamin, Walter, *The Origin of the German Tragic Drama*, trans. John Osborne, London: Verso, 1998
    'The Task of the Translator: An Introduction to the Translation of Baudelaire's *Tableaux parisiens*', *Illuminations*, ed. Hannah Arendt, trans. Harry Zohn, New York: Schocken Books, 1969

Berg, Alban, *Letters to his Wife*, trans. Bernard Grun, New York: St Martin's Press, 1971

Berio, Luciano, 'Requies (1984)', booklet to *Luciano Berio: World Premiere Recordings*: *Requies – Voci – Corale*, London Sinfonietta, cond. Berio, RCA Victor, Red Seal RD87898. © BMG Music

Bernard, Jonathan W., 'An Interview with Elliott Carter', *Perspectives of New Music*, 28/2 (1990), 180–214

Boehm, Gottfried, 'Prekäre Balance', *Cézanne Vollendet Unvollendet*, ed. F. Baumann *et al.*, Zurich: Kunsthaus, 2000, pp. 29–39

Borio, Gianmario, 'Sull'interazione fra la studio degli schizzi e l'analisi dell'opera', *La nuova ricerca sull'opera di Luigi Nono*, ed. Gianmario Borio, Giovanni Morelli and Veniero Rizzardi, Venice: Leo S. Olschki, 1999, pp. 1–21

Borio, Gianmario and Hermann Danuser (eds.), *Im Zenit der Moderne. Die Internationalen Ferienkurse für Neue Musik Darmstadt 1946–1966*, Freiburg im Breisgau: Rombach, 1997

Borries, Melchior von, *Alban Bergs Drei Orchesterstücke Op. 6 als ein Meisterwerk atonaler Symphonik*, Weimar: Verlag und Datenbank für Geisteswissenschaften, 1996

Boulez, Pierre, *Penser la musique aujourd'hui*, Geneva: Gonthier, 1964; English translation, Pierre Boulez, *Boulez on Music Today*, trans. Susan Bradshaw and Richard Rodney Bennett, Cambridge Mass.: Harvard University Press, 1971

    Relevés d'apprenti, Paris: Seuil, 1966; English translation, Pierre Boulez, *Stocktakings from an Apprenticeship*, trans. Stephen Walsh, Oxford: Clarendon Press, 1991

Brand, Juliane and Christopher Hailey, *The Berg–Schoenberg Correspondence*: *Selected Letters*, New York: Norton, 1987

Březina, Aleš, 'Die Martinů-Manuskripte in der Paul Sacher Stiftung', *Schweizer Jahrbuch für Musikwissenschaft/Annales Suisses de Musicologie*, 13–14 (1993–4), 157–274

Brooks, Philip C., *Research in Archives*: *The Use of Unpublished Primary Sources*, University of Chicago Press, 1969

Burkholder, J. Peter, *All Made of Tunes*: *Charles Ives and the Uses of Musical Borrowing*, New Haven: Yale University Press, 1995

Cadenbach, Rainer, *Max Reger und seine Zeit*, Laaber Verlag, 1991

Cage, John, 'Four Musicians at Work', *Trans Formation: Arts, Communication, Environment: A World Review*, 1/3 (1952), 164–174

    'Notes on Compositions II (1950–1963)', *John Cage: Writer*, selected and introduced by Richard Kostelanetz, New York: Limelight Editions, 1993

    Williams Mix, New York: Henmar Press, 1960

Canto d'Amore: *Classicism in Modern Art and Music 1914–1935*, ed. Gottried Boehm, Ulrich Mosch and Katharina Schmidt, Basle: Kunstmuseum, 1996

Carter, Elliott, *Harmony Book*, ed. Nicholas Hopkins and John F. Link, New York: Carl Fischer, 2002

Chadabe, Joel, *Electric Sound*, Upper Saddle River, NJ: Prentice Hall, 1997

Cone, Edward T., 'Stravinsky: The Progress of a Method', *Perspectives of New Music*, 1/1 (1962), 18–26

Cooper, Barry, *Beethoven and the Creative Process*, Oxford: Clarendon Press, 1990

Cyr, Louis (ed.), *Igor Stravinsky, L'oiseau de feu: fac-similé du manuscript Saint-Pétersbourg 1909/1910*, Geneva: Minkoff, 1985

Dahlhaus, Carl, *Foundations of Music History*, trans. J. B. Robinson, Cambridge University Press, 1985

    'Plea for a Romantic Category: The concept of the Work of Art in the Newest Music', in Carl Dahlhaus, *Schoenberg and the New Music*, trans. Derrick Puffett and Alfred Clayton, Cambridge University Press, 1987

Danuser, Hermann, *Gustav Mahler und seine Zeit*, Laaber Verlag, 1991

Decroupet, Pascal, 'Renverser la vapeur . . . Zu Musikdenken und Kompositionen von Boulez aus den fünfziger Jahren', *Musik-Konzepte,* 89/90 (1995), 112–31

'Une genèse, une œuvre, une pensée musicale – en mouvement. *Zeitmaße* de Karlheinz Stockhausen', *Revue belge de musicologie*, 52 (1998), 347–61

Decroupet, Pascal and Elena Ungeheuer, 'Through the Sensory Looking-Glass: The Aesthetic and Serial Foundations of *Gesang der Jünglinge*', *Perspectives of New Music*, 36/1 (1998), 97–142

Dessauer, Guido, 'Das Papier, im Archiv', *Das Papier*, 43/11 (1989), 607–15

Eco, Umberto, *The Open Work*, trans. Anna Cancogni, Cambridge Mass.: Harvard University Press, 1989

Edwards, Allen, *Flawed Words and Stubborn Sounds*: *A Conversation with Elliott Carter*, New York: Norton, 1971

Eimert, Herbet (ed.), *die Reihe 2. Information über serielle Musik. Anton Webern*, 2nd edn, Vienna: Universal Edition, 1955

Fanning, David, 'Berg's Sketches for *Wozzeck*: A Commentary and Inventory (Includes Appendices)', *Journal of the Royal Music Association*, 112/2 (1986–7), 280–322

Feder, Georg, *Musikphilologie. Eine Einführung in die musikalische Textkritik, Hermeneutik und Editionstechnik*, Darmstadt: Wissenschaftliche Buchgesellschaft, 1987

Feller, Ross, 'Elevated Bug Fixing: Brian Ferneyhough in Conversation with Ross Feller', forthcoming

'Multicursal Labyrinths in the Work of Brian Ferneyhough', Ann Arbor: UMI Dissertation Services, 1994

'Strategic Defamiliarization: The Process of Difficulty in Brian Ferneyhough's Music', *The Open Space*, 2 (Spring 2000), 197–202

Ferneyhough, Brian, 'Temporal Patterning and Process Mapping', an unpublished paper read at IRCAM, Paris, April 1996

Brian Ferneyhough: Collected Writings, ed. James Boros and Richard Toop, Contemporary Music Studies 10, Amsterdam: Harwood Academic Publishers, 1995

Gillies, Malcolm, 'Stylistic Integrity and Influence in Bartók's Works: The Case of Szymanowski', *International Journal of Musicology*, 1 (1992), 139–60

Goehr, Lydia, *The Imaginary Museum of Musical Works*: *An Essay in the Philosophy of Music*, Oxford University Press, 1992

Gombocz, Adrienne and László Somfai, 'Bartók Briefe an Calvocoressi (1914–1930)', *Studia Musicologica*, 24 (1982), 199–231

Grier, James, *The Critical Editing of Music*: *History, Method and Practice*, Cambridge University Press, 1996

Gülke, Peter, 'Neue Beiträge zur Kenntnis des Sinfonikers Schubert', *Franz Schubert*, Musik-Konzepte Sonderband [Special Issue], ed. Heinz-Klaus Metzger and Rainer Riehn, Munich: edition text+kritik, 1979, pp. 193–220

Gurewitsch, Matthew, 'Finding the Truth in the Composer's Hand', *The New York Times* (14 May 2000)

György Kurtág: Musikmanuskripte, Inventare der Paul Sacher Stiftung, ed. Friedemann Sallis, Ulrich Mosch and Christina Dreier, Mainz: Schott Musik International, forthcoming

Haas, Georg Friedrich, 'Disziplin oder Indisziplin? Anmerkungen zu der von Ulrich Mosch veröffentlichten Reihentabelle von Pierre Boulez', *Musiktheorie*, 5/3 (1990), 271–3

Haberditzl, Anna, 'Kleine Mühen – große Wirkung: Maßnahmen der passiven Konservierung bei der Lagerung, Verpackung und Nutzung von Archiv- und Bibliotheksgut', *Bestandserhaltung in Archiven und Bibliotheken*, ed. Hartmut Weber, Stuttgart: W. Kohlhammer, 1992, pp. 71–83

Hall, Patricia, *A View of Berg's Lulu Through the Autograph Sources*, Berkeley: University of California Press, 1996

  'The Inception of *Wozzeck*: 1914–18', forthcoming

  'Two Sketches for Alban Berg's *Lulu*', *Music History from Primary Sources: A Guide to the Moldenhauer Archives*, ed. Jon Newsom and Alfred Mann, Washington: Library of Congress, 2000

Häusler, Jopsef, 'Klangfelder und Formflächen. Kompositorische Grundprinzipien im II. Band der *Structures* von Pierre Boulez', text accompanying the record Wergo 60011, 1965

Hay, Louis, 'History of Genesis?' *Yale French Studies*, 89 (1996), 191–207

Hefling, Stephen, 'The Making of Mahler's *Todenfeier*', Ph.D. diss., Yale University, 1996

Hilmar, Ernst, *Wozzeck von Alban Berg*, Vienna: Universal Edition, 1975

Hilmar, Rosemary, *Katalog der Musikhandschriften, Schriften und Studien Alban Bergs im Fond Alban Berg und der weiteren handschriftlichen Quellen im Besitz der Österreichischen Nationalbibliothek*, Alban Berg Studien 1, Vienna: Universal Edition, 1980

Hobsbawm, Eric, *Age of Extremes: The Short Twentieth Century 1914–1991*, London: Abacus, 1995

Horlacher, Gretchen, 'Sketches and Superimposition in Stravinsky's *Symphony of Psalms*', *Mitteilungen der Paul Sacher Stiftung*, 12 (1999), 22–6

Huang, Alfred, *The Complete I Ching*, Rochester, Vermont: Inner Traditions, 1998

Hyde, Martha, 'Format and Function of Schoenberg's Twelve-Tone Sketches', *Journal of the American Musicological Society*, 36/3 (1983), 453–80

  'Musical Form and the Development of Schoenberg's Twelve-Tone Method', *Journal of Music Theory*, 29/1 (1985), 85–144

Ingarden, Roman, *Das literarische Kunstwerk: eine Untersuchung aus dem Grenzgebiet der Ontologie, Logik und Literaturwissenschaft*, Halle: Niemeyer, 1931

  The Work of Music and the Problem of its Identity, ed. J. G. Harrell, London: Macmillan Press, 1986

Jacobi, Jolande, *The Pyschology of C. G. Jung*, New Haven: Yale University Press, 1962

Jans, Hans Jörg, 'Strawinskys Musik und ihr Schrift-Bild', *Strawinsky. Sein Nachlass. Sein Bild*, Basle: Kunstmuseum, 1984

Jans, Hans Jörg, Felix Meyer and Ingrid Westin (eds.), *Komponisten des 20. Jahrhunderts in der Paul Sacher Stiftung*, Basle: Kunstmuseum, 1986

Jenny, Laurent, 'Genetic Criticism and its Myths', *Yale French Studies*, 89 (1996), 9–25

Johnson, Douglas, 'Beethoven Scholars and Beethoven Sketches', *Nineteenth Century Music*, 2 (1978–9), 3–17

Johnson, Douglas, Alan Tyson and Robert Winter, *The Beethoven Sketchbooks: History, Reconstruction, Inventory*, Berkeley: University of California Press, 1985

Kerman, Joseph, *Concerto Conversations*, Cambridge, Mass.: Harvard University Press, 1999

  Musicology in the 1980s: Methods, Goals, Opportunities, New York: Da Capo Press, 1982

Krämer, Ulrich, *Alban Berg als Schüler Arnold Schoenberg*, Vienna: Universal Edition, 1996

Kobrin, Ed, 'I Ching', *Source* (Composer/Performer), 7/4–2 (1970), 1–7

Koblyakov, Lev, *Pierre Boulez: A World of Harmony*, Contemporary Music Studies 2, Chur: Harwood Academic Publishers, 1990

  'Pierre Boulez: *Le marteau sans maître* – Analysis of the Pitch Structure', *Zeitschrift für Musiktheorie*, 8/1 (1977), 24–39

Kostelanetz, Richard, *Conversing with Cage*, New York: Limelight Editions, 1988

  John Cage (Ex)plain(ed), New York: Schirmer Books, 1996

Kostelanetz, Richard (ed.), *John Cage: An Anthology*, New York: Da Capo Press, 1970

Kosztolányi, Dezső, [Interview with Béla Bartók], *Pesti Hírlap* (31 May 1925)

Küppers, Harald, *DuMont's Farbenatlas*, Cologne: DuMont Buchverlag, 1999

Kurtág, György, *Játékok VI zongorára. Naplójegyzetek, személyes üzenetek* [Games VI for piano. Diary entries, personal messages], Budapest: Editio Musica, 1997

Lack, Graham (ed.), *The Future in the Present: Composer Institutes in the 21st Century*, Munich: Orff-Zentrum, 2000

Lebrave, Jean-Louis, 'La critique génétique: une discipline nouvelle ou un avatar moderne de la philologie?' *Genesis: manuscrits, recherche, invention*, 1 (1992), 33–72

Lichtenhahn, Ernst and Tilman Seebass (eds.), *Musikhandschriften aus der Sammlung Paul Sacher: Festschrift zu Paul Sachers siebzigstem Geburtstag*, Basle: Editiones Roche, 1976

Ligeti, György, 'Pierre Boulez. Entscheidung und Automatik in der Structure Ia', *die Reihe*, 4 (Vienna: Universal Edition, 1958), 38–63

Loetscher, Hugo, 'Vorläufiges zu einer Hinterlassenschaft: Ein Archivar in eigener Sache', *Neue Zürcher Zeitung*, 219/225 (29 September 1997), 29

Luciano Berio: Musikmanuskripte, Inventare der Paul Sacher Stiftung 2, ed. René Karlen, Winterthur: Amadeus, 1988

Luciano Berio: Musikmanuskripte, Inventare der Paul Sacher Stiftung 2, revised and enlarged second edition, ed. Ulrich Mosch, Mainz: Schott Musik International, forthcoming.

Macleod, Joseph Todd Gordon, *The Sisters d'Arányi*, London: Allen & Unwin, 1969

Mäkelä, Tomi, 'Comprehending Chromaticism: Structural Semantics in Anton Webern's *Wiese im Park* Op. 13 No. 1', *Hudební Veda a Výchova* 8, Acta Universitas Palackianæ Olomucenisis Facultas Pædagogica, Musica VI, Olomouc: Univerzita Palackého v Olomouci, 2000, pp. 95–104

'Die Konfigurierung des Klanges. Die Angaben zur Instrumentation von *Ragtime* für elf Instrumente und *Pribaoutki* in Igor Strawinskys Skizzen', *Mitteilungen der Paul Sacher Stiftung*, 13 (2000), 26–32

'"Verunglückt auf der Reise". Das "Erste Concert" (Fragment) von Max Reger mit Blick auf sein Klavierkonzert opus 114', *Musikalische Moderne und Tradition*, ed. Alexander Becker, Gabriele Gefäller and Susanne Popp, Wiesbaden: Breitkopf & Härtel, 2000, pp. 37–54

'Viewpoints on Orchestration – Talks about Texture', *Finnish Musical Quarterly*, 3 (1992), 40–5

Marston, Nicholas, 'Sketch', *The New Grove Dictionary of Music and Musicians*, vol. 23, ed. Stanley Sadie and John Tyrrell, London: Macmillan, 2001, p. 472

McLean, Donald, 'A Documentary and Analytical Study of Alban Berg's Three Pieces for Orchestra', Ph.D. diss., University of Toronto, 1997

Meyer, Felix (ed.), *Quellenstudien II Zwölf Komponisten des 20. Jahrhunderts*, Winterthur: Amadeus, 1993

Settling New Scores: Music Manuscripts from the Paul Sacher Foundation, Mainz: Schott, 1998

Michel, Pierre, *György Ligeti. Compositeur d'aujourd'hui*, Paris: Minerve, 1985

Mies, Paul, *Die Bedeutung der Skizzen Beethovens zur Erkenntnis seines Stils*, Leipzig: Breitkopf & Härtel, 1925

Moldenhauer, Hans, *Anton von Webern: Sketches (1926–1945)*, with a commentary by Ernst Krenek, New York: Carl Fischer, 1968

Moldenhauer, Hans and Rosaleen, *Anton von Webern. Chronik seines Lebens und Werks*, Zurich and Freiburg im Breisgau: Atlantis, 1980

Mosch, Ulrich, 'Disziplin und Indisziplin. Zum seriellen Komponieren im 2. Satz des *Marteau sans maître* von Pierre Boulez', *Musiktheorie*, 5/1 (1990), 39–66

'Musikverlage, "Komponisten-Institute" und das zeitgenössische Schaffen', *Der Musikverlag und seine Komponisten im 21. Jahrhundert*: *Zum 100-jährigen Jubiläum der Universal Edition*, Studien zur Wertungsvorschung 41, ed. Otto Kolleritsch, Vienna and Graz: Universal Edition, 2002, pp. 30–43

Nattiez, Jean-Jacques (ed.), *The Boulez–Cage Correspondence*, trans. Robert Samuels, Cambridge University Press, 1993. For the original, non-translated edition of this correspondence, see Pierre Boulez and John Cage, *Correspondance et Documents*, ed. Jean-Jacques Nattiez *et al.*, Winterthur: Amadeus, 1990

Newbould, Brian, *Schubert: The Music and the Man*, Berkeley: University of California Press, 1999

Osmond-Smith, David, *Berio*, Oxford University Press, 1991

'La mesure de la distance: *Rendering* de Berio', *Inharmoniques*, 7 (1991), 147–52

Osmond-Smith, David (ed. and trans.), *Luciano Berio: Two Interviews with Rossana Dalmonte and Bálint András Varga*, New York and London: Boyars, 1985

Owens, Jessie Ann, *Composers at Work*: *The Craft of Musical Composition 1450–1600*, Oxford University Press, 1997

Perkins, David, *Is Literary History Possible?* Baltimore: The Johns Hopkins University Press, 1993

Peterson, Peter, *Alban Berg: Wozzeck*, Munich: edition text + kritik, 1985

Piencikowski, Robert, 'Nature morte avec guitare', in *Pierre Boulez. Eine Festschrift zum 60. Geburtstag am 26. März 1985*, ed. Josef Häusler, Vienna: Universal Edition, 1985, pp. 66–81

Poe, Edgar Allan, *Marginalia*, Charlottesville: University Press of Virginia, 1981

Retallack, Joan (ed.), *MUSICAGE: Cage Muses on Words, Art, Music*, Hanover and London: Wesleyan University Press, 1996

Reuß, Roland, 'Schicksal der Handschrift, Schicksal der Druckschrift. Notizen zur "Textgenese"', *Textkritische Beiträge* (Textgenese 1), 5 (1999), 1–25

'Textkritische Editionen und Dateiformate. Notizen', in *Jahrbuch für Computerphilologie*, ed. Volker Deubel, Karl Eibl and Fotis Jannidis, Paderborn: Mentis, 1999, pp. 101–6

Rimsky-Korsakov, Nicolai, *Grundlagen der Orchestration mit Notenbeispielen aus eigenen Werken*, trans. Alexandr Elukhen, Berlin: Russischer Musikverlag, 1922

Sallis, Friedemann, 'Reading György Ligeti's *Lux aeterna*: An Exercise in Musicological Border-Crossing', *Muualla, täällä. Kirjoituksia elämästä, kuttuurista, musiikista. Juhlakirja Erkki Salmenhaara (Festschrift for Erkki Salmenhaara)*, ed. Helena Tyrväinen, Seija Lappalainen, Tomi Mäkelä and Irma Vierimaa, Jyväskylä: Atena Kustannus Oy Jyväskylä, 2001, pp. 137–52

'The Genealogy of György Kurtág's *Hommage à R. Sch*, op. 15d', *Studia Musicologica*, 43/3–4 (2002), 311–22

Scherliess, Volker, *Igor Strawinsky und seine Zeit*, Laaber Verlag, 1983

Schleiermacher, Friedrich, *Vorlesungen über die Ästhetik*, Berlin: Walter de Gruyter, 1974

Schubert, Franz, *Symphony No. 10 in D major D. 936A*, ed. Brian Newbould, London: Faber Music, 1995

Schumann, Robert, *Gesammelte Schriften über Musik und Musiker*, vol. 2, ed. Gustav Jansen, Leipzig: Breitkopf & Härtel, 1891

Seebass, Tilman (ed.), *Musikhandschriften der Bodmeriana: Katalog*, Cologny-Geneva: Fondation Martin Bodmer, 1986

Shreffler, Anne C., '"*Mein Weg geht jetzt vorüber*": The Vocal Origins of Webern's Twelve-tone Composition', *Journal of the American Musicological Society*, 47/2 (1994), 275–339

Sibelius, Jean, 'Diary 1909–1943' Jean Sibelius Collection, Helsinki: The National Archives of Finland

Somfai, László, *Béla Bartók*: *Compositions, Concepts, and Autograph Sources*, Berkeley: University of California Press, 1996

Tizennyolc Bartók-tanulmány [Eighteen Bartók studies], Budapest: Zeneműkiadó, 1981

'Bartók vázlatok II.' [Bartók sketches II], *Zenetudományi Dolgozatok*, Budapest: MTA Zenetudományi Intézet, 1985, pp. 30–5

'Progressive Music via Peasant Music? Revisiting the Sources of Bartók's Style and Compositional Process', *The Past in the Present*, Proceedings of the IMS Inter-congressional Symposium and the 10th Meeting of the Cantus Planus, Budapest & Viségrad, 2000, ed. László Dobszay, Budapest: Liszt Ferenc Academy of Music, 2003, pp. 499–513

Somfai, László (ed.), *Béla Bartók*: *Black Pocket-book. Sketches 1907–1922* (facsimile edition), Editio Musica Budapest, 1987

Stein, Leonard, 'Schoenberg: Five Statements', *Perspectives of New Music* (Fall/Winter 1975), 161–173

Stockhausen, Karlheinz, 'Gruppenkomposition: Klavierstück I (Anleitung zum Hören)', *Texte 1*, Cologne: DuMont Verlag, 1963

Stravinsky, Igor, *Poétique musicale sous forme de six leçons*, Cambridge, Mass.: Harvard University Press, 1942; in English, Igor Stravinsky, *Poetics in the Form of Six Lessons*, trans. Arthur Knodel and Ingolf Dahl, Cambridge, Mass.: Harvard University Press, 1979

Stravinsky, Igor and Robert Craft, *The Rite of Spring: Sketches 1911–1913*, London: Boosey & Hawkes, 1969

Stuckenschmidt, Hans Heinz, *Schönberg: Leben, Umwelt, Werk*, Zurich: Atlantis, 1974

Süss, Harald, *Deutsche Schreibschrift*, Augsburg: Augustus Verlag, 1995

Taruskin, Richard, 'Reply to Brown and Dempster', *Journal of Music Theory*, 33/1 (1989), 155–64
Stravinsky and the Russian Traditions: *A Biography of the Works through 'Marva'*, Oxford University Press, 1996

Tedeschi, Massimo Gentili (ed.), *Guida a una descrizione catalografica uniforme dei manoscritti musicali*, Rome: Instituto centrale per il catalogo unico delle biblioteche italiane e per le informazione bibliografiche, 1984

Thomas, Christiane, 'Was erwarten Archivarinnen und Archivare von Restauratoren', *Dritte Tagung der Österreichischen Archivrestauratorinnen und Restauratoren, 18–19 November 1996*, Vienna: Österreichisches Staatsarchiv, 1996

Thomas, Gavin, 'Musica e musica . . . ', *Musical Times*, 137/1 (1996), 15

Toop, Richard, 'On Complexity', *Perspectives of New Music*, 31/1 (Winter 1993), 42–57

Ungeheuer, Elena, 'Statistical Gestalts – Perceptible Features in Serial Music', *Music, Gestalt, and Computing*, ed. Marc Leman, Berlin: Springer, 1997, pp. 103–13

Virtanen, Timo, 'Pohjola's Daughter – "L'aventure d'un héros"', *Sibelius Studies*, ed. Timothy L. Jackson and Veijo Murtomäki, Cambridge University Press, 2001, pp. 139–74

Weber, Max, *Die rationalen und soziologischen Grundlagen der Musik*, Tübingen: J. C. B. Mohr, 1972; in English, Max Weber, *The Rational and Social Foundations of Music*, Carbondale: Southern Illinois University Press, 1958

Webern, Anton, *Kinderstück* opus postumum, New York: Carl Fischer, 1967

Webern, Anton, *Klavierstück* opus postumum, Vienna: Universal Edition, 1966

Weiss, Günther, *et al.*, *Gustav Mahler: Briefe und Musikautographen aus den Moldenhauer-Archiven in der Bayerischen Staatsbibliothek*, Patrimonia 157, Munich: Kulturstiftung der Länder, 2003

Whelan, Thomas, *Towards a History and Theory of Sketch Studies*, Ann Arbor: UMI, 1990

Whittall, Arnold, 'Music Analysis as Human Science? Le Sacre du Printemps in Theory and Practice', *Music Analysis*, 1/1 (1982), 33–54

Wightman, Alistair, 'Szymanowski, Bartók and the Violin', *Musical Times*, 122 (1981), 159–63

Wilkinson, Marc, 'Pierre Boulez' Structure Ia. Bemerkungen zur Zwölfton-Technik', *Gravesaner Blätter*, 4/10 (1958), 12–29

Index